# EUROPE AND ELSEWHERE

AND I ROSE TO RECEIVE MY GUEST, AND BRACED MYSELF FOR THE
THUNDERCRASH AND THE BRIMSTONE STENCH WHICH
SHOULD ANNOUNCE HIS ARRIVAL

(See p. 326)

# EUROPE AND ELSEWHERE

By
MARK TWAIN

WITH AN APPRECIATION BY
BRANDER MATTHEWS
AND AN INTRODUCTION BY
ALBERT BIGELOW PAINE

HARPER & BROTHERS, PUBLISHERS
NEW YORK AND LONDON

EUROPE AND ELSEWHERE

*First Edition*
E-X

# CONTENTS

# AN APPRECIATION

(This "Biographical Criticism" was prepared by Prof. Brander Matthews, as an introduction to the Uniform Edition of Mark Twain's Works, published in 1899).

IT is a common delusion of those who discuss contemporary literature that there is such an entity as the "reading public," possessed of a certain uniformity of taste. There is not one public; there are many publics—as many, in fact, as there are different kinds of taste; and the extent of an author's popularity is in proportion to the number of these separate publics he may chance to please. Scott, for example, appealed not only to those who relished romance and enjoyed excitement, but also to those who appreciated his honest portrayal of sturdy characters. Thackeray is preferred by ambitious youth who are insidiously flattered by his tacit compliments to their knowledge of the world, by the disenchanted who cannot help seeing the petty meannesses of society, and by the less sophisticated in whom sentiment has not gone to seed in sentimentality. Dickens in his own day bid for the approval of those who liked broad caricature (and were therefore pleased with Stiggins and Chadband), of those who fed greedily on plentiful pathos (and were therefore delighted with the deathbeds of Smike and Paul Dombey and

Little Nell) and also of those who asked for unexpected adventure (and were therefore glad to disentangle the melodramatic intrigues of Ralph Nickleby).

In like manner the American author who has chosen to call himself Mark Twain has attained to an immense popularity because the qualities he possesses in a high degree appeal to so many and so widely varied publics—first of all, no doubt, to the public that revels in hearty and robust fun, but also to the public which is glad to be swept along by the full current of adventure, which is sincerely touched by manly pathos, which is satisfied by vigorous and exact portrayal of character, and which respects shrewdness and wisdom and sanity and a healthy hatred of pretense and affectation and sham. Perhaps no one book of Mark Twain's—with the possible exception of *Huckleberry Finn*—is equally a favorite with all his readers; and perhaps some of his best characteristics are absent from his earlier books or but doubtfully latent in them. Mark Twain is many sided; and he has ripened in knowledge and in power since he first attracted attention as a wild Western funny man. As he has grown older he has reflected more; he has both broadened and deepened. The writer of "comic copy" for a mining-camp newspaper has developed into a liberal humorist, handling life seriously and making his readers think as he makes them laugh, until to-day Mark Twain has perhaps the largest audience of any author now using the English language. To trace the stages of this evolution and to count the steps

whereby the sagebrush reporter has risen to the rank
of a writer of world-wide celebrity, is as interesting
as it is instructive.

I

Samuel Langhorne Clemens was born November
30, 1835, at Florida, Missouri. His father was a
merchant who had come from Tennessee and who
removed soon after his son's birth to Hannibal, a
little town on the Mississippi. What Hannibal was
like and what were the circumstances of Mr. Clemens's boyhood we can see for ourselves in the convincing pages of *Tom Sawyer*. Mr. Howells has
called Hannibal "a loafing, out-at-elbows, down-at-
the-heels, slave-holding Mississippi town"; and
Mr. Clemens, who silently abhorred slavery, was of
a slave-owning family.

When the future author was but twelve his father
died, and the son had to get his education as best
he could. Of actual schooling he got little and of
book learning still less, but life itself is not a bad
teacher for a boy who wants to study, and young
Clemens did not waste his chances He spent six
years in the printing office of the little local paper,
—for, like not a few others on the list of Americnn
authors that stretches from Benjamin Franklin to
William Dean Howells, he began his connection with
literature by setting type. As a journeyman printer
the lad wandered from town to town and rambled
even as far east as New York.

When he was nineteen he went back to the home
of his boyhood and presently resolved to become a

pilot on the Mississippi. How he learned the river he has told us in *Life on the Mississippi*, wherein his adventures, his experiences, and his impressions while he was a cub pilot are recorded with a combination of precise veracity and abundant humor which makes the earlier chapters of that marvelous book a most masterly fragment of autobiography. The life of a pilot was full of interest and excitement and opportunity, and what young Clemens saw and heard and divined during the years when he was going up and down the mighty river we may read in the pages of *Huckleberry Finn* and *Pudd'nhead Wilson*. But toward the end of the 'fifties the railroads began to rob the river of its supremacy as a carrier; and in the beginning of the 'sixties the Civil War broke out and the Mississippi no longer went unvexed to the sea. The skill, slowly and laboriously acquired, was suddenly rendered useless, and at twenty-five the young man found himself bereft of his calling. As a border state, Missouri was sending her sons into the armies of the Union and into the armies of the Confederacy, while many a man stood doubting, not knowing which way to turn. The ex-pilot has given us the record of his very brief and inglorious service as a soldier of the South. When this escapade was swiftly ended, he went to the Northwest with his brother, who had been appointed Territorial Secretary of Nevada. Thus the man who had been born on the borderland of North and South, who had gone East as a jour-printer, who had been again and again up and down the Mississippi, now went West while he was still plastic and impressionable; and he had thus another chance to increase that intimate knowledge of American life and American character which is one of the most precious of his possessions.

While still on the river he had written a satiric letter or two which found their way into print. In Nevada he went to the mines and lived the life he has described in *Roughing It*, but when he failed to "strike it rich," he naturally drifted into journalism and back into a newspaper office again. The *Virginia City Enterprise* was not overmanned, and the newcomer did all sorts of odd jobs, finding time now and then to write a sketch which seemed important enough to permit of his signature. He now began to sign himself Mark Twain, taking the name from a call of the man who heaves the lead on a Mississippi River steamboat, and who cries, "By the mark, three," "Mark Twain," and so on. The name of Mark Twain soon began to be known to those who were curious in newspaper humor. After a while he was drawn across the mountains to San Francisco, where he found casual employment on the *Morning Call*, and where he joined himself to a little group of aspiring *literators* which included Mr. Bret Harte, Mr. Noah Brooks, Mr. Charles Henry Webb, and Mr. Charles Warren Stoddard.

It was in 1867 that Mr. Webb published Mark Twain's first book, *The Celebrated Jumping Frog of Calaveras;* and it was in 1867 that the proprietors of the *Alta California* supplied him with the funds necessary to enable him to become one of the passengers on the steamer *Quaker City*, which had been chartered to take a select party on what is now known as the Mediterranean trip. The weekly letters, in which he set forth what befell him on this journey, were printed in the *Alta* Sunday after Sunday, and were copied freely by the other Californian papers. These letters served as the foundation of a book published in 1869 and called *The Innocents Abroad*, a book which instantly brought to the author celebrity and cash.

Both of these valuable aids to ambition were increased by his next step, his appearance on the lecture platform. Mr. Noah Brooks, who was present at his first attempt, has recorded that Mark Twain's "method as a lecturer was distinctly unique and novel. His slow, deliberate drawl, the anxious and perturbed expression of his visage, the apparently painful effort with which he framed his sentences, the surprise that spread over his face when the audience roared with delight or rapturously applauded the finer passages of his word painting, were unlike anything of the kind they had ever known." In the thirty years since that first appearance the method has not changed, although it has probably matured. Mark Twain is one of the most effective of platform speakers and one of the most artistic, with an art of his own which is very individual and very elaborate in spite of its seeming simplicity.

Although he succeeded abundantly as a lecturer, and although he was the author of the most widely circulated book of the decade, Mark Twain still thought of himself only as a journalist; and when he gave up the West for the East he became an editor of the Buffalo *Express*, in which he had bought an interest. In 1870 he married; and it is perhaps not indiscreet to remark that his was another of those happy unions of which there have been so many in the annals of American authorship. In 1871 he removed to Hartford, where his home has been ever since; and at the same time he gave up newspaper work.

In 1872 he wrote *Roughing It*, and in the following year came his first sustained attempt at fiction, *The Gilded Age*, written in collaboration with Mr. Charles Dudley Warner. The character of "Colonel Mulberry Sellers" Mark Twain soon took out of this book to make it the central figure of a play which the late John T. Raymond acted hundreds of times throughout the United States, the playgoing public pardoning the inexpertness of the dramatist in favor of the delicious humor and the compelling veracity with which the chief character was presented. So universal was this type and so broadly recognizable its traits that there were few towns wherein the play was presented in which some one did not accost the actor who impersonated the ever-hopeful schemer to declare: "I'm the original of Sellers! Didn't Mark ever tell you? Well, he took the Colonel from me!"

Encouraged by the welcome accorded to this first attempt at fiction, Mark Twain turned to the days of his boyhood and wrote *Tom Sawyer*, published in 1875. He also collected his sketches, scattered here and there in newspapers and magazines. Toward the end of the 'seventies he went to Europe again with his family; and the result of this journey is recorded in *A Tramp Abroad*, published in 1880. Another volume of sketches, *The Stolen White Elephant*, was put forth in 1882; and in the same year Mark Twain first came forward as a historical novelist—if *The Prince and the Pauper* can fairly be called a historical novel. The year after, he sent forth the volume describing his *Life on the Mississippi;* and in 1884 he followed this with the story in which that life has been crystallized forever, *Huckleberry Finn*, the finest of his books, the deepest in its insight, and the widest in its appeal.

This Odyssey of the Mississippi was published by a new firm, in which the author was a chief partner, just as Sir Walter Scott had been an associate of Ballantyne and Constable. There was at first a period of prosperity in which the house issued the *Personal Memoirs* of Grant, giving his widow checks for $350,000 in 1886, and in which Mark Twain himself published *A Connecticut Yankee at King Arthur's Court*, a volume of *Merry Tales*, and a story called *The American Claimant*, wherein "Colonel Sellers" reappears. Then there came a succession of hard years; and at last the publishing house in which Mark Twain was a partner failed, as the publishing house in which Walter Scott was a partner had formerly failed. The author of *Huckleberry Finn* at sixty found himself suddenly saddled with a load of debt, just as the author of *Waverley* had been burdened full threescore years earlier; and Mark Twain stood up stoutly under it, as Scott had done before him. More fortunate than the Scotchman, the American has lived to pay the debt in full.

Since the disheartening crash came, he has given to the public a third Mississippi River tale, *Pudd'nhead Wilson*, issued in 1894; and a third historical novel *Joan of Arc*, a reverent and sympathetic study of the bravest figure in all French history, printed anonymously in *Harper's Magazine* and then in a volume acknowledged by the author in 1896. As one of the results of a lecturing tour around the world he prepared another volume of travels, *Following the Equator*, published toward the end of 1897. Mention must also be made of a fantastic tale called *Tom Sawyer Abroad*, sent forth in 1894, of a volume of sketches, *The Million Pound Bank-Note*, assembled in 1893, and also of a collection of literary essays, *How to Tell a Story*, published in 1897.

This is but the barest outline of Mark Twain's life —such a brief summary as we must have before us if we wish to consider the conditions under which the author has developed and the stages of his growth. It will serve, however, to show how various have been his forms of activity—printer, pilot, miner, journalist, traveler, lecturer, novelist, publisher— and to suggest the width of his experience of life.

## II

A humorist is often without honor in his own country. Perhaps this is partly because humor is likely to be familiar, and familiarity breeds contempt.

# AN APPRECIATION

Perhaps it is partly because (for some strange reason) we tend to despise those who make us laugh, while we respect those who make us weep—forgetting that there are formulas for forcing tears quite as facile as the formulas for forcing smiles. Whatever the reason, the fact is indisputable that the humorist must pay the penalty of his humor; he must run the risk of being tolerated as a mere fun maker, not to be taken seriously, and unworthy of critical consideration. This penalty has been paid by Mark Twain. In many of the discussions of American literature he is dismissed as though he were only a competitor of his predecessors, Artemus Ward and John Phœnix, instead of being, what he is really, a writer who is to be classed—at whatever interval only time may decide—rather with Cervantes and Molière.

Like the heroines of the problem plays of the modern theater, Mark Twain has had to live down his past. His earlier writing gave but little promise of the enduring qualities obvious enough in his later works. Mr. Noah Brooks has told us how he was advised, if he wished to "see genuine specimens of American humor, frolicsome, extravagant, and audacious," to look up the sketches which the then almost unknown Mark Twain was printing in a Nevada newspaper. The humor of Mark Twain is still American, still frolicsome, extravagant, and audacious; but it is riper now and richer, and it has taken unto itself other qualities existing only in germ in these firstlings of his muse. The sketches in *The Jumping Frog* and the letters which made up *The*

*Innocents Abroad* are "comic copy," as the phrase is in newspaper offices—comic copy not altogether unlike what John Phœnix had written and Artemus Ward, better indeed than the work of these newspaper humorists (for Mark Twain had it in him to develop as they did not), but not essentially dissimilar.

And in the eyes of many who do not think for themselves, Mark Twain is only the author of these genuine specimens of American humor. For when the public has once made up its mind about any man's work, it does not relish any attempt to force it to unmake this opinion and to remake it. Like other juries, it does not like to be ordered to reconsider its verdict as contrary to the facts of the case. It is always sluggish in beginning the necessary readjustment, and not only sluggish, but somewhat grudging. Naturally it cannot help seeing the later works of a popular writer from the point of view it had to take to enjoy his earlier writings. And thus the author of *Huckleberry Finn* and *Joan of Arc* is forced to pay a high price for the early and abundant popularity of *The Innocents Abroad*.

No doubt, a few of his earlier sketches were inexpensive in their elements; made of materials worn threadbare by generations of earlier funny men, they were sometimes cut in the pattern of his predecessors. No doubt, some of the earliest of all were crude and highly colored, and may even be called forced, not to say violent. No doubt, also, they did not suggest the seriousness and the melancholy which always must underlie the deepest humor, as we find it in Cervantes and Molière, in Swift and in

Lowell. But even a careless reader, skipping through the book in idle amusement, ought to have been able to see in *The Innocents Abroad* that the writer of that liveliest of books of travel was no mere merry-andrew, grinning through a horse collar to make sport for the groundlings; but a sincere observer of life, seeing through his own eyes and setting down what he saw with abundant humor, of course, but also with profound respect for the eternal verities.

George Eliot in one of her essays calls those who parody lofty themes "debasers of the moral currency." Mark Twain is always an advocate of the sterling ethical standard. He is ready to overwhelm an affectation with irresistible laughter, but he never lacks reverence for the things that really deserve reverence. It is not at the Old Masters that he scoffs in Italy, but rather at those who pay lip service to things which they neither enjoy nor understand. For a ruin or a painting or a legend that does not seem to him to deserve the appreciation in which it is held he refuses to affect an admiration he does not feel; he cannot help being honest—he was born so. For meanness of all kinds he has a burning contempt; and on Abelard he pours out the vials of his wrath. He has a quick eye for all humbugs and a scorching scorn for them; but there is no attempt at being funny in the manner of the cockney comedians when he stands in the awful presence of the Sphinx. He is not taken in by the glamour of Palestine; he does not lose his head there; he keeps his feet: but he knows that he is standing on holy ground; and there is never a hint of irreverence in his attitude.

*A Tramp Abroad* is a better book than *The Innocents Abroad;* it is quite as laughter-provoking, and its manner is far more restrained. Mark Twain was then master of his method, sure of himself, secure of his popularity; and he could do his best and spare no pains to be certain that it was his best. Perhaps there is a slight falling off in *Following the Equator;* a trace of fatigue, of weariness, of disenchantment. But the last book of travels has passages as broadly humorous as any of the first; and it proves the author's possession of a pithy shrewdness not to be suspected from a perusal of its earliest predecessor. The first book was the work of a young fellow rejoicing in his own fun and resolved to make his readers laugh with him or at him; the latest book is the work of an older man, who has found that life is not all laughter, but whose eye is as clear as ever and whose tongue is as plain-spoken.

These three books of travel are like all other books of travel in that they relate in the first person what the author went forth to see. Autobiographic also are *Roughing It* and *Life on the Mississippi*, and they have always seemed to me better books than the more widely circulated travels. They are better because they are the result of a more intimate knowledge of the material dealt with. Every traveler is of necessity but a bird of passage; he is a mere carpetbagger; his acquaintance with the countries he visits is external only; and this acquaintanceship is made only when he is a full-grown man. But

Mark Twain's knowledge of the Mississippi was acquired in his youth; it was not purchased with a price; it was his birthright; and it was internal and complete. And his knowledge of the mining camp was achieved in early manhood when the mind is open and sensitive to every new impression. There is in both these books a fidelity to the inner truth, a certainty of touch, a sweep of vision, not to be found in the three books of travels. For my own part I have long thought that Mark Twain could securely rest his right to survive as an author on those opening chapters in *Life on the Mississippi* in which he makes clear the difficulties, the seeming impossibilities, that fronted those who wished to learn the river. These chapters are bold and brilliant, and they picture for us forever a period and a set of conditions, singularly interesting and splendidly varied, that otherwise would have had to forego all adequate record.

### III

It is highly probable that when an author reveals the power of evoking views of places and of calling up portraits of people such as Mark Twain showed in *Life on the Mississippi*, and when he has the masculine grasp of reality Mark Twain made evident in *Roughing It*, he must needs sooner or later turn from mere fact to avowed fiction and become a story-teller. The long stories which Mark Twain has written fall into two divisions—first, those of which the scene is laid in the present, in reality, and mostly in the Mississippi Valley, and second, those of which the scene is laid in the past, in fantasy mostly, and in Europe.

As my own liking is a little less for the latter group, there is no need for me now to linger over them. In writing these tales of the past Mark Twain was making up stories in his head; personally I prefer the tales of his in which he has his foot firm on reality. *The Prince and the Pauper* has the essence of boyhood in it; it has variety and vigor; it has abundant humor and plentiful pathos; and yet I for one would give the whole of it for the single chapter in which Tom Sawyer lets the contract for whitewashing his aunt's fence.

Mr. Howells has declared that there are two kinds of fiction he likes almost equally well—"a real novel and a pure romance"; and he joyfully accepts *A Connecticut Yankee at King Arthur's Court* as "one of the greatest romances ever imagined." It is a humorous romance overflowing with stalwart fun; and it is not irreverent, but iconoclastic, in that it breaks not a few disestablished idols. It is intensely American and intensely nineteenth century and intensely democratic—in the best sense of that abused adjective. The British critics were greatly displeased with the book;—and we are reminded of the fact that the Spanish still somewhat resent *Don Quixote* because it brings out too truthfully the fatal gap in the Spanish character between the ideal and the real. So much of the feudal still survives in British society that Mark Twain's merry and elucidating assault on the past seemed to some almost an insult to the present.

But no critic, British or American, has ventured to discover any irreverence in *Joan of Arc*, wherein, indeed, the tone is almost devout and the humor almost too much subdued. Perhaps it is my own distrust of the so-called historical novel, my own disbelief that it can ever be anything but an inferior form of art, which makes me care less for this worthy effort to honor a noble figure. And elevated and dignified as is the *Joan of Arc*, I do not think that it shows us Mark Twain at his best; although it has many a passage that only he could have written, it is perhaps the least characteristic of his works. Yet it may well be that the certain measure of success he has achieved in handling a subject so lofty and so serious, will help to open the eyes of the public to see the solid merits of his other stories, in which his humor has fuller play and in which his natural gifts are more abundantly displayed.

Of these other stories three are "real novels," to use Mr. Howells's phrase; they are novels as real as any in any literature. *Tom Sawyer* and *Huckleberry Finn* and *Pudd'nhead Wilson* are invaluable contributions to American literature—for American literature is nothing if it is not a true picture of American life and if it does not help us to understand ourselves. *Huckleberry Finn* is a very amusing volume, and a generation has read its pages and laughed over it immoderately; but it is very much more than a funny book; it is a marvelously accurate portrayal of a whole civilization. Mr. Ormsby, in an essay which accompanies his translation of *Don Quixote*, has pointed out that for a full century

# AN APPRECIATION

after its publication that greatest of novels was
enjoyed chiefly as a tale of humorous misadventure,
and that three generations had laughed over it
before anybody suspected that it was more than a
mere funny book. It is perhaps rather with the
picaresque romances of Spain that *Huckleberry Finn*
is to be compared than with the masterpiece of
Cervantes; but I do not think it will be a century
or take three generations before we Americans generally discover how great a book *Huckleberry Finn*
really is, how keen its vision of character, how close
its observation of life, how sound its philosophy, and
how it records for us once and for all certain phases of
Southwestern society which it is most important for
us to perceive and to understand. The influence of
slavery, the prevalence of feuds, the conditions and
the circumstances that make lynching possible—all
these things are set before us clearly and without
comment. It is for us to draw our own moral, each
for himself, as we do when we see Shakespeare
acted.

*Huckleberry Finn*, in its art, for one thing, and
also in its broader range, is superior to *Tom Sawyer*
and to *Pudd'nhead Wilson*, fine as both these are in
their several ways. In no book in our language,
to my mind, has the boy, simply as a boy, been
better realized than in *Tom Sawyer*. In some
respects *Pudd'nhead Wilson* is the most dramatic
of Mark Twain's longer stories, and also the most
ingenious; like *Tom Sawyer* and *Huckleberry Finn*,
it has the full flavor of the Mississippi River, on
which its author spent his own boyhood, and

from contact with the soil of which he always rises reinvigorated.

It is by these three stories, and especially by *Huckleberry Finn*, that Mark Twain is likely to live longest. Nowhere else is the life of the Mississippi Valley so truthfully recorded. Nowhere else can we find a gallery of Southwestern characters as varied and as veracious as those Huck Finn met in his wanderings. The histories of literature all praise the *Gil Blas* of Le Sage for its amusing adventures, its natural characters, its pleasant humor, and its insight into human frailty; and the praise is deserved. But in everyone of these qualities *Huckleberry Finn* is superior to *Gil Blas*. Le Sage set the model of the picaresque novel, and Mark Twain followed his example; but the American book is richer than the French—deeper, finer, stronger. It would be hard to find in any language better specimens of pure narrative, better examples of the power of telling a story and of calling up action so that the reader cannot help but see it, than Mark Twain's account of the Shepherdson-Grangerford feud, and his description of the shooting of Boggs by Sherburn and of the foiled attempt to lynch Sherburn afterward.

These scenes, fine as they are, vivid, powerful, and most artistic in their restraint, can be matched in the two other books. In *Tom Sawyer* they can be paralleled by the chapter in which the boy and the girl are lost in the cave, and Tom, seeing a gleam of light in the distance, discovers that it is a candle carried by Indian Joe, the one enemy he has in the

world. In *Pudd'nhead Wilson* the great passages
of *Huckleberry Finn* are rivaled by that most pathetic
account of the weak son willing to sell his own
mother as a slave "down the river." Although
no one of the books is sustained throughout on this
high level, and although, in truth, there are in each of
them passages here and there that we could wish
away (because they are not worthy of the association in which we find them), I have no hesitation in
expressing here my own conviction that the man who
has given us four scenes like these is to be compared
with the masters of literature; and that he can abide
the comparison with equanimity.

## IV

Perhaps I myself prefer these three Mississippi
Valley books above all Mark Twain's other writings
(although with no lack of affection for those also)
partly because these have the most of the flavor of
the soil about them. After veracity and the sense
of the universal, what I best relish in literature is this
native aroma, pungent, homely, and abiding. Yet
I feel sure that I should not rate him so high if
he were the author of these three books only. They
are the best of him, but the others are good also,
and good in a different way. Other writers have
given us this local color more or less artistically,
more or less convincingly: one New England and
another New York, a third Virginia, and a fourth
Georgia, and a fifth Wisconsin; but who so well as
Mark Twain has given us the full spectrum of the

Union? With all his exactness in reproducing the Mississippi Valley, Mark Twain is not sectional in his outlook; he is national always. He is not narrow; he is not Western or Eastern; he is American with a certain largeness and boldness and freedom and certainty that we like to think of as befitting a country so vast as ours and a people so independent.

In Mark Twain we have "the national spirit as seen with our own eyes," declared Mr. Howells; and, from more points of view than one, Mark Twain seems to me to be the very embodiment of Americanism. Self-educated in the hard school of life, he has gone on broadening his outlook as he has grown older. Spending many years abroad, he has come to understand other nationalities, without enfeebling his own native faith. Combining a mastery of the commonplace with an imaginative faculty, he is a practical idealist. No respecter of persons, he has a tender regard for his fellow man. Irreverent toward all outworn superstitions, he has ever revealed the deepest respect for all things truly worthy of reverence. Unwilling to take pay in words, he is impatient always to get at the root of the matter, to pierce to the center, to see the thing as it is. He has a habit of standing upright, of thinking for himself, and of hitting hard at whatsoever seems to him hateful and mean; but at the core of him there is genuine gentleness and honest sympathy, brave humanity and sweet kindliness. Perhaps it is boastful for us to think that these characteristics which we see in Mark Twain are characteristics also of the American people as a whole; but it is pleasant to think so.

# AN APPRECIATION

Mark Twain has the very marrow of Americanism. He is as intensely and as typically American as Franklin or Emerson or Hawthorne. He has not a little of the shrewd common sense and the homely and unliterary directness of Franklin. He is not without a share of the aspiration and the elevation of Emerson; and he has a philosophy of his own as optimistic as Emerson's. He possesses also somewhat of Hawthorne's interest in ethical problems, with something of the same power of getting at the heart of them; he, too, has written his parables and apologues wherein the moral is obvious and unobtruded. He is uncompromisingly honest; and his conscience is as rugged as his style sometimes is.

No American author has to-day at his command a style more nervous, more varied, more flexible, or more various than Mark Twain's. His colloquial ease should not hide from us his mastery of all the devices of rhetoric. He may seem to disobey the letter of the law sometimes, but he is always obedient to the spirit. He never speaks unless he has something to say; and then he says it tersely, sharply, with a freshness of epithet and an individuality of phrase, always accurate, however unacademic. His vocabulary is enormous, and it is deficient only in the dead words; his language is alive always, and actually tingling with vitality. He rejoices in the daring noun and in the audacious adjective. His instinct for the exact word is not always unerring, and now and again he has failed to exercise it; but there is in his prose none of the flatting and sharping he censured in Fenimore Cooper's. His style has none of the cold perfection of an antique statue; it is too modern and too American for that, and too completely the expression of the man himself, sincere and straightforward. It is not free from slang, although this is far less frequent than one might expect; but it does its work swiftly and cleanly. And it is capable of immense variety. Consider the tale of the Blue Jay in *A Tramp Abroad*, wherein the humor is sustained by unstated pathos; what could be better told than this, with every word the right word and in the right place? And take Huck Finn's description of the storm when he was alone on the island, which is in dialect, which will not parse, which bristles with double negatives, but which none the less is one of the finest passages of descriptive prose in all American literature.

## V

After all, it is as a humorist pure and simple that Mark Twain is best known and best beloved. In the preceding pages I have tried to point out the several ways in which he transcends humor, as the word is commonly restricted, and to show that he is no mere fun maker. But he is a fun maker beyond all question, and he has made millions laugh as no other man of our century has done. The laughter he has aroused is wholesome and self-respecting; it clears the atmosphere. For this we cannot but be grateful. As Lowell said, "let us not be ashamed to confess that, if we find the tragedy a bore, we take the profoundest satisfaction in the farce. It is a mark of sanity." There is no laughter in Don Quixote, the noble enthusiast whose wits are unsettled; and there is little on the lips of Alceste the misanthrope of Molière; but for both of them life would have been easier had they known how to laugh. Cervantes himself, and Molière also, found relief in laughter for their melancholy; and it was the sense of humor which kept them tolerantly interested in the spectacle of humanity, although life had pressed hardly on them both. On Mark Twain also life has left its scars; but he has bound up his wounds and battled forward with a stout heart, as Cervantes did, and Molière. It was Molière who declared that it was a strange business to undertake to make people laugh; but even now, after two centuries, when the best of Molière's plays are acted, mirth breaks out again and laughter overflows.

It would be doing Mark Twain a disservice to liken him to Molière, the greatest comic dramatist of all time; and yet there is more than one point of similarity. Just as Mark Twain began by writing comic copy which contained no prophecy of a masterpiece like *Huckleberry Finn*, so Molière was at first the author only of semiacrobatic farces on the Italian model in no wise presaging *Tartuffe* and *The Misanthrope*. Just as Molière succeeded first of all in pleasing the broad public that likes robust fun, and then slowly and step by step developed into a dramatist who set on the stage enduring figures plucked out of the abounding life about him, so also has Mark Twain grown, ascending from *The Jumping Frog* to *Huckleberry Finn*, as comic as its elder brother and as laughter-provoking, but charged also with meaning and with philosophy. And like Molière again, Mark Twain has kept solid hold of the material world; his doctrine is not of the earth earthy, but it is never sublimated into sentimentality. He sympathizes with the spiritual side of humanity, while never ignoring the sensual. Like Molière, Mark Twain takes his stand on common sense and thinks scorn of affectation of every sort. He understands sinners and strugglers and weaklings; and he is not harsh with them, reserving his scorching hatred for hypocrites and pretenders and frauds.

At how long an interval Mark Twain shall be rated after Molière and Cervantes it is for the future to declare. All that we can see clearly now is that it is with them that he is to be classed—with Molière and Cervantes, with Chaucer and Fielding, humorists all of them, and all of them manly men.

*Brander Matthews*

# INTRODUCTION

A NUMBER of articles in this volume, even the more important, have not heretofore appeared in print. Mark Twain was nearly always writing—busily trying to keep up with his imagination and enthusiasm: A good many of his literary undertakings remained unfinished or were held for further consideration, in time to be quite forgotten. Few of these papers were unimportant, and a fresh interest attaches to them to-day in the fact that they present some new detail of the author's devious wanderings, some new point of observation, some hitherto unexpressed angle of his indefatigable thought.

The present collection opens with a chapter from a book that was never written, a book about England, for which the author made some preparation, during his first visit to that country, in 1872. He filled several notebooks with brief comments, among which appears this single complete episode, the description of a visit to Westminster Abbey by night. As an example of what the book might have been we may be sorry that it went no farther.

It was not, however, quite in line with his proposed undertaking, which had been to write a more or less satirical book on English manners and customs. Arriving there, he found that he liked the people and their country too well for that, besides he was so busy entertaining, and being entertained, that he had little time for critical observation. In a letter home he wrote:

> I came here to take notes for a book, but I haven't done much but attend dinners and make speeches. I have had a jolly good time, and I do hate to go away from these English folks; they make a stranger feel entirely at home, and they laugh so easily that it is a comfort to make after-dinner speeches here.

England at this time gave Mark Twain an even fuller appreciation than he had thus far received in his own country. To hunt out and hold up to ridicule the foibles of hosts so hospitable would have been quite foreign to his nature. The notes he made had little satire in them, being mainly memoranda of the moment. . . .

"Down the Rhône," written some twenty years later, is a chapter from another book that failed of completion. Mark Twain, in Europe partly for his health, partly for financial reasons, had agreed to write six letters for the New York *Sun*, two of which —those from Aix and Marienbad—appear in this volume. Six letters would not make a book of sufficient size and he thought he might supplement them by making a drifting trip down the Rhône, the "river of angels," as Stevenson called it, and turning it into literature.

The trip itself proved to be one of the most delightful excursions of his life, and his account of it, so far as completed, has interest and charm. But he was alone, with only his boatman (the "Admiral") and his courier, Joseph Very, for company, a monotony of human material that was not inspiring. He

made some attempt to introduce fictitious characters, but presently gave up the idea. As a whole
the excursion was too drowsy and comfortable to
stir him to continuous effort; neither the notes nor
the article, attempted somewhat later, ever came to
conclusion.

Three articles in this volume, beginning with "To
the Person Sitting in Darkness," were published in
the *North American Review* during 1901-02, at a
period when Mark Twain had pretty well made up
his mind on most subjects, and especially concerning the interference of one nation with another on
matters of religion and government. He had
recently returned from a ten years' sojourn in Europe
and his opinion was eagerly sought on all public
questions, especially upon those of international
aspect. He was no longer regarded merely as a
humorist, but as a sort of Solon presiding over a
court of final conclusions. A writer in the *Evening
Mail* said of this later period:

> Things have reached the point where, if Mark Twain is not at
> a public meeting or banquet, he is expected to console it with one
> of his inimitable letters of advice and encouragement.

His old friend, W. D. Howells, expressed an
amused fear that Mark Twain's countrymen, who in
former years had expected him to be merely a
humorist, should now, in the light of his wider
acceptance abroad, demand that he be mainly
serious.

He was serious enough, and fiercely humorous as
well, in his article "To the Person Sitting in Dark-

ness" and in those which followed it. It seemed to him that the human race, always a doubtful quantity, was behaving even worse than usual. On New Year's Eve, 1900-01, he wrote:

## A GREETING FROM THE NINETEENTH TO THE TWENTIETH CENTURY

I bring you the stately nation named Christendom, returning, bedraggled, besmirched, and dishonored, from pirate raids in Kiao-Chau, Manchuria, South Africa, and the Philippines, with her soul full of meanness, her pocket full of boodle, and her mouth full of pious hypocracies. Give her soap and a towel, but hide the looking-glass.

Certain missionary activities in China, in particular, invited his attention, and in the first of the *Review* articles he unburdened himself. A masterpiece of pitiless exposition and sarcasm, its publication stirred up a cyclone. Periodicals more or less orthodox heaped upon him denunciation and vituperation. "To My Missionary Critics," published in the *Review* for April, was his answer. He did not fight alone, but was upheld by a vast following of liberal-minded readers, both in and out of the Church. Edward S. Martin wrote him:

How gratifying it is to feel that we have a man among us who understands the rarity of plain truth, and who delights to utter it, and has the gift of doing so without cant, and with not too much seriousness.

The principals of the primal human drama, our biblical parents of Eden, play a considerable part in Mark Twain's imaginative writings. He wrote "Diaries" of both Adam and Eve, that of the latter

# INTRODUCTION

being among his choicest works. He was generally planning something that would include one or both of the traditional ancestors, and results of this tendency express themselves in the present volume. Satan, likewise, the picturesque angel of rebellion and defeat, the Satan of *Paradise Lost*, made a strong appeal and in no less than three of the articles which follow the prince of error variously appears. For the most part these inventions offer an aspect of humor; but again the figure of the outcast angel is presented to us in an attitude of sorrowful kinship with the great human tragedy.

ALBERT BIGELOW PAINE.

EUROPE AND ELSEWHERE

# A MEMORABLE MIDNIGHT EXPERIENCE

(1872)

"COME along—and hurry. Few people have got originality enough to think of the expedition I have been planning, and still fewer could carry it out, maybe, even if they *did* think of it. Hurry, now. Cab at the door."

It was past eleven o'clock and I was just going to bed. But this friend of mine was as reliable as he was eccentric, and so there was not a doubt in my mind that his "expedition" had merit in it. I put on my coat and boots again, and we drove away.

"Where is it? Where are we going?"

"Don't worry. You'll see."

He was not inclined to talk. So I thought this must be a weighty matter. My curiosity grew with the minutes, but I kept it manfully under the surface. I watched the lamps, the signs, the numbers, as we thundered down the long streets, but it was of no use—I am always lost in London, day or night. It was very chilly—almost bleak. People leaned against the gusty blasts as if it were the dead of winter. The crowds grew thinner and thinner and the noises waxed faint and seemed far away. The sky was overcast and threatening. We drove on, and still on, till I wondered if we were ever going to stop. At last we passed by a spacious bridge and a vast building with a lighted clock tower, and presently entered a gateway, passed through a sort of tunnel, and stopped in a court surrounded by the black outlines of a great edifice. Then we alighted, walked a dozen steps or so, and waited. In a little while footsteps were heard and a man emerged from the darkness and we dropped into his wake without saying anything. He led us under an archway of masonry, and from that into a roomy tunnel, through a tall iron gate, which he locked behind us. We followed him down this tunnel, guided more by his footsteps on the stone flagging than by anything we could very distinctly see. At the end of it we came to another iron gate, and our conductor stopped there and lit a little bull's-eye lantern. Then he unlocked the gate—and I wished he had oiled it first, it grated so dismally. The gate swung open and we stood on the threshold of what seemed a limitless domed and pillared cavern carved out of the solid darkness. The conductor and my friend took off their hats reverently, and I did likewise. For the moment that we stood thus there was not a sound, and the silence seemed to add to the solemnity of the gloom. I *looked* my inquiry!

"It is the tomb of the great dead of England— *Westminster Abbey.*"

(One cannot express a start—in words.) Down among the columns—ever so far away, it seemed— a light revealed itself like a star, and a voice came echoing through the spacious emptiness:

"Who goes there!"

"Wright!"

2

# MEMORABLE MIDNIGHT EXPERIENCE

The star disappeared and the footsteps that accompanied it clanked out of hearing in the distance. Mr. Wright held up his lantern and the vague vastness took something of form to itself—the stately columns developed stronger outlines, and a dim pallor here and there marked the places of lofty windows. We were among the tombs; and on every hand dull shapes of men, sitting, standing, or stooping, inspected us curiously out of the darkness—reached out their hands toward us—some appealing, some beckoning, some warning us away. Effigies, they were—statues over the graves; but they looked human and natural in the murky shadows. Now a little half-grown black-and-white cat squeezed herself through the bars of the iron gate and came purring lovingly about us, unawed by the time or the place—unimpressed by the marble pomp that sepulchers a line of mighty dead that ends with a great author of yesterday and began with a sceptered monarch away back in the dawn of history more than twelve hundred years ago. And she followed us about and never left us while we pursued our work. We wandered hither and thither, uncovered, speaking in low voices, and stepping softly by instinct, for any little noise rang and echoed there in a way to make one shudder. Mr. Wright flashed his lantern first upon this object and then upon that, and kept up a running commentary that showed that there was nothing about the venerable Abbey that was trivial in his eyes or void of interest. He is a man in authority—being superintendent of the works—and his daily business keeps him familiar

3

with every nook and corner of the great pile. Casting a luminous ray now here, now yonder, he would say:

"Observe the height of the Abbey—one hundred and three feet to the base of the roof—I measured it myself the other day. Notice the base of this column—old, very old—hundreds and hundreds of years; and how well they knew how to build in those old days. Notice it—every stone is laid horizontally—that is to say, just as nature laid it originally in the quarry—not set up edgewise; in our day some people set them on edge, and then wonder why they split and flake. Architects cannot teach nature anything. Let me remove this matting—it is put there to preserve the pavement; now, there is a bit of pavement that is seven hundred years old; you can see by these scattering clusters of colored mosaics how beautiful it was before time and sacrilegious idlers marred it. Now there, in the border, was an inscription once; see, follow the circle—you can trace it by the ornaments that have been pulled out—here is an A, and there is an O, and yonder another A—all beautiful old English capitals—there is no telling what the inscription was—no record left, now. Now move along in this direction, if you please. Yonder is where old King Sebert the Saxon, lies—his monument is the oldest one in the Abbey; Sebert died in 616, and that's as much as twelve hundred and fifty years ago—think of it!—twelve hundred and fifty years. Now yonder is the last one—Charles Dickens—there on the floor with the brass letters on the slab—and to this day

4

the people come and put flowers on it. Why, along
at first they almost had to *cart* the flowers out, there
were so many. Could not *leave* them there, you
know, because it's where everybody walks—and
a body wouldn't want them trampled on, anyway.
All this place about here, now, is the Poet's
Corner. There is Garrick's monument, and Addi-
son's, and Thackeray's bust—and Macaulay lies
there. And here, close to Dickens and Garrick, lie
Sheridan and Doctor Johnson—and here is old Parr
—Thomas Parr—you can read the inscription:

> "Tho: Par of Y Covnty of Sallop Borne A :1483. He
> Lived in Y Reignes of Ten Princes, viz: K. Edw. 4
> K. Ed. 5. K. Rich 3. K. Hen. 7. K. Hen. 8. Edw. 6. QVV. Ma.
> Q. Eliz. K. IA. and K. Charles, Aged 152 Yeares, And
> Was Buryed Here Novemb. 15. 1635.

"Very old man indeed, and saw a deal of life.
(Come off the grave, Kitty, poor thing; she keeps
the rats away from the office, and there's no harm
in her—her and her mother.) And here—this is
Shakespeare's statue—leaning on his elbow and
pointing with his finger at the lines on the scroll:

> "The cloud-capt towers, the gorgeous palaces,
> The solemn temples, the great globe itself,
> Yea, all which it inherit shall dissolve,
> And, like the baseless fabric of a vision,
> Leave not a wrack behind.

"That stone there covers Campbell the poet.
Here are names you know pretty well—Milton, and
Gray who wrote the 'Elegy,' and Butler who wrote
'Hudibras,' and Edmund Spencer, and Ben Jonson—
there are three tablets to him scattered about the

5

Abbey, and all got 'O Rare Ben Jonson' cut on them—you were standing on one of them just now—he is buried standing up. There used to be a tradition here that explains it. The story goes that he did not dare ask to be buried in the Abbey, so he asked King James if he would make him a present of eighteen inches of English ground, and the king said yes, and asked him where he would have it, and he said in Westminster Abbey. Well, the king wouldn't go back on his word, and so there he is sure enough—stood up on end. Years ago, in Dean Buckland's time—before my day—they were digging a grave close to Jonson and they uncovered him and his head fell off. Toward night the clerk of the works hid the head to keep it from being stolen, as the ground was to remain open till next day. Presently the dean's son came along and he found a head, and hid it away for Jonson's. And by and by along comes a stranger, and *he* found a head, too, and walked off with it under his cloak, and a month or so afterward he was heard to boast that he had Ben Jonson's head. Then there was a deal of correspondence about it, in the *Times*, and everybody distressed. But Mr. Frank Buckland came out and comforted everybody by telling how he saved the true head, and so the stranger must have got one that wasn't of any consequence. And then up speaks the clerk of the works and tells how *he* saved the right head, and so *Dean Buckland* must have got a wrong one. Well, it was all settled satisfactorily at last, because the clerk of the works *proved* his head. And then I believe they got that head from the

6

stranger—so now we have three. But it shows you what regiments of people you are walking over—been collecting here for twelve hundred years—in some places, no doubt, the bones are fairly matted together.

"And here are some unfortunates. Under this place lies Anne, queen of Richard III, and daughter of the Kingmaker, the great Earl of Warwick—murdered she was—poisoned by her husband. And here is a slab which you see has once had the figure of a man in armor on it, in brass or copper, let into the stone. You can see the shape of it—but it is all worn away now by people's feet; the man has been dead five hundred years that lies under it. He was a knight in Richard II's time. His enemies pressed him close and he fled and took sanctuary here in the Abbey. Generally a man was safe when he took sanctuary in those days, but this man was not. The captain of the Tower and a band of men pursued him and his friends and they had a bloody fight here on this floor; but this poor fellow did not stand much of a chance, and they butchered him right before the altar."

We wandered over to another part of the Abbey, and came to a place where the pavement was being repaired. Every paving stone has an inscription on it and covers a grave. Mr. Wright continued:

"Now, you are standing on William Pitt's grave —you can read the name, though it is a good deal worn—and you, sir, are standing on the grave of Charles James Fox. I found a very good place here the other day—nobody suspected it—been curiously overlooked, somehow—but—it is a very nice place indeed, and very comfortable" (holding his bull's eye to the pavement and searching around). "Ah, here it is—this is the stone—nothing under here— nothing at all—a very nice place indeed—and very comfortable."

Mr. Wright spoke in a professional way, of course, and after the manner of a man who takes an interest in his business and is gratified at any piece of good luck that fortune favors him with; and yet will all that silence and gloom and solemnity about me, there was something about his idea of a nice, comfortable place that made the cold chills creep up my back. Presently we began to come upon little chamberlike chapels, with solemn figures ranged around the sides, lying apparently asleep, in sumptuous marble beds, with their hands placed together above their breasts—the figures and all their surroundings black with age. Some were dukes and earls, some where kings and queens, some were ancient abbots whose effigies had lain there so many centuries and suffered such disfigurement that their faces were almost as smooth and featureless as the stony pillows their heads reposed upon. At one time while I stood looking at a distant part of the pavement, admiring the delicate tracery which the now flooding moonlight was casting upon it through a lofty window, the party moved on and I lost them. The first step I made in the dark, holding my hands before me, as one does under such circumstances, I touched a cold object, and stopped to feel its shape. I made out a thumb, and then delicate fingers. It was the clasped, appealing hands of one of those reposing images—a lady, a queen. I touched the face—by accident, not design—and shuddered inwardly, if not outwardly; and then something rubbed against my leg, and I shuddered outwardly and inwardly both. It was the cat. The friendly creature meant well, but, as the English say, she gave me "such a turn." I took her in my arms for company and wandered among the grim sleepers till I caught the glimmer of the lantern again. Presently, in a little chapel, we were looking at the sarcophagus, let into the wall, which contains the bones of the infant princes who were smothered in the Tower. Behind us was the stately monument of Queen Elizabeth, with her effigy dressed in the royal robes, lying as if at rest. When we turned around, the cat, with stupendous simplicity, was coiled up and sound asleep upon the feet of the Great Queen! Truly this was reaching far toward the millennium when the lion and the lamb shall lie down together. The murderer of Mary and Essex, the conqueror of the Armada, the imperious ruler of a turbulent empire, become a couch, at last, for a tired kitten! It was the most eloquent sermon upon the vanity of human pride and human grandeur that inspired Westminster preached to us that night.

We would have turned puss out of the Abbey, but for the fact that her small body made light of railed gates and she would have come straight back again. We walked up a flight of half a dozen steps and, stopping upon a pavement laid down in 1260, stood in the core of English history, as it were—upon the

holiest ground in the British Empire, if profusion of
kingly bones and kingly names of old renown make
holy ground. For here in this little space were the
ashes, the monuments and gilded effigies, of ten of
the most illustrious personages who have worn
crowns and borne scepters in this realm. This
royal dust was the slow accumulation of hundreds of
years. The latest comer entered into his rest four
hundred years ago, and since the earliest was sep-
ulchered, more than eight centuries have drifted by.
Edward the Confessor, Henry the Fifth, Edward the
First, Edward the Third, Richard the Second, Henry
the Third, Eleanor, Philippa, Margaret Woodville—
it was like bringing the collossal myths of history
out of the forgotten ages and speaking to them face
to face. The gilded effigies were scarcely marred—
the faces were comely and majestic, old Edward the
First looked the king—one had no impulse to be
familiar with him. While we were contemplating the figure of Queen Eleanor lying in state, and
calling to mind how like an ordinary human being
the great king mourned for her six hundred years
ago, we saw the vast illuminated clock face of the
Parliament House tower glowering at us through a
window of the Abbey and pointing with both hands to
midnight. It was a derisive reminder that we were a
part of this present sordid, plodding, commonplace
time, and not august relics of a bygone age and the
comrades of kings—and then the booming of the
great bell tolled twelve, and with the last stroke
the mocking clock face vanished in sudden darkness
and left us with the past and its grandeurs again.

We descended, and entered the nave of the splendid Chapel of Henry VII. Mr. Wright said:

"Here is where the order of knighthood was conferred for centuries; the candidates sat in these seats; these brasses bear their coats of arms; these are their banners overhead, torn and dusty, poor old things, for they have hung there many and many a long year. In the floor you see inscriptions—kings and queens that lie in the vault below. When this vault was opened in our time they found them lying there in beautiful order—all quiet and comfortable—the red velvet on the coffins hardly faded any. And the bodies were sound—I saw them myself. They were embalmed, and looked natural, although they had been there such an awful time. Now in this place here, which is called the chantry, is a curious old group of statuary—the figures are mourning over George Villiers, Duke of Buckingham, who was assassinated by Felton in Charles I's time. Yonder, Cromwell and his family used to lie. Now we come to the south aisle and this is the grand monument to Mary Queen of Scots, and her effigy—you easily see they get all the portraits from this effigy. Here in the wall of the aisle is a bit of a curiosity pretty roughly carved:

Wm. WEST TOOME

SHOWER

1698

"William West, tomb shower, 1698. That fellow carved his name around in several places about the Abbey."

This was a sort of revelation to me. I had been wandering through the Abbey, never imagining but that its shows were created only for us—the people of the nineteenth century. But here is a man (become a show himself now, and a curiosity) to whom all these things were sights and wonders a hundred and seventy-five years ago. When curious idlers from the country and from foreign lands came here to look, he showed them old Sebert's tomb and those of the other old worthies I have been speaking of, and called them ancient and venerable; and he showed them Charles II's tomb as the newest and latest novelty he had; and he was doubtless present at the funeral. Three hundred years before his time some ancestor of his, perchance, used to point out the ancient marvels, in the immemorial way and then say: "This, gentlemen, is the tomb of his late Majesty Edward the Third—and I wish I could see him alive and hearty again, as I saw him twenty years ago; yonder is the tomb of Sebert the Saxon king—he has been lying there well on to eight hundred years, they say. And three hundred years before *this* party, Westminster was still a show, and Edward the Confessor's grave was a novelty of some thirty years' standing—but old "Sebert" was hoary and ancient still, and people who spoke of Alfred the Great as a comparatively recent man pondered over Sebert's grave and tried to take in all the tremendous meaning of it when the "toome shower" said, "This man has lain here well nigh five hundred years." It does seem as if all the generations that have lived and died since the world was

created have visited Westminster to stare and wonder
—and still found ancient things there. And some
day a curiously clad company may arrive here in a
balloon ship from some remote corner of the globe,
and as they follow the verger among the monuments
they may hear him say: "This is the tomb of Victoria the Good Queen; battered and uncouth as it
looks, it once was a wonder of magnificence—but
twelve hundred years work a deal of damage to these
things."

As we turned toward the door the moonlight was
beaming in at the windows, and it gave to the
sacred place such an air of restfulness and peace
that Westminster was no longer a grisly museum of
moldering vanities, but her better and worthier self
—the deathless mentor of a great nation, the guide
and encourager of right ambitions, the preserver of
just fame, and the home and refuge for the nation's
best and bravest when their work is done.

# TWO MARK TWAIN EDITORIALS

(Written 1869 and 1870, for the Buffalo *Express*, of which Mark Twain became editor and part owner)

I

## "SALUTATORY"

BEING a stranger, it would be immodest and unbecoming in me to suddenly and violently assume the associate editorship of the *Buffalo Express* without a single explanatory word of comfort or encouragement to the unoffending patrons of the paper, who are about to be exposed to constant attacks of my wisdom and learning. But this explanatory word shall be as brief as possible. I only wish to assure parties having a friendly interest in the prosperity of the journal, that I am not going to hurt the paper deliberately and intentionally at any time. I am not going to introduce any startling reforms, or in any way attempt to make trouble. I am simply going to do my plain, unpretending duty, when I cannot get out of it; I shall work diligently and honestly and faithfully at all times and upon all occasions, when privation and want shall compel me to do it; in writing, I shall always confine myself strictly to the truth, except when it is attended with inconvenience; I shall witheringly rebuke all forms of crime and misconduct, except when com-

14

mitted by the party inhabiting my own vest; I shall not make use of slang or vulgarity upon any occasion or under any circumstances, and shall never use profanity except in discussing house rent and taxes. Indeed, upon second thought, I will not even use it then, for it is unchristian, inelegant, and degrading —though to speak truly I do not see how house rent and taxes are going to be discussed worth a cent without it. I shall not often meddle with politics, because we have a political editor who is already excellent, and only needs to serve a term in the penitentiary in order to be perfect. I shall not write any poetry, unless I conceive a spite against the subscribers.

Such is my platform. I do not see any earthly use in it, but custom is law, and custom must be obeyed, no matter how much violence it may do to one's feelings. And this custom which I am slavishly following now is surely one of the least necessary that ever came into vogue. In private life a man does not go and trumpet his crime before he commits it, but your new editor is such an important personage that he feels called upon to write a "salutatory" at once, and he puts into it all that he knows, and all that he don't know, and some things he thinks he knows but isn't certain of. And he parades his list of wonders which he is going to perform; of reforms which he is going to introduce, and public evils which he is going to exterminate; and public blessings which he is going to create; and public nuisances which he is going to abate. He spreads this all out with oppressive solemnity over a column and a half of large print, and feels that the country is saved. His satisfaction over it, something enormous. He then settles down to his miracles and inflicts profound platitudes and impenetrable wisdom upon a helpless public as long as they can stand it, and then they send him off consul to some savage island in the Pacific in the vague hope that the cannibals will like him well enough to eat him. And with an inhumanity which is but a fitting climax to his career of persecution, instead of packing his trunk at once he lingers to inflict upon his benefactors a "valedictory." If there is anything more uncalled for than a "salutatory," it is one of those tearful, blubbering, long-winded "valedictories"—wherein a man who has been annoying the public for ten years cannot take leave of them without sitting down to cry a column and a half. Still, it is the custom to write valedictories, and custom should be respected. In my secret heart I admire my predecessor for declining to print a valedictory, though in public I say and shall continue to say sternly, it is custom and he ought to have printed one. People never read them any more than they do the "salutatories," but nevertheless he ought to have honored the old fossil—he ought to have printed a valedictory. I said as much to him, and he replied:

"I have resigned my place—I have departed this life—I am journalistically dead, at present, ain't I?"

"Yes."

"Well, wouldn't you consider it disgraceful in a corpse to sit up and comment on the funeral?"

I record it here, and preserve it from oblivion, as

the briefest and best "valedictory" that has yet come under my notice.     MARK TWAIN.

P. S.—I am grateful for the kindly way in which the press of the land have taken notice of my irruption into regular journalistic life, telegraphically or editorially, and am happy in this place to express the feeling.

## II

### A TRIBUTE TO ANSON BURLINGAME
(February, 1870)

ON Wednesday, in St. Petersburg, Mr. Burlingame died after a short illness. It is not easy to comprehend, at an instant's warning, the exceeding magnitude of the loss which mankind sustains in this death—the loss which all nations and all peoples sustain in it. For he had outgrown the narrow citizenship of a state and become a citizen of the world; and his charity was large enough and his great heart warm enough to feel for all its races and to labor for them. He was a true man, a brave man, an earnest man, a liberal man, a just man, a generous man, in all his ways and by all his instincts a noble man; he was a man of education and culture, a finished conversationalist, a ready, able, and graceful speaker, a man of great brain, a broad and deep and weighty thinker. He was a great man—a very, very great man. He was imperially endowed by nature; he was faithfully befriended by circumstances, and he wrought gallantly always, in whatever station he found himself.

He was a large, handsome man, with such a face as children instinctively trust in, and homeless and friendless creatures appeal to without fear. He was courteous at all times and to all people, and he had the rare and winning faculty of being always *interested* in whatever a man had to say—a faculty which he possessed simply because nothing was trivial to him which any man or woman or child had at heart. When others said harsh things about even unconscionable and intrusive bores after they had retired from his presence, Mr. Burlingame often said a generous word in their favor, but never an unkind one.

A chivalrous generosity was his most marked characteristic—a large charity, a noble kindliness that could not comprehend narrowness or meanness. It is this that shows out in his fervent abolitionism, manifested at a time when it was neither very creditable nor very safe to hold such a creed; it was this that prompted him to hurl his famous Brooks-and-Sumner speech in the face of an astonished South at a time when all the North was smarting under the sneers and taunts and material aggressions of admired and applauded Southerners. It was this that made him so warmly espouse the cause of Italian liberty—an espousal so pointed and so vigorous as to attract the attention of Austria, which empire afterward declined to receive him when he was appointed Austrian envoy by Mr. Lincoln. It was this trait which prompted him to punish Americans in China when they imposed upon the Chinese. It was this trait which moved him, in framing treaties, to frame them in the broad interest of the world, instead of selfishly seeking to acquire advantages for his own country alone and at the expense of the other party to the treaty, as had always before been the recognized "diplomacy." It was this trait which was and is the soul of the crowning achievements of his career, the treaties with America and England in behalf of China. In every labor of this man's life there was present a good and noble motive; and in nothing that he ever did or said was there anything small or base. In real greatness, ability, grandeur of character, and achievement, he stood head and shoulders above all the Americans of to-day, save one or two.

Without any noise, or any show, or any flourish, Mr. Burlingame did a score of things of shining mark during his official residence in China. They were hardly heard of away here in America. When he first went to China, he found that with all their kingly powers, American envoys were still not of much consequence in the eyes of their countrymen of either civil or official position. But he was a man who was always "posted." He knew all about the state of things he would find in China before he sailed from America. And so he took care to demand and receive additional powers before he turned his back upon Washington. When the customary consular irregularities placidly continued and he notified those officials that such irregularities must instantly cease, and they inquired with insolent flippancy what the consequence might be in case they did not cease, he answered blandly that he would *dismiss* them, from the highest to the lowest!

(He had quietly come armed with absolute authority
over their official lives.) The consular irregularities ceased. A far healthier condition of American commercial interests ensued there.

To punish a foreigner in China was an unheard-of
thing. There was no way of accomplishing it. Each
Embassy had its own private district or grounds,
forced from the imperial government, and into that
sacred district Chinese law officers could not in-
trude. All foreigners guilty of offenses against
Chinamen were tried by their own countrymen, in
these holy places, and as no Chinese testimony was
admitted, the culprit almost always went free. One
of the very first things Mr. Burlingame did was
to make a Chinaman's oath as good as a foreigner's;
and in his ministerial court, through Chinese and
American testimony combined, he very shortly
convicted a noted American ruffian of murdering a
Chinaman. And now a community accustomed to
light sentences were naturally startled when, under
Mr. Burlingame's hand, and bearing the broad seal
of the American Embassy, came an order to take
him out and hang him!

Mr. Burlingame broke up the "extra-territorial"
privileges (as they were called), as far as our country
was concerned, and made justice as free to all and
as untrammeled in the metes and bounds of its jurisdiction, in China, as ever it was in any land.

Mr. Burlingame was the leading spirit in the co-
operative policy. He got the Imperial College established. He procured permission for an American
to open the coal mines of China. Through his efforts

China was the first country to close her ports against the war vessels of the Southern Confederacy; and Prince Kung's order, in this matter, was singularly energetic, comprehensive, and in earnest. The ports were closed then, and never opened to a Southern warship afterward.

Mr. Burlingame "construed" the treaties existing between China and the other nations. For many years the ablest diplomatists had vainly tried to come to a satisfactory understanding of certain obscure clauses of these treaties, and more than once powder had been burned in consequences of failure to come to such understandings. But the clear and comprehensive intellect of the American envoy reduced the wordy tangle of diplomatic phrases to a plain and honest handful of paragraphs, and these were unanimously and thankfully accepted by the other foreign envoys, and officially declared by them to be a thorough and satisfactory elucidation of all the uncertain clauses in the treaties.

Mr. Burlingame did a mighty work, and made official intercourse with China lucid, simple, and systematic, thenceforth for all time, when he persuaded that government to adopt and accept the code of international law by which the civilized nations of the earth are guided and controlled.

It is not possible to specify all the acts by which Mr. Burlingame made himself largely useful to the world during his official residence in China. At least it would not be possible to do it without making this sketch too lengthy and pretentious for a newspaper article.

Mr. Burlingame's short history—for he was only forty-seven—reads like a fairy tale. Its successes, its surprises, its happy situations, occur all along, and each new episode is always an improvement upon the one which went before it.

He begins life an assistant in a surveying party away out on the Western frontier; then enters a branch of a Western college; then passes through Harvard with the honors; becomes a Boston lawyer and looks back complacently from his high perch upon the old days when he was a surveyor nobody in the woods; becomes a state senator, and makes laws; still advancing, goes to the Constitutional Convention and makes regulations wherewith to rule the makers of laws; enters Congress and smiles back upon the Legislature and the Boston lawyer, and from these smiles still back upon the country surveyor, recognizes that he is known to fame in Massachusetts; challenges Brooks and is known to the nation; next, with a long stride upward, he is clothed with ministerial dignity and journeys to the under side of the world to represent the youngest in the court of the oldest of the nations; and finally, after years go by, we see him moving serenely among the crowned heads of the Old World, a magnate with secretaries and undersecretaries about him, a retinue of quaint, outlandish Orientals in his wake, and a long following of servants—and the world is aware that his salary is unbelievably enormous, not to say imperial, and likewise knows that he is invested with power to make treaties with all the chief nations of the earth, and that he bears the stately title of Ambassador, and in his person represents the mysterious and awful grandeur of that vague colossus, the Emperor of China, his mighty empire and his four hundred millions of subjects! Down what a dreamy vista his backward glance must stretch, now, to reach the insignificant surveyor in the Western woods!

He was a good man, and a very, very great man. America lost a son, and all the world a servant. when he died.

# THE TEMPERANCE CRUSADE AND
# WOMAN'S RIGHTS

## (1873)

THE women's crusade against the rum sellers continues. It began in an Ohio village early in the new year, and has now extended itself eastwardly to the Atlantic seaboard, 600 miles, and westwardly (at a bound, without stopping by the way,) to San Francisco, about 2,500 miles. It has also scattered itself along down the Ohio and Mississippi rivers southwardly some ten or twelve hundred miles. Indeed, it promises to sweep, eventually, the whole United States, with the exception of the little cluster of commonwealths which we call New England. Puritan New England is sedate, reflective, conservative, and very hard to inflame.

The method of the crusaders is singular. They contemn the use of force in the breaking up of the whisky traffic. They only assemble before a drinking shop, or within it, and sing hymns and pray, hour after hour—and day after day, if necessary— until the publican's business is broken up and he surrenders. This is not force, at least they do not consider it so. After the surrender the crusaders march back to headquarters and proclaim the victory, and ascribe it to the powers above. They rejoice together awhile, and then go forth again in their strength and conquer another whisky shop with their prayers and hymns and their staying capacity (pardon the rudeness), and spread *that* victory upon the battle flag of the powers above. In this generous way the crusaders have parted with the credit of not less than three thousand splendid triumphs, which some carping people say they gained their own selves, without assistance from any quarter. If I am one of these, I am the humblest. If I seem to doubt that prayer is the agent that conquers these rum sellers, I do it honestly, and not in a flippant spirit. If the crusaders were to stay at home and pray for the rum seller and for his adoption of a better way of life, or if the crusaders even assembled together in a church and offered up such a prayer with a united voice, and it accomplished a victory, I would then feel that it was the praying that moved Heaven to do the miracle; for I believe that if the prayer is the agent that brings about the desired result, it cannot be necessary to pray the prayer in any particular place in order to get the ear, or move the grace, of the Deity. When the crusaders go and invest a whisky shop and fall to praying, one suspects that they are praying rather less to the Deity than *at* the rum man. So I cannot help feeling (after carefully reading the details of the rum sieges) that as much as nine tenths of the credit of each of the 3,000 victories achieved thus far belongs of right to the crusaders themselves, and it grieves me to see them give it away with such spendthrift generosity.

I will not afflict you with statistics, but I desire to say just a word or two about the character of this

crusade. The crusaders are young girls and women
—not the inferior sort, but the very best in the village
communities. The telegraph keeps the newspapers
supplied with the progress of the war, and thus the
praying infection spreads from town to town, day
after day, week after week. When it attacks a
community it seems to seize upon almost everybody in it at once. There is a meeting in a church,
speeches are made, resolutions are passed, a purse
for expenses is made up, a "praying band" is appointed; if it be a large town, half a dozen praying
bands, each numbering as many as a hundred women,
are appointed, and the working district of each band
marked out. Then comes a grand assault in force, all
along the line. Every stronghold of rum is invested;
first one and then another champion ranges up before
the proprietor and offers up a special petition for
him; he has to stand meekly there behind his bar,
under the eyes of a great concourse of ladies who are
better than he is and are aware of it, and hear all the
secret iniquities of his business divulged to the angels
above, accompanied by the sharp sting of wishes for
his regeneration, which imply an amount of need for
it which is in the last degree uncomfortable to him.
If he holds out bravely, the crusaders hold out more
bravely still—or at least more persistently; though
I doubt if the grandeur of the performance would
not be considerably heightened if one solitary
crusader were to try praying at a hundred rum
sellers in a body for a while, and see how it felt to
have everybody against her instead of for her. If
the man holds out the crusaders camp before his

place and keep up the siege till they wear him out. In one case they besieged a rum shop two whole weeks. They built a shed before it and kept up the praying all night and all day long every day of the fortnight, and this in the bitterest winter weather, too. They conquered.

You may ask if such an investment and such interference with a man's business (in cases where he is "protected" by a license) is lawful? By no means. But the whole community being with the crusaders, the authorities have usually been overawed and afraid to execute the laws, the authorities being, in too many cases, mere little politicians, and more given to looking to chances of re-election than fearlessly discharging their duty according to the terms of their official oaths.

Would you consider the conduct of these crusaders justifiable? I do—thoroughly justifiable. They find themselves voiceless in the making of laws and the election of officers to execute them. Born with brains, born in the country, educated, having large interests at stake, they find their tongues tied and their hands fettered, while every ignorant whisky-drinking foreign-born savage in the land may hold office, help to make the laws, degrade the dignity of the former and break the latter at his own sweet will. They see their fathers, husbands, and brothers sit inanely at home and allow the scum of the country to assemble at the "primaries," name the candidates for office from their own vile ranks, and, unrebuked, elect them. They live in the midst of a country where there is no end to the laws and no beginning to the execution of them. And when the laws intended to protect their sons from destruction by intemperance lie torpid and without sign of life year after year, they recognize that here is a matter which interests them personally—a matter which comes straight home to them. And since they are allowed to lift no legal voice against the outrageous state of things they suffer under in this regard, I think it is no wonder that their patience has broken down at last, and they have contrived to persuade themselves that they are justifiable in breaking the law of trespass when the laws that should make the trespass needless are allowed by the voters to lie dead and inoperative.

I cannot help glorying in the pluck of these women, sad as it is to see them displaying themselves in these unwomanly ways; sad as it is to see them carrying their grace and their purity into places which should never know their presence; and sadder still as it is to see them trying to save a set of men who, it seems to me, there can be no reasonable object in saving. It does not become us to scoff at the crusaders, remembering what it is they have borne all these years, but it does become us to admire their heroism—a heroism that boldly faces jeers, curses, ribald language, obloquy of every kind and degree—in a word, every manner of thing that pure-hearted, pure-minded women such as these are naturally dread and shrink from, and remains steadfast through it all, undismayed, patient, hopeful, giving no quarter, asking none, determined to conquer and succeeding. It is the same old superb spirit that animated that other devoted, magnificent, mistaken crusade of six hundred years ago. The sons of such women as these must surely be worth saving from the destroying power of rum.

The present crusade will doubtless do but little work against intemperance that will be really permanent, but it will do what is as much, or even more, to the purpose, I think. I think it will suggest to more than one man that if women could vote they would vote on the side of morality, even if they did vote and speak rather frantically and furiously; and it will also suggest that when the women once made up their minds that it was not good to leave the all-powerful "primaries" in the hands of loafers, thieves, and pernicious little politicians, they would not sit indolently at home as their husbands and brothers do now, but would hoist their praying banners, take the field in force, pray the assembled political scum back to the holes and slums where they belong, and set up some candidates fit for decent human beings to vote for.

I dearly want the women to be raised to the political altitude of the negro, the imported savage, and the pardoned thief, and allowed to vote. It is our last chance, I think. The women will be voting before long, and then if a B. F. Butler can still continue to lord it in Congress; if the highest offices in the land can still continue to be occupied by perjurers and robbers; if another Congress (like the forty-second) consisting of 15 honest men and 296 of the other kind can once more be created, it will at

last be time, I fear, to give over trying to save the
country by human means, and appeal to Providence.
Both the great parties have failed. I wish we might
have a woman's party now, and see how that would
work. I feel persuaded that in extending the suffrage
to women this country could lose absolutely nothing
and might gain a great deal. For thirty centuries
history has been iterating and reiterating that in a
moral fight woman is simply dauntless, and we all
know, even with our eyes shut upon Congress and
our voters, that from the day that Adam ate of the
apple and told on Eve down to the present day,
man, in a moral fight, has pretty uniformly shown
himself to be an arrant coward.

I will mention casually that while I cannot bring
myself to find fault with the women whom we call
the crusaders, since I feel that they, being politically
fettered, have the natural right of the oppressed to
rebel, I have a very different opinion about the
clergymen who have in a multitude of instances
attached themselves to the movement, and by voice
and act have countenanced and upheld the women
in unlawfully trespassing upon whisky mills and
interrupting the rum sellers' business. It seems to
me that it would better become clergymen to teach
their flocks to respect the laws of the land, and urge
them to refrain from breaking them. But it is not
a new thing for a thoroughly good and well-meaning
preacher's soft heart to run away with his soft head.

# O'SHAH

(A series of news letters describing a visit to England by the Shah of Persia)

## I

### THE ARRIVAL IN ENGLAND

LONDON, *June 18, 1873.*

"WOULD you like to go over to Belgium and help bring the Shah to England?"

I said I was willing.

"Very well, then; here is an order from the Admiralty which will admit you on board Her Majesty's ship *Lively*, now lying at Ostend, and you can return in her day after to-morrow."

That was all. That was the end of it. Without stopping to think, I had in a manner taken upon myself to bring the Shah of Persia to England. I could not otherwise regard the conversation I had just held with the London representative of the New York *Herald*. The amount of discomfort I endured for the next two or three hours cannot be set down in words. I could not eat, sleep, talk, smoke with any satisfaction. The more I thought the thing over the more oppressed I felt. What was the Shah to me, that I should go to all this worry and trouble on his account? Where was there the least occasion for taking upon myself such a responsibility? If I got him over all right, well. But if I lost him? if he died

31

on my hands? if he got drowned? It was depressing, any way I looked at it. In the end I said to myself, "If I get this Shah over here safe and sound I never will take charge of another one." And yet, at the same time I kept thinking: "This country has treated me well, stranger as I am, and this foreigner is the country's guest—that is enough, I will help him out; I will fetch him over; I will land him in London, and say to the British people, 'Here is your Shah; give me a receipt.'"

I felt easy in my mind now, and was about to go to bed, but something occurred to me. I took a cab and drove downtown and routed out that *Herald* representative.

"Where is Belgium?" said I.

"Where is Belgium? I never heard such a question!"

"That doesn't make any difference to me. If I have got to fetch this Shah I don't wish to go to the wrong place. Where is Belgium? Is it a shilling fare in a cab?"

He explained that it was in foreign parts—the first place I have heard of lately which a body could not go to in a cab for a shilling.

I said I could not go alone, because I could not speak foreign languages well, could not get up in time for the early train without help, and could not find my way. I said it was enough to have the Shah on my hands; I did not wish to have everything piled on me. Mr. Blank was then ordered to go with me. I do like to have somebody along to talk to when I go abroad.

32

When I got home I sat down and thought the thing all over. I wanted to go into this enterprise understandingly. What was the main thing? That was the question. A little reflection informed me. For two weeks the London papers had sung just one continual song to just one continual tune, and the idea of it all was "how to impress the Shah." These papers had told all about the St. Petersburg splendors, and had said at the end that splendors would no longer answer; that England could not outdo Russia in that respect; therefore some other way of impressing the Shah must be contrived. And these papers had also told all about the Shahstic reception in Prussia and its attendant military pageantry. England could not improve on that sort of thing— she could not impress the Shah with soldiers; something else must be tried. And so on. Column after column, page after page of agony about how to "impress the Shah." At last they had hit upon a happy idea—a grand naval exhibition. That was it! A man brought up in Oriental seclusion and simplicity, a man who had never seen anything but camels and such things, could not help being surprised and delighted with the strange novelty of ships. The distress was at an end. England heaved a great sigh of relief; she knew at last how to impress the Shah.

My course was very plain, now, after that bit of reflection. All I had to do was to go over to Belgium and impress the Shah. I failed to form any definite plan as to the process, but I made up my mind to manage it somehow. I said to myself, "I will impress this Shah or there shall be a funeral that will be worth contemplating."

I went to bed then, but did not sleep a great deal, for the responsibilities were weighing pretty heavily upon me. At six o'clock in the morning Mr. Blank came and turned me out. I was surprised at this, and not gratified, for I detest early rising. I never like to say severe things, but I was a good deal tried this time. I said I did not mind getting up moderately early, but I hated to be called day before yesterday. However, as I was acting in a national capacity and for a country that I liked, I stopped grumbling and we set out. A grand naval review is a good thing to impress a Shah with, but if he would try getting up at six o'clock in the morning—but no matter; we started.

We took the Dover train and went whistling along over the housetops at the rate of fifty miles an hour, and just as smoothly and pleasantly, too, as if we were in a sleigh. One never can have anything but a very vague idea of what speed is until he travels over an English railway. Our "lightning" expresses are sleepy and indolent by comparison. We looked into the back windows of the endless ranks of houses abreast and below us, and saw many a homelike little family of early birds sitting at their breakfasts. New views and new aspects of London were about me; the mighty city seemed to spread farther and wider in the clear morning air than it had ever done before. There is something awe-inspiring about the mere look of the figures that express the population of London when one comes to set them down in a good

34

large hand—4,000,000! It takes a body's breath away, almost.

We presently left the city behind. We had started drowsy, but we did not stay so. How could we, with the brilliant sunshine pouring down, the balmy wind blowing through the open windows, and the Garden of Eden spread all abroad? We swept along through rolling expanses of growing grain—not a stone or a stump to mar their comeliness, not an unsightly fence or an ill-kept hedge; through broad meadows covered with fresh green grass as clean swept as if a broom had been at work there—little brooks wandering up and down them, noble trees here and there, cows in the shade, groves in the distance and church spires projecting out of them; and there were the quaintest old-fashioned houses set in the midst of smooth lawns or partly hiding themselves among fine old forest trees; and there was one steep-roofed ancient cottage whose walls all around, and whose roof, and whose chimneys, were clothed in a shining mail of ivy leaves!—so thoroughly, indeed, that only one little patch of roof was visible to prove that the house was not a mere house of leaves, with glass windows in it. Imagine those dainty little homes surrounded by flowering shrubs and bright green grass and all sorts of old trees—and then go on and try to imagine something more bewitching.

By and by we passed Rochester, and, sure enough, right there, on the highest ground in the town and rising imposingly up from among clustering roofs, was the gray old castle—roofless, ruined, ragged, the sky beyond showing clear and blue through the glassless windows, the walls partly clad with ivy—a time-scarred, weather-beaten old pile, but ever so picturesque and ever so majestic, too. There it was, a whole book of English history. I had read of Rochester Castle a thousand times, but I had never really believed there was any such building before.

Presently we reached the sea and came to a stand far out on a pier; and here was Dover and more history. The chalk cliffs of England towered up from the shore and the French coast was visible. On the tallest hill sat Dover Castle, stately and spacious and superb, looking just as it has always looked any time these ten or fifteen thousand years— I do not know its exact age, and it does not matter, anyway.

We stepped aboard the little packet and steamed away. The sea was perfectly smooth, and painfully brilliant in the sunshine. There were no curiosities in the vessel except the passengers and a placard in French setting forth the transportation fares for various kinds of people. The lithographer probably considered that placard a triumph. It was printed in green, blue, red, black, and yellow; no individual line in one color, even the individual letters were separately colored. For instance, the first letter of a word would be blue, the next red, the next green, and so on. The placard looked as if it had the small-pox or something. I inquired the artist's name and place of business, intending to hunt him up and kill him when I had time; but no one could tell me. In the list of prices first-class passengers were set down at fifteen shillings and four pence, and dead bodies at one pound ten shillings and eight pence—just double price! That is Belgian morals, I suppose. I never say a harsh thing unless I am greatly stirred; but in my opinion the man who would take advantage of a dead person would do almost any odious thing. I publish this scandalous discrimination against the most helpless class among us in order that people intending to die abroad may come back by some other line.

We skimmed over to Ostend in four hours and went ashore. The first gentleman we saw happened to be the flag lieutenant of the fleet, and he told me where the *Lively* lay, and said she would sail about six in the morning. Heavens and earth. He said he would give my letter to the proper authority, and so we thanked him and bore away for the hotel. Bore away is good sailor phraseology, and I have been at sea portions of two days now. I easily pick up a foreign language.

Ostend is a curious, comfortable-looking, massively built town, where the people speak both the French and the Flemish with exceeding fluency, and yet I could not understand them in either tongue. But I will write the rest about Ostend in to-morrow's letter.

We idled about this curious Ostend the remainder of the afternoon and far into the long-lived twilight, apparently to amuse ourselves, but secretly I had a deeper motive. I wanted to see if there was anything here that might "impress the Shah." In the end I was reassured and content. If Ostend could impress him, England could amaze the head clear off

his shoulders and have marvels left that not even
the trunk could be indifferent to.

These citizens of Flanders—Flounders, I think they
call them, though I feel sure I have eaten a creature
of that name or seen it in an aquarium or a menagerie,
or in a picture or somewhere—are a thrifty, industrious race, and are as commercially wise and far-
sighted as they were in Edward the Third's time,
and as enduring and patient under adversity as they
were in Charles the Bold's. They are prolific in the
matter of children; in some of the narrow streets
every house seemed to have had a freshet of children,
which had burst through and overflowed into the
roadway. One could hardly get along for the pack
of juveniles, and they were all soiled and all healthy.
They all wore wooden shoes, which clattered noisily
on the stone pavements. All the women were hard
at work; there were no idlers about the houses.
The men were away at labor, no doubt. In nearly
every door women sat at needlework or something
of that marketable nature—they were knitting principally. Many groups of women sat in the street,
in the shade of walls, making point lace. The lace
maker holds a sort of pillow on her knees with a strip
of cardboard fastened on it, on which the lace pattern
has been punctured. She sticks bunches of pins in
the punctures and about them weaves her web of
threads. The numberless threads diverge from the
bunch of pins like the spokes of a wheel, and the
spools from which the threads are being unwound
form the outer circle of the wheel. The woman
throws these spools about her with flying fingers, in

and out, over and under one another, and so fast that you can hardly follow the evolutions with your eyes. In the chaos and confusion of skipping spools you wonder how she can possibly pick up the right one every time, and especially how she can go on gossiping with her friends all the time and yet never seem to miss a stitch. The laces these ingenious Flounders were making were very dainty and delicate in texture and very beautiful in design.

Most of the shops in Ostend seemed devoted to the sale of sea shells. All sorts of figures of men and women were made of shells; one sort was composed of grotesque and ingenious combinations of lobster claws in the human form. And they had other figures made of stuffed frogs—some fencing, some barbering each other, and some were not to be described at all without indecent language. It must require a barbarian nature to be able to find humor in such nauseating horrors as these last. These things were exposed in the public windows where young girls and little children could see them, and in the shops sat the usual hairy-lipped young woman waiting to sell them.

There was a contrivance attached to the better class of houses which I had heard of before, but never seen. It was an arrangement of mirrors outside the window, so contrived that the people within could see who was coming either up or down the street—see all that might be going on, in fact—without opening the window or twisting themselves into uncomfortable positions in order to look.

A capital thing to watch for unwelcome (or welcome) visitors with, or to observe pageants in cold or rainy weather. People in second and third stories had, also, another mirror which showed who was passing underneath.

The dining room at our hotel was very spacious and rather gorgeous. One end of it was composed almost entirely of a single pane of plate glass, some two inches thick—for this is the plate-glass manufacturing region, you remember. It was very clear and fine. If one were to enter the place in such a way as not to catch the sheen of the glass, he would suppose that the end of the house was wide open to the sun and the storms. A strange boyhood instinct came strongly upon me, and I could not really enjoy my dinner, I wanted to break that glass so badly. I have no doubt that every man feels so, and I know that such a glass must be simply torture to a boy.

This dining room's walls were almost completely covered with large oil paintings in frames.

It was an excellent hotel; the utmost care was taken that everything should go right. I went to bed at ten and was called at eleven to "take the early train." I said I was not the one, so the servant stirred up the next door and he was not the one; then the next door and the next—no success—and so on till the reverberations of the knocking were lost in the distance down the hall, and I fell asleep again. They called me at twelve to take another early train, but I said I was not the one again, and asked as a favor that they would be particular to call the rest next time, but never mind me. However, they could not understand my English; they only said something in reply to signify that, and then went on banging up the boarders, none of whom desired to take the early train.

When they called me at one, it made my rest seem very broken, and I said if they would skip me at two I would call myself—not really intending to do it, but hoping to beguile the porter and deceive him. He probably suspected that and was afraid to trust me, because when he made his rounds at that hour he did not take any chances on me, but routed me out along with the others. I got some more sleep after that, but when the porter called me at three I felt depressed and jaded and greatly discouraged. So I gave it up and dressed myself. The porter got me a cup of coffee and kept me awake while I drank it. He was a good, well-meaning sort of Flounder, but really a drawback to the hotel, I should think.

Poor Mr. Blank came in then, looking worn and old. He had been called for all the different trains, too, just as I had. He said it was a good enough hotel, but they took too much pains. While we sat there talking we fell asleep and were called again at four. Then we went out and dozed about town till six, and then drifted aboard the *Lively*.

She was trim and bright, and clean and smart; she was as handsome as a picture. The sailors were in brand-new man-of-war costume, and plenty of officers were about the decks in the state uniform of the service—cocked hats, huge epaulettes, claw-hammer coats lined with white silk—hats and coats and trousers all splendid with gold lace. I judged that these were all admirals, and so got afraid and went ashore again. Our vessel was to carry the Shah's brother, also the Grand Vizier, several Persian princes, who were uncles to the Shah, and other dignitaries of more or less consequence. A vessel alongside was to carry the luggage, and a vessel just ahead (the *Vigilant*) was to carry nobody but just the Shah and certain Ministers of State and servants and the Queen's special ambassador, Sir Henry Rawlinson, who is a Persian scholar and talks to the Shah in his own tongue.

I was very glad, for several reasons, to find that I was not to go in the same ship with the Shah. First, with him not immediately under my eye I would feel less responsibility for him; and, secondly, as I was anxious to impress him, I wanted to practice on his brother first.

## THE SHAH'S QUARTERS

On the afterdeck of the *Vigilant*—very handsome ship—a temporary cabin had been constructed for the sole and special use of the Shah, temporary but charmingly substantial and graceful and pretty. It was about thirty feet long and twelve wide, beautifully gilded, decorated and painted within and without. Among its colors was a shade of light green, which reminds me of an anecdote about the Persian party, which I will speak of in to-morrow's letter.

It was getting along toward the time for the Shah to arrive from Brussels, so I ranged up alongside my own ship. I do not know when I ever felt so ill at ease and undecided. It was a sealed letter which I had brought from the Admiralty, and I could not guess what the purport of it might be. I supposed I was intended to command the ship—that is, I had supposed it at first, but, after seeing all those splendid officers, I had discarded that idea. I cogitated a good deal, but to no purpose. Presently a regiment of Belgian troops arrived and formed in line along the pier. Then a number of people began to spread down carpets for fifty yards along the pier, by the railway track, and other carpets were laid from these to the ships. The gangway leading on board my ship was now carpeted and its railings were draped with bright-colored signal flags. It began to look as if I was expected; so I walked on board. A sailor immediately ran and stopped me, and made another sailor bring a mop for me to wipe my feet on, lest I might soil the deck, which was wonderfully clean and nice. Evidently I was not the person expected, after all. I pointed to the group of officers and asked the sailor what the naval law would do to a man if he were to go and speak to some of those admirals— for there was an awful air of etiquette and punctilio about the premises; but just then one of those officers came forward and said that if his instinct was cor- rect an Admiralty order had been received giving me a passage in the ship; and he also said that he was the first lieutenant, and that I was very welcome and he would take pains to make me feel at home, and furthermore there was champagne and soda waiting down below; and furthermore still, all the

London correspondents, to the number of six or seven, would arrive from Brussels with the Shah, and would go in our ship, and if our passage were not a lively one, and a jolly and enjoyable one, it would be a very strange thing indeed. I could have jumped for joy if I had not been afraid of breaking some rule of naval etiquette and getting hanged for it.

Now the train was signaled, and everybody got ready for the great event. The Belgian regiment straightened itself up, and some two hundred Flounders arrived and took conspicuous position on a little mound. I was a little afraid that this would impress the Shah; but I was soon occupied with other interests. The train of thirteen cars came tearing in, and stopped abreast the ships. Music and guns began an uproar. Odd-looking Persian faces and felt hats (brimless stovepipes) appeared at the car windows.

Some gorgeous English officials fled down the carpet from the *Vigilant*. They stopped at a long car with the royal arms upon it, uncovered their heads, and unlocked the car door. Then the Shah stood up in it and gave us a good view. He was a handsome, strong-featured man, with a rather European fairness of complexion; had a mustache, wore spectacles, seemed of a good height and graceful build and carriage, and looked about forty or a shade less. He was very simply dressed—brimless stovepipe and close-buttoned dark-green military suit, without ornament. No, not wholly without ornament, for he had a band two inches wide worn over his shoulder and down across his breast, scarf fashion, which band was one solid glory of fine diamonds.

A Persian official appeared in the Shah's rear and enveloped him in an ample quilt—or cloak, if you please—which was lined with fur. The outside of it was of a whitish color and elaborately needle-worked in Persian patterns like an India shawl. The Shah stepped out and the official procession formed about him and marched him down the carpet and on board the *Vigilant* to slow music. Not a Flounder raised a cheer. All the small fry swarmed out of the train now.

The Shah walked back alongside his fine cabin, looking at the assemblage of silent, solemn Flounders; the correspondent of the London *Telegraph* was hurrying along the pier and took off his hat and bowed to the "King of Kings," and the King of Kings gave a polite military salute in return. This was the commencement of the excitement. The success of the breathless *Telegraph* man made all the other London correspondents mad, every man of whom flourished his stovepipe recklessly and cheered lustily, some of the more enthusiastic varying the exercise by lowering their heads and elevating their coat tails. Seeing all this, and feeling that if I was to "impress the Shah" at all, now was my time, I ventured a little squeaky yell, quite distinct from the other shouts, but just as hearty. His Shahship heard and saw and saluted me in a manner that was, I considered, an acknowledgment of my superior importance. I do not know that I ever felt so ostentatious and absurd before. All the correspondents came

45

aboard, and then the Persian baggage came also, and was carried across to the ship alongside of ours. When she could hold no more we took somewhere about a hundred trunks and boxes on board our vessel. Two boxes fell into the water, and several sailors jumped in and saved one, but the other was lost. However, it probably contained nothing but a few hundred pounds of diamonds and things.

At last we got under way and steamed out through a long slip, the piers on either side being crowded with Flounders; but never a cheer. A battery of three guns on the starboard pier boomed a royal salute, and we swept out to sea, the *Vigilant* in the lead, we right in her wake, and the baggage ship in ours. Within fifteen minutes everybody was well acquainted; a general jollification set in, and I was thoroughly glad I had come over to fetch the Shah.

## II

### MARK TWAIN EXECUTES HIS CONTRACT AND DELIVERS THE SHAH IN LONDON

LONDON, *June 19, 1873.*

#### SOME PERSIAN FINERY

LEAVING Ostend, we went out to sea under a clear sky and upon smooth water—so smooth, indeed, that its surface was scarcely rippled. I say the sky was clear, and so it was, clear and sunny; but a rich haze lay upon the water in the distance—a soft, mellow mist, through which a scattering sail or two loomed vaguely. One may call such a morning perfect.

The corps of correspondents were well jaded with their railway journey, but after champagne and soda downstairs with the officers, everybody came up refreshed and cheery and exceedingly well acquainted all around. The Persian grandees had meantime taken up a position in a glass house on the after-deck, and were sipping coffee in a grave, Oriental way. They all had much lighter complexions and a more European cast of features than I was pre-pared for, and several of them were exceedingly handsome, fine-looking men.

They all sat in a cricle on a sofa (the deckhouse being circular), and they made a right gaudy spec-tacle. Their breasts were completely crusted with gold bullion embroidery of a pattern resembling frayed and interlacing ferns, and they had large jeweled ornaments on their breasts also. The Grand Vizier came out to have a look around. In addition to the sumptuous gold fernery on his breast he wore a jeweled star as large as the palm of my hand, and about his neck hung the Shah's miniature, reposing in a bed of diamonds, that gleamed and flashed in a wonderful way when touched by the sunlight. It was said that to receive the Shah's portrait from the Shah was the highest compliment that could be conferred upon a Persian subject. I did not care so much about the diamonds, but I would have liked to have the portrait very much. The Grand Vizier's sword hilt and the whole back of the sheath from end to end were composed of a neat and simple combination of some twelve or fifteen thousand emeralds and diamonds.

### "IMPRESSING" A PERSIAN GENERAL

Several of the Persians talked French and English. One of them, who was said to be a general, came up on the bridge where some of us were standing, pointed to a sailor, and asked me if I could tell him what that sailor was doing?

I said he was communicating with the other ships by means of the optical telegraph—that by using the three sticks the whole alphabet could be expressed. I showed him how A, B and C were made, and so forth. Good! This Persian was "impressed"! He showed it by his eyes, by his gestures, by his manifest surprise and delight. I said to myself, if the Shah were only here now, the grand desire of Great Britain could be accomplished. The general immediately called the other grandees and told them about this telegraphic wonder. Then he said:

"Now does everyone on board acquire this knowledge?"

"No, only the officers."

"And this sailor?"

"He is only the signalman. Two or three sailors on board are detailed for this service, and by order and direction of the officers they communicate with the other ships."

"Very good! very fine! Very great indeed!"

These men were unquestionably impressed. I got

the sailor to bring the signal book, and the matter
was fully explained, to their high astonishment;
also the flag signals, and likewise the lamp signals
for night telegraphing. Of course, the idea came
into my head, in the first place, to ask one of the
officers to conduct this bit of instruction, but I at
once dismissed it. I judged that this would all go
to the Shah, sooner or later. I had come over on
purpose to "impress the Shah," and I was not going
to throw away my opportunity. I wished the Queen
had been there; I would have been knighted, sure.
You see, they knight people here for all sorts of
things—knight them, or put them into the peerage
and make great personages of them. Now, for
instance, a king comes over here on a visit; the Lord
Mayor and sheriffs do him becoming honors in the
city, and straightway the former is created a baronet
and the latter are knighted. When the Prince of
Wales recovered from his illness one of his chief
physicians was made a baronet and the other was
knighted. Charles II made duchesses of one or two
female acquaintances of his for something or other—
I have forgotten now what it was. A London shoe-
maker's apprentice became a great soldier—indeed,
a Wellington—won prodigious victories in many
climes and covered the British arms with glory all
through a long life; and when he was 187 years old
they knighted him and made him Constable of the
Tower. But he died next year and they buried him
in Westminster Abbey. There is no telling what
that man might have become if he had lived. So
you see what a chance I had; for I have no doubt in

the world that I have been the humble instrument, under Providence, of "impressing the Shah." And I really believe that if the Queen comes to hear of it I shall be made a duke.

Friends intending to write will not need to be reminded that a duke is addressed as "Your Grace"; it is considered a great offense to leave that off.

### A PICTURESQUE NAVAL SPECTACLE

When we were a mile or so out from Ostend conversation ceased, an expectant look came into all faces, and opera glasses began to stand out from above all noses. This impressive hush lasted a few minutes, and then some one said:

"There they are!"

"Where?"

"Away yonder ahead—straight ahead."

Which was true. Three huge shapes smothered in the haze—the *Vanguard*, the *Audacious*, and the *Devastation*—all great ironclads. They were to do escort duty. The officers and correspondents gathered on the forecastle and waited for the next act. A red spout of fire issued from the *Vanguard's* side, another flashed from the *Audacious*. Beautiful these red tongues were against the dark haze. Then there was a long pause—ever so long a pause and not a sound, not the suspicion of a sound; and now, out of the stillness, came a deep, solemn "boom! boom!" It had not occurred to me that at so great a distance I would not hear the report as soon as I saw the flash. The two crimson jets were very beautiful, but not more so than the rolling volumes of white smoke that plunged after them, rested a moment over the water, and then went wreathing and curling up among the webbed rigging and the tall masts, and left only glimpses of these things visible, high up in the air, projecting as if from a fog.

Now the flashes came thick and fast from the black sides of both vessels. The muffled thunders of the guns mingled together in one continued roll, the two ships were lost to sight, and in their places two mountains of tumbled smoke rested upon the motionless water, their bases in the hazy twilight and their summits shining in the sun. It was good to be there and see so fine a spectacle as that.

### THE NAVAL SALUTE

We closed up fast upon the ironclads. They fell apart to let our flotilla come between, and as the *Vigilant* ranged up the rigging of the ironclads was manned to salute the Shah. And, indeed, that was something to see. The shrouds, from the decks clear to the trucks, away up toward the sky, were black with men. On the lower rounds of these rope ladders they stood five abreast, holding each other's hands, and so the tapering shrouds formed attenuated pyramids of humanity, six pyramids of them towering into the upper air, and clear up on the top of each dizzy mast stood a little creature like a clothes pin—a mere black peg against the sky—and that mite was a sailor waving a flag like a postage stamp. All at once the pyramids of men burst into a cheer, and followed it with two more, given with a will; and if the Shah was not impressed he must be the offspring of a mummy.

And just at this moment, while we all stood there gazing ——

However breakfast was announced and I did not wait to see.

### THE THIRTY-FOUR-TON GUNS SPEAK

If there is one thing that is pleasanter than another it is to take breakfast in the wardroom with a dozen naval officers. Of course, that awe-inspiring monarch, the captain, is aft, keeping frozen state with the Grand Viziers when there are any on board, and so there is nobody in the wardroom to maintain naval etiquette. As a consequence none is maintained. One officer, in a splendid uniform, snatches a champagne bottle from a steward and opens it himself; another keeps the servants moving; another opens soda; everybody eats, drinks, shouts, laughs in the most unconstrained way, and it does seem a pity that ever the thing should come to an end. No individual present seemed sorry he was not in the ship with the Shah. When the festivities had been going on about an hour, some tremendous booming was heard outside. Now here was a question between duty and broiled chicken. What might that booming mean? Anguish sat upon the faces of the correspondents. I watched to see what they would do, and the precious moments were flying. Somebody cried down a companionway:

"The *Devastation* is saluting!"

The correspondents tumbled over one another, over chairs, over everything in their frenzy to get on deck, and the last gun reverberated as the last heel disappeared on the stairs. The *Devastation*, the pride of England, the mightiest war vessel afloat, carrying guns that outweigh any metal in any service, it is said (thirty-five tons each), and these boys had missed that spectacle—at least I knew that some of them had. I did not go. Age has taught me wisdom. If a spectacle is going to be particularly imposing I prefer to see it through somebody else's eyes, because that man will always exaggerate. Then I can exaggerate his exaggeration, and my account of the thing will be the most impressive.

But I felt that I had missed my figure this time, because I was not sure which of these gentlemen reached the deck in time for a glimpse and which didn't. And this morning I cannot tell by the London papers. They all have imposing descriptions of that thing, and no one of them resembles another. Mr. X's is perhaps the finest, but he was singing a song about "Spring, Spring, Gentle Spring," all through the bombardment, and was overexcited, I fear.

The next best was Mr. Y's; but he was telling about how he took a Russian battery, along with another man, during the Crimean War, and he was not fairly through the story till the salute was over, though I remember he went up and saw the smoke. I will not frame a description of the *Devastation's* salute, for I have no material that I can feel sure is reliable.

## THE GRAND SPECTACULAR CLIMAX

When we first sailed away from Ostend I found myself in a dilemma; I had no notebook. But "any port in a storm," as the sailors say. I found a fair, full pack of ordinary playing cards in my overcoat pocket—one always likes to have something along to amuse children with—and really they proved excellent to take notes on, although bystanders were a bit inclined to poke fun at them and ask facetious questions. But I was content; I made all the notes I needed. The aces and low "spot" cards are very good indeed to write memoranda on, but I will not recommend the Kings and Jacks.

## SPEAKING BY THE CARDS

Referring to the seven of hearts, I find that this naval exhibition and journey from Ostend to Dover is going to cost the government £500,000. Got it from a correspondent. It is a round sum.

Referring to the ace of diamonds, I find that along in the afternoon we sighted a fresh fleet of men-of-war coming to meet us. The rest of the diamonds, down to the eight spot (nines and tens are no good for notes) are taken up with details of that spectacle. Most of the clubs and hearts refer to matters immediately following that, but I really can hardly do anything with them because I have forgotten what was trumps.

## THE SPECTACLE

But never mind. The sea scene grew little by little, until presently it was very imposing. We drew up into the midst of a waiting host of vessels. Enormous five-masted men-of-war, great turret ships, steam packets, pleasure yachts—every sort of craft, indeed—the sea was thick with them; the yards and riggings of the warships loaded with men, the packets crowded with people, the pleasure ships rainbowed with brilliant flags all over and over—some with flags strung thick on lines stretching from bowsprit to foremast, thence to mainmast, thence to mizzenmast, and thence to stern. All the ships were in motion—gliding hither and thither, in and out, mingling and parting—a bewildering whirl of flash and color. Our leader, the vast, black, ugly, but very formidable *Devastation*, plowed straight through the gay throng, our Shah-ships following, the lines of big men-of-war saluting, the booming of the guns drowning the cheering, stately islands of smoke towering everywhere. And so, in this condition of unspeakable grandeur, we swept into the harbor of Dover, and saw the English princes and the long ranks of red-coated soldiers waiting on the pier, civilian multitudes behind them, the lofty hill front by the castle swarming with spectators, and there was the crash of cannon and a general hurrah all through the air. It was rather a contrast to silent Ostend and the unimpressible Flanders.

### THE SHAH "IMPRESSED" AT LAST

The Duke of Edinburgh and Prince Arthur received the Shah in state, and then all of us—princes, Shahs, ambassadors, Grand Viziers and newspaper correspondents—climbed aboard the train and started off to London just like so many brothers.

From Dover to London it was a sight to see. Seventy miles of human beings in a jam—the gaps were not worth mentioning—and every man, woman, and child waving hat or handkerchief and cheering. I wondered—could not tell—could not be sure—could only wonder—would this "impress the Shah"? I would have given anything to know. But—well, it ought—but—still one could not tell.

And by and by we burst into the London Railway station—a very large station it is—and found it wonderfully decorated and all the neighboring streets packed with cheering citizens. Would this impress the Shah? I—I—well, I could not yet feel certain.

The Prince of Wales received the Shah—ah, you should have seen how gorgeously the Shah was dressed now—he was like the sun in a total eclipse of rainbows—yes, the Prince received him, put him in a grand open carriage, got in and made him sit over further and not "crowd," the carriage clattered out of the station, all London fell apart on either side and lifted a perfectly national cheer, and just at that instant the bottom fell out of

the sky and forty deluges came pouring down at
once!

The great strain was over, the crushing suspense
at an end. I said, "Thank God, this will impress
the Shah."

Now came the long files of Horse Guards in silver
armor. We took the great Persian to Buckingham
Palace. I never stirred till I saw the gates open
and close upon him with my own eyes and knew he
was there. Then I said:

"England, here is your Shah; take him and be
happy, but don't ever ask me to fetch over another
one."

This contract has been pretty straining on me.


### III
#### THE SHAH AS A SOCIAL STAR

LONDON, *June 21, 1873.*

AFTER delivering the Shah at the gates of that
unsightly pile of dreary grandeur known as
Buckingham Palace I cast all responsibility for him
aside for the time being, and experienced a sense of
relief and likewise an honest pride in my success,
such as no man can feel who has not had a Shah at
nurse (so to speak) for three days.

It is said by those who ought to know that when
Buckingham Palace was being fitted up as a home
for the Shah one of the chief rooms was adorned
with a rich carpet which had been designed and
manufactured especially to charm the eye of His
Majesty. The story goes on to say that a couple of

the Persian suite came here a week ago to see that all things were in readiness and nothing overlooked, and that when they reached that particular room and glanced at the lovely combination of green figures and white ones in that carpet they gathered their robes carefully up about their knees and then went elaborately tiptoeing about the floor with the aspect and anxiety of a couple of cats hunting for dry ground in a wet country, and they stepped only on the white figures and almost fainted whenever they came near touching a green one. It is said that the explanation is that these visiting Persians are all Mohammedans, and green being a color sacred to the descendants of the Prophet, and none of these people being so descended, it would be dreadful profanation for them to defile the holy color with their feet. And the general result of it all was that carpet had to be taken up and is a dead loss.

Man is a singular sort of human being, after all, and his religion does not always adorn him. Now, our religion is the right one, and has fewer odd and striking features than any other; and yet my ancestors used to roast Catholics and witches and warm their hands by the fire; but they would be blanched with horror at the bare thought of breaking the Sabbath, and here is a Persian monarch who never sees any impropriety in chopping a subject's head off for the mere misdemeanor of calling him too early for breakfast, and yet would be consumed with pious remorse if unheeding foot were to chance to step upon anything so green as you or I, my reader.

Oriental peoples say that women have no souls to save and, almost without my memory, many American Protestants said the same of babies. I thought there was a wide gulf between the Persians and ourselves, but I begin to feel that they are really our brothers after all.

After a day's rest the Shah went to Windsor Castle and called on the Queen. What that suggests to the reader's mind is this:—That the Shah took a hand satchel and an umbrella, called a cab and said he wanted to go to the Paddington station; that when he arrived there the driver charged him sixpence too much, and he paid it rather than have trouble; that he tried now to buy a ticket, and was answered by a ticket seller as surly as a hotel clerk that he was not selling tickets for that train yet; that he finally got his ticket, and was beguiled of his satchel by a railway porter at once, who put it into a first-class carriage and got a sixpence, which the company forbids him to receive; that presently when the guard (or conductor) of the train came along the Shah slipped a shilling into his hand and said he wanted to smoke, and straightway the guard signified that it was all right; that when the Shah arrived at Windsor Castle he rang the bell, and when the girl came to the door asked her if the Queen was at home, and she left him standing in the hall and went to see; that by and by she returned and said would he please sit down in the front room and Mrs. Guelph would be down directly; that he hung his hat on the hatrack, stood his umbrella up in the corner, entered the front room and sat down on a

59

haircloth chair; that he waited and waited and got
tired; that he got up and examined the old piano,
the depressing lithographs on the walls and the
album of photographs of faded country relatives
on the center table, and was just about to fall
back on the family Bible when the Queen entered
briskly and begged him to sit down and apologized
for keeping him waiting, but she had just got a
new girl and everything was upside down, and so
forth and so on; but how are the family, and
when did he arrive, and how long should he stay
and why didn't he bring his wife. I knew that
that was the picture which would spring up in the
American reader's mind when it was said the Shah
went to visit the Queen, because that was the
picture which the announcement suggested to
my own mind.

But it was far from the facts, very far. Nothing
could be farther. In truth, these people made as
much of a to do over a mere friendly call as anybody else would over a conflagration. There were
special railway trains for the occasion; there was
a general muster of princes and dukes to go along,
each one occupying room 40; there were regiments of cavalry to clear the way; railway stations
were turned into flower gardens, sheltered with
flags and all manner of gaudy splendor; there were
multitudes of people to look on over the heads of
interminable ranks of policemen standing shoulder
to shoulder and facing front; there was braying of
music and booming of cannon. All that fuss, in
sober truth, over a mere off-hand friendly call.

Imagine what it would have been if he had brought another shirt and was going to stay a month.

### AT THE GUILDHALL

Truly, I am like to suffocate with astonishment at the things that are going on around me here. It is all odd, it is all queer enough, I can tell you; but last night's work transcends anything I ever heard of in the way of—well, how shall I express it? how can I word it? I find it awkward to get at it. But to say it in a word—and it is a true one, too, as hundreds and hundreds of people will testify—last night the Corporation of the City of London, with a simplicity and ignorance which almost rise to sublimity, actually gave a ball to a Shah who does not dance. If I would allow myself to laugh at a cruel mistake, this would start me. It is the oddest thing that has happened since I have had charge of the Shah. There is some excuse for it in the fact that the Aldermen of London are simply great and opulent merchants, and cannot be expected to know much about the ways of high life—but then they could have asked some of us who have been with the Shah.

The ball was a marvel in its way. The historical Guildhall was a scene of great magnificence. There was a high dais at one end, on which were three state chairs under a sumptuous canopy; upon the middle one sat the Shah, who was almost a Chicago conflagration of precious stones and gold bullion lace. Among other gems upon his breast were a number of emeralds of marvelous size, and from

a loop hung an historical diamond of great size
and wonderful beauty. On the right of the Shah
sat the Princess of Wales, and on his left the wife
of the Crown Prince of Russia. Grouped about
the three stood a full jury of minor princes,
princesses, and ambassadors hailing from many
countries.

### THE TWO CORRALS

The immense hall was divided in the middle by a
red rope. The Shah's division was sacred to blue
blood, and there was breathing room there; but the
other corral was but a crush of struggling and per-
spiring humanity. The place was brilliant with gas
and was a rare spectacle in the matter of splendid
costumes and rich coloring. The lofty stained-glass
windows, pictured with celebrated episodes in the
history of the ancient city, were lighted from the
outside, and one may imagine the beauty of the effect.
The great giants, Gog and Magog (whose origin and
history, curiously enough, are unknown even to
tradition), looked down from the lofty gallery, but
made no observation. Down the long sides of the
hall, with but brief spaces between, were imposing
groups of marble statuary; and, contrasted with the
masses of life and color about them, they made a
picturesque effect. The groups were statues (in
various attitudes) of the Duke of Wellington. I do
not say this knowingly, but only supposingly; but
I never have seen a statue in England yet that
represented anybody but the Duke of Wellington,

and, as for the streets and terraces and courts and
squares that are named after him or after selections
from his 797 titles, they are simply beyond the
grasp of arithmetic. This reminds me that, having
named everything after Wellington that there was
left to name in England (even down to Wellington
boots), our British brothers, still unsatisfied, still
oppressed with adulation, blandly crossed over
and named our Californian big trees Wellington,
and put it in Latin at that. They did that, calmly
ignoring the fact that we, the discoverers and owners
of the trees, had long ago named them after a larger
man. However, if the ghost of Wellington enjoys
such a proceeding, possibly the ghost of Washington
will not greatly trouble itself about the matter. But
what really disturbs me is that, while Wellington is
justly still in the fashion here, Washington is fading
out of the fashion with us. It is not a good sign. The
idols we have raised in his stead are not to our
honor.

Some little dancing was done in the sacred corral
in front of the Shah by grandees belonging mainly
to "grace-of-God" families, but he himself never
agitated a foot. The several thousand commoner
people on the other side of the rope could not dance
any more than sardines in a box. Chances to view
the Guildhall spectacle were so hungered for that
people offered £5 for the privilege of standing three
minutes in the musicians' gallery and were refused.
I cannot convey to you an idea of the inordinate
desire which prevails here to see the Shah better than
by remarking that speculators who held four-seat

opera boxes at Covent Garden Theater to-night were able to get $250 for them. Had all the seats been sold at auction the opera this evening would have produced not less than one hundred and twenty-five thousand dollars in gold! I am below the figures rather than above them. The greatest house (for money) that America ever saw was gathered together upon the occasion of Jenny Lind's first concert at Castle Garden. The seats were sold at auction and produced something over twenty thousand dollars.

I am by no means trying to describe the Guildhall affair of last night. Such a crush of titled swells; such a bewildering array of jeweled uniforms and brilliant feminine costumes; such solemn and awful reception ceremonies in the library; such grim and stately imposing addresses and Persian replies; such imposing processional pageantry later on; such depressing dancing before the apathetic Shah; such ornate tables and imperial good cheer at the banquet —it makes a body' tired to merely think of trying to put all that on paper. Perhaps you, sir, will be good enough to imagine it, and thus save one who respects you and honors you five columns of solid writing.

THE LUNATIC ASYLUM IS BLESSED WITH A GLIMPSE

As regards the momentous occasion of the opera, this evening, I found myself in a grievous predicament, for a republican. The tickets were all sold long ago, so I must either go as a member of the royal family or not at all. After a good deal of reflection it seemed best not to mix up with that class lest a political significance might be put upon it. But a queer arrangement had been devised whereby I might have a glimpse of the show, and I took advantage of that. There is an immense barn-like glass house attached to the rear of the theater, and that was fitted up with seats, carpets, mirrors, gas, columns, flowers, garlands, and a meager row of shrubs strung down the sides on brackets—to create an imposing forest effect, I suppose. The place would seat ten or twelve hundred people. All but a hundred paid a dollar and a quarter a seat—for what? To look at the Shah three quarters of a minute, while he walked through to enter the theater. The remaining hundred paid $11 a seat for the same privilege, with the added luxury of rushing on the stage and glancing at the opera audience for one single minute afterward, while the chorus sung "God Save the Queen!" We are all gone mad, I do believe. Eleven hundred five-shilling lunatics and a hundred two-guinea maniacs. The *Herald* purchased a ticket and created me one of the latter, along with two or three more of the staff.

Our cab was about No. 17,342 in the string that worked its slow way through London and past the theater. The Shah was not to come till nine o'clock, and yet we had to be at the theater by half past six, or we would not get into the glass house at all, they said. We were there on time, and seated in a small gallery which overlooked a very brilliantly dressed throng of people. Every seat was occupied. We sat there two hours and a half gazing and melting.

The wide, red-carpeted central aisle below offered good display ground for officials in fine uniforms, and they made good use of it.

By and by a band in showy uniform came in and stood opposite the entrance. At the end of a tedious interval of waiting trumpets sounded outside, there was some shouting, the band played half of "God Save the Queen," and then the Duke and Duchess of Cambridge and a dozen gorgeous Persian officials entered. After a little the young Prince Arthur came, in a blue uniform, with a whole broadside of gold and silver medals on his breast—for good behavior, punctuality, accurate spelling, penman-ship, etc., I suppose, but I could not see the inscrip-tions. The band gave him some bars of "God Save the Queen," too, while he stood under us talking, with altogether unroyal animation, with the Persians —the crowd of people staring hungrily at him the while—country cousins, maybe, who will go home and say, "I was as close to him as I am to that chair this minute."

Then came the Duke of Teck and the Princess Mary, and the band God-Save-the-Queen'd them also. Now came the Prince of Wales and the Russian Tsarina—the royal anthem again, with an extra blast at the end of it. After them came a young, handsome, mighty giant, in showy uniform, his breast covered with glittering orders, and a general's chapeau, with a flowing white plume, in his hand—

the heir to all the throne of all the Russias. The band greeted him with the Russian national anthem, and played it clear through. And they did right; for perhaps it is not risking too much to say that this is the only national air in existence that is really worthy of a great nation.

And at last came the long-expected millennium himself, His Imperial Majesty the Shah, with the charming Princess of Wales on his arm. He had all his jewels on, and his diamond shaving brush in his hat front. He shone like a window with the westering sun on it.

### WHAT THE ASYLUM SAW

The small space below us was full now—it could accommodate no more royalty. The august procession filed down the aisle in double rank, the Shah and the Princess of Wales in the lead, and cheers broke forth and a waving of handkerchiefs as the Princess passed—all said this demonstration was meant for her. As the procession disappeared through the farther door, the hundred eleven-dollar maniacs rushed through a small aperture, then through an anteroom, and gathered in a flock on the stage, the chorus striking up "God Save the Queen" at the same moment.

We stood in a mighty bandbox, or a Roman coliseum, with a sea of faces stretching far away over the ground floor, and above them rose five curving tiers of gaudy humanity, the dizzy upper tier in the far distance rising sharply up against the roof, like a flower garden trying to hold an earth-quake down and not succeeding. It was a magnificent spectacle, and what with the roaring of the chorus, the waving of handkerchiefs, the cheering of the people, the blazing gas, and the awful splendor of the long file of royalty, standing breast to breast in the royal box, it was wonderfully exhilarating, not to say exciting.

The chorus sang only three-quarters of a minute—one stanza—and down came the huge curtain and shut out the fairyland. And then all those eleven-dollar people hunted their way out again.

### A NATION DEMENTED

We are certainly gone mad. We scarcely look at the young colossus who is to reign over 70,000,000 of people and the mightiest empire in extent which exists to-day. We have no eyes but for this splendid barbarian, who is lord over a few deserts and a modest ten million of ragamuffins—a man who has never done anything to win our gratitude or excite our admiration, except that he managed to starve a million of his subjects to death in twelve months. If he had starved the rest I suppose we would set up a monument to him now.

The London theaters are almost absolutely empty these nights. Nobody goes, hardly. The managers are being ruined. The streets for miles are crammed with people waiting whole long hours for a chance glimpse of the Shah. I never saw any man "draw" like this one.

Is there any truth in the report that your bureaus are trying to get the Shah to go over there and lecture? He could get $100,000 a night here and choose his own subject.

I know a showman who has got a pill that belonged to him, and which for some reason he did not take. That showman will not take any money for that pill. He is going to travel with it. And let me tell you he will get more engagements than he can fill in a year.

IV

MARK TWAIN HOOKS THE PERSIAN OUT OF
THE ENGLISH CHANNEL

LONDON, *June 26, 1873.*

I SUPPOSE I am the only member of the Shah's family who is not wholly broken down and worn out; and, to tell the truth, there is not much of me left. If you have ever been limited to four days in Paris or Rome or Jerusalem and been "rushed" by a guide you can form a vague, far-away sort of conception of what the Shah and the rest of us have endured during these late momentous days. If this goes on we may as well get ready for the imperial inquest.

When I was called at five o'clock the other morning to go to Portsmouth, and remembered that the Shah's incessant movements had left me only three hours' sleep that night, nothing but a sense of duty drove me forth. A cab could not be found, nor a

carriage in all London. I lost an hour and a half
waiting and trying, then started on foot and lost
my way; consequently I missed one train by a
good while, another one by three minutes, and then
had more than half an hour to spare before another
would go. Most people had had a similar experience,
and there was comfort in that. We started at last,
and were more than three hours going seventy-two
miles. We stopped at no stations, hardly, but we
halted every fifteen minutes out in the woods and
fields for no purpose that we could discover. Never
was such an opportunity to look at scenery. There
were five strangers in our car, or carriage, as the
English call it, and by degrees their English reserve
thawed out and they passed around their sherry
and sandwiches and grew sociable.

One of them had met the Russian General of
Police in St. Petersburg, and found him a queer old
simple-hearted soldier, proud of his past and devoted
to his master, the present Tsar, and to the memory
of his predecessor, Nicholas. The English gentleman
gave an instance of the old man's simplicity which
one would not expect in a chief of police. The
general had been visiting London and been greatly
impressed by two things there—the admirable police
discipline and the museum. It transpired that the
museum he referred to was not that mighty collection of marvels known to all the world as the British
Museum, but Mme. Toussaud's Waxworks Show;
and in this waxwork show he had seen a figure of
the Emperor Nicholas. And did it please him? Yes,
as to the likeness; for it was a good likeness and a

commanding figure; but—"*Mon Dieu!* try to fancy it, m'sieu—dressed in the uniform of a simple colonel of infantry!—the great Nicholas of Russia, my august late master, dressed in a colonel's uniform!"

The old general could not abide that. He went to the proprietor and remonstrated against this wanton indignity. The proprietor was grieved; but it was the only Russian uniform he could get, and——

"Say no more!" said the general. "May I get you one?"

The proprietor would be most happy. The general lost not a moment; he wrote it once to the Emperor Alexander, describing with anguish the degradation which the late great Nicholas was suffering day by day through his infamously clothed waxen representative, and imploring His Majesty to send suitable raiment for the imperial dummy, and also a letter to authenticate the raiment. And out of regard for the old servant and respect for his outraged feelings the Emperor of all the Russias descended from his Alpine altitude to send to the Toussaud waxwork the general's uniform worn last by his father, and to write with his own hand an authenticating letter to go with it. So the simple-hearted police chief was happy once more, and never once thought of charging the "museum" $10,000 for these valuable additions to the show, which he might easily have done, and collected the money, too. How like our own chiefs of police this good old soul is!

Another of these English gentlemen told an anecdote, which, he said, was old, but which I had not heard before. He said that one day St. Peter and the devil chanced to be thrown together, and found it pretty dull trying to pass the time. Finally they got to throwing dice for a lawyer. The devil threw sixes. Then St. Peter threw sixes. The devil threw sixes again. St. Peter threw sixes again. The devil threw sixes once more. Then St. Peter threw sevens, and the devil said, "Oh, come now, Your Honor, cheat fair. None of your playing miracles here!" I thought there was a nice bit of humor in that suggestion to "cheat fair."

### A SMALL PRIVATE NAUTICAL RACE

I am getting to Portsmouth about as fast in this letter as I did in that train. The Right Honorable the Mayor of Portsmouth had had a steamer placed at his disposal by the Admiralty, and he had invited the Lord Mayor of London and other guests to go in her. This was the ship I was to sail in, and she was to leave her pier at 9 A.M. sharp. I arrived at that pier at ten minutes to eleven exactly. There was one chance left, however. The ship had stopped for something and was floating at ease about a mile away.

A rusty, decayed, little two-oared skiff, the size of a bathtub, came floating by, with a fisherman and his wife and child in it. I entreated the man to come in and take me to the ship. Presently he consented and started toward me. I stood impatient and all ready to jump the moment he should get within thirty yards of me; he halted at the distance of thirty-five and said it would be a long pull; did I think I could pay him two shillings for it, seeing it was a holiday? All this palaver and I in such a state of mind! I jumped aboard and told him to rush, which he did; at least he threw his whole heart into his little, useless oars, and we moved off at the rate of a mile a week. This was solid misery. When we had gone a hundred and nine feet and were gaining on the tenth a long, trim, graceful man-of-war's boat came flying by, bound for the flagship. Without expecting even the courtesy of a response, I hailed and asked the coxswain to take me to the mayor's vessel. He said, "Certainly, sir!—ease her, boys!" I could not have been more astonished at anything in the world. I quickly gave my man his two shillings, and he started to pull me to the boat. Then there was a movement of discontent among the sailors, and they seemed about to move on. I thought—well, you are not such generous fellows, after all, as I took you to be, or so polite, either; but just then the coxswain hailed and said:

"The boys don't mind the pull, and they're perfectly willing to take you, but they say they ain't willing to take the fisherman's job away from him."

Now that was genuine manliness and right conduct. I shall always remember that honorable act. I told them the fisherman was already paid, and I was in their boat the next moment. Then ensued the real fun of the day, as far as I was personally concerned. The boys glanced over their shoulders to measure the distance, and then at the order to "Give way!" they bent to it and the boat sped through the water like an arrow. We passed all kinds of craft and steadily shortened the distance that lay between us and the ship. Presently the coxswain said:

"No use! Her wheels have begun to turn over. Lively now, lively!"

Then we flew. We watched the ship's movement with a sharp interest and calculated our chances.

"Can you steer?" said the coxswain.

"Can a duck swim?" said I.

"Good—we'll make her yet!"

I took the helm and he the stroke oar, and that one oar did appear to add a deal to that boat's speed. The ship was turning around to go out to sea, and she did seem to turn unnecessarily fast, too; but just as she was pointed right and both her wheels began to go ahead our boat's bow touched her companionway and I was aboard. It was a handsome race, and very exciting. If I could have had that dainty boat and those eight white-shirted, blue-trousered sailors for the day I would not have gone in any ship, but would have gone about in vast naval style and experienced the feelings of an admiral.

### OLD HISTORICAL MEN-OF-WAR

Our ship sailed out through a narrow way, bordered by piers that swarmed with people, and likewise by prodigious men-of-war of the fashion of a hundred years ago. There were, perhaps, a dozen of the stately veterans, these relics of an historic past; and not looking aged and seedy, either, but as bright and fresh as if they had been launched and painted yesterday. They were the noblest creatures to look upon; hulls of huge proportion and great length; four long tiers of cannon grinning from their tall sides; vast sterns that towered into the air like the gable end of a church; graceful bows and figure-heads; masts as trim and lofty as spires—surely no spectacle could be so imposing as a sea fight in the old times, when such beautiful and such lordly ships as these ruled the seas. And how it must have stirred the heart of England when a fleet of them used to come sailing in from victory, with ruined sides and tattered spars and sails, while bells and cannon pealed a welcome!

One of the grandest of these veterans was the very one upon whose deck Nelson himself fell in the moment of triumph. I suppose England would rather part with ten colonies than with that illustrious old ship. We passed along within thirty steps of her, and I was just trying to picture in my mind the tremendous scenes that had transpired upon her deck upon that day, the proudest in England's naval history, when the venerable craft, stirred by the boom of saluting cannon, perhaps, woke up out of her long sleep and began to vomit smoke and thunder herself, and then she looked her own natural self again, and no doubt the spirit of Nelson was near. Still it would have been pleasanter to be on her decks than in front of her guns; for, as the white

volumes of smoke burst in our faces, one could not help
feeling that a ball might by accident have got mixed
up with a blank cartridge, and might chip just enough
off the upper end of a man to disfigure him for life;
and, besides, the powder they use in cannon is in
grains as large as billiard chalks, and it does not
all explode—suppose a few should enter one's system? The crash and roar of these great guns was
as unsettling a sound as I have ever heard at short
range. I took off my hat and acknowledged the
salute, of course, though it seemed to me that it
would have been better manners if they had
saluted the Lord Mayor, inasmuch as he was on
board.

### THE WORLD'S GREATEST NAVY ON VIEW

We went out to the Spithead and sailed up and
down there for four hours through four long ranks
of stately men-of-war—formidable ironclads they
were—the most insignificant of which would make
a breakfast of a whole fleet of Nelson's prodigious
ships and still be hungry. The show was very fine,
for there were forty-nine of the finest ironclads the
world can show, and many gunboats besides. Indeed,
here in its full strength was the finest navy in the
world, and this the only time in history that just
such a spectacle has been seen, and none who saw
it that day is likely to live long enough to see its like
again. The vessels were all dressed out with flags,
and all about them frolicked a bewildering host of
bannered yachts, steamers, and every imaginable sort
of craft. It would be hard to contrive a gayer scene.

One of the royal yachts came flying along presently
and put the Shah on board one of the ironclads, and
then the yards of the whole fleet were manned
simultaneously, and such another booming and bellowing of great guns ensued as I cannot possibly
describe. Within two minutes the huge fleet was
swallowed up in smoke, with angry red tongues of
fire darting through it here and there. It was wonderful to look upon. Every time the *Devastation*
let off one of her thirty-five-ton guns it seemed as
if an entire London fog issued from her side, and
the report was so long coming that if she were to
shoot a man he would be dead before he heard it,
and would probably go around wondering through
all eternity what it was that happened to him. I
returned to London in a great hurry by a train that
was in no way excited by it, but failed in the end
and object I had in view after all, which was to
go to the grand concert at Albert Hall in honor
of the Shah. I had a strong desire to see that
building filled with people once. Albert Hall is one
of the many monuments erected to the memory
of the late Prince Albert. It is a huge and costly
edifice, but the architectural design is old, not to
say in some sense a plagiarism; for there is but little
originality in putting a dome on a gasometer. It
is said to seat 13,000 people, and surely that is a
thing worth seeing—at least to a man who was not
at the Boston Jubilee. But no tickets were to be
had—every seat was full, they said. It was no
particular matter, but what made me mad was to
come so extremely close and then miss. Indeed, I

was madder than I can express, to think that if the architect had only planned the place to hold 13,001 I could have got in. But, after all, I was not the only person who had occasion to feel vexed. Colonel X, a noted man in America, bought a seat some days ago for $10 and a little afterward met a knowing person who said the Shah would be physically worn out before that concert night and would not be there, and consequently nobody else; so the seat was immediately sold for $5. Then came another knowing one, who said the Shah would unquestionably be at the concert, so the colonel went straight and bought his ticket back again. The temporary holder of it only charged him $250 for carrying it around for him during the interval! The colonel was at the concert, and took the Shah's head clerk for the Shah all the evening. Vexation could go no further than that.

V

MARK TWAIN GIVES THE ROYAL PERSIAN
A "SEND-OFF"

LONDON, *June 30, 1873.*

FOR the present we are done with the Shah in London. He is gone to the country to be further "impressed." After all, it would seem that he was more moved and more genuinely entertained by the military day at Windsor than by even the naval show at Portsmouth. It is not to be wondered at, since he is a good deal of a soldier himself and not much of a sailor. It has been estimated that there were 300,000 people assembled at Windsor—some say 500,000. That was a show in itself. The Queen of England was there; so was Windsor Castle; also an imposing array of cavalry, artillery, and infantry. And the accessories to these several shows were the matchless rural charms of England—a vast expanse of green sward, walled in by venerable forest trees, and beyond them glimpses of hills clothed in Summer vegetation. Upon such a theater a bloodless battle was fought and an honorable victory won by trained soldiers who have not always been carpet knights, but whose banners bear the names of many historic fights.

England is now practically done with the Shah. True, his engagement is not yet completed, for he is still billed to perform at one or two places; but curiosity is becoming sated, and he will hardly draw as good houses as heretofore. Whenever a star has to go to the provinces it is a bad sign. The poor man is well nigh worn out with hard work. The other day he was to have performed before the Duke of Buccleuch and was obliged to send an excuse. Since then he failed of his engagement at the Bank of England. He does not take rest even when he might. He has a telegraphic apparatus in his apartments in Buckingham Palace, and it is said that he sits up late, talking with his capital of Persia by telegraph. He is so fascinated with the wonderful contrivance that he cannot keep away from it. No doubt it is the only homelike thing the exile finds in the hard, practical West, for it is the next of kin to the enchanted carpets that figure in the romance and traditions of his own land, and which carry the wanderer whither he will about the earth, circumscribing the globe in the twinkling of an eye, propelled by only the force of an unspoken wish.

### GOSSIP ABOUT THE SHAH

This must be a dreary, unsatisfactory country to him, where one's desires are thwarted at every turn. Last week he woke up at three in the morning and demanded of the Vizier on watch by his bedside that the ballet dancers be summoned to dance before him. The Vizier prostrated himself upon the floor and said:

"O king of kings, light of the world, source of human peace and contentment, the glory and admiration of the age, turn away thy sublime countenance, let not thy fateful frown wither thy slave; for behold the dancers dwell wide asunder in the desert wastes of London, and not in many hours could they be gathered together."

The Shah could not even speak, he was so astounded with the novelty of giving a command that could not be obeyed. He sat still a moment, suffering, then wrote in his tablets these words:

"MEM.—Upon arrival in Teheran, let the Vizier have the coffin which has just been finished for the late general of the household troops—it will save time."

He then got up and set his boots outside the door to be blacked and went back to bed, calm and comfortable, making no more to-do about giving away that costly coffin than I would about spending a couple of shillings.

### THE LESSON OF HIS JOURNEY

If the mountains of money spent by civilized Europe in entertaining the Shah shall win him to adopt some of the mild and merciful ways that prevail in Christian realms it will have been money well and wisely laid out. If he learns that a throne may rest as firmly upon the affections of a people as upon their fears; that charity and justice may go hand in hand without detriment to the authority of the sovereign; that an enlarged liberty granted to the subject need not impair the power of the monarch; if he learns these things Persia will be the gainer by his journey, and the money which Europe has expended in entertaining him will have been profitably invested. That the Shah needs a hint or two in these directions is shown by the language of the following petition, which has just reached him from certain Parsees residing here and in India:

### THE PETITION

1. A heavy and oppressive poll tax, called the Juzia, is imposed upon the remnant of the ancient Zoroastrian race now residing in Persia. A hundred years ago, when the Zoroastrian population was 30,000 families, and comparatively well-to-do, the tax was only 250 toomans; now, when there are scarcely six thousand souls altogether, and stricken with poverty, they have to pay 800 toomans. In addition to the crushing effect of this tax, the government officials oppress these poor people in enforcing the tax.

2. A Parsee desirous of buying landed property is obliged to pay twenty per cent. on the value of the property as fee to the Kazee and other authorities.

3. When a Parsee dies any member of his family, no matter however distant, who may have previously been converted to Mohammedanism, claims and obtains the whole property of the deceased, to the exclusion of all the rightful heirs. In enforcing this claim the convert is backed and supported by government functionaries.

4. When a Parsee returns to Persia from a foreign country he is harassed with all sorts of exactions at the various places he has to pass through in Persia.

5. When any dispute arises, whether civil or criminal, between a Mohammedan and a Parsee, the officials invariably side with the former, and the testimony of one Mohammedan—no matter how false on its very face—receives more credit than that of a dozen or any number of Parsee witnesses. If a Mohammedan kills a Parsee he is only fined about eight toomans, or four pounds sterling; but on the contrary, if a Parsee wounds or murders a Mohammedan he is not only cut to pieces himself, but all his family and children are put to the sword, and sometimes all the Parsees living in the same street are harassed in a variety of ways. The Parsees are prevented from dressing themselves well and from riding a horse or donkey. No matter, even if he were ill and obliged to ride, he is compelled to dismount in the presence of a Mohammedan rider, and is forced to walk to the place of his destination. The Parsees are not allowed to trade in European articles, nor are they allowed to deal in domestic produce, as grocers, dyers, or oilmen, tailors, dairymen, &c., on the ground that their touch would pollute the articles and supplies and make them unfit for the use of Mohammedans.

6. The Parsees are often insulted and abused in every way by the Mohammedans, and their children are stolen or forcibly taken away from them by the Mohammedans. These children are concealed in Mohammedan houses, their names are changed, and they are forced to become Mohammedans, and when they refuse to embrace the Mohammedan faith they are maltreated in various ways. When a man is forcibly converted, his wife and family are also forced to join him as Mohammedans. The Mohammedans desecrate the sacred places of worship of the Zoroastrians and the places for the disposal of their dead.

7. In general the Parsees are heavily taxed in various ways, and are subjected to great oppression. In consequence of such persecution the Parsee population of Persia has, during this century, considerably decreased and is now so small that it consists of a few thousand families only. It is possible that these persecutions are practiced on the Zoroastrian inhabitants of Persia without the knowledge of His Majesty the Shah.

### THE INGENIOUS BARON REUTER

It is whispered that the Shah's European trip was not suggested by the Shah himself, but by the noted telegraphic newsman, Baron Reuter. People who pretend to know say that Reuter began life very poor; that he was an energetic spirit and improved such opportunities as fell in his way; that he learned several languages, and finally became a European guide, or courier, and employed himself in conducting all sorts of foreigners through all sorts of countries and wearing them out with the usual frantic system of sight-seeing. That was a good education for him; it also gave him an intimate knowledge of all the routes of travel and taught him how certain long ones might be shortened. By and by he got some carrier pigeons and established a news express, which necessarily prospered, since it furnished journals and commercial people with all matters of importance considerably in advance of the mails. When railways came into vogue he obtained concessions which enlarged his facilities and still enabled him to defy competition. He was ready for the telegraph and seized that, too; and now for years

## "REUTER'S TELEGRAMS"

has stood in brackets at the head of the telegraphic column of all European journals. He became rich; he bought telegraph lines and built others, purchased a second-hand German baronetcy, and finally sold out his telegraphic property to his government for $3,000,000 and was out of business for once. But he could not stay out.

After building himself a sort of a palace, he looked around for fresh game, singled out the Shah of Persia and "went for him," as the historian Josephus phrases it. He got an enormous "concession" from him and then conceived the admirable idea of exhibiting a Shah of Persia in the capitals of Europe and thus advertising his concession before needful capitalists. It was a sublimer idea than any that any showman's brain has ever given birth to. No Shah had ever voluntarily traveled in Europe before; but then no Shah had ever fallen into the hands of a European guide before.

## THE FAT "CONCESSION"

The baron's "concession" is a financial curiosity. It allows him the sole right to build railways in Persia for the next seventy years; also street railroads; gives all the land necessary, free of charge, for double tracks and fifty or sixty yards on each side; all importations of *material*, etc., free of duty; all the baron's exports free of duty also. The baron may appropriate and work all mines (except those

84

of the precious metals) free of charge, the Shah to
have 15 per cent of the profits. Any private mine
may be "gobbled" (the Persian word is *akbamarish*)
by the baron if it has not been worked during
five years previously. The baron has the exclu-
sive privilege of making the most of all government forests, he giving the Shah 15 per cent of the
profits from the wood sold. After a forest is removed, the baron is to be preferred before all other
purchasers if he wants to buy the land. The baron
alone may dig wells and construct canals, and
he is to own all the land made productive by
such works. The baron is empowered to raise
$30,000,000 on the capital stock for working pur-
poses, and the Shah agrees to pay 7 per cent interest
on it; and Persia is wholly unencumbered with debt.
The Shah hands over to the baron the management
of his customs for twenty years, and the baron
engages to pay for this privilege $100,000 a year
more than the Shah now receives, so the baron
means to wake up that sleepy Persian commerce.
After the fifth year the baron is to pay the Shah an
additional 60 per cent of the profits, if his head is
still a portion of his person then. The baron is to
have first preference in the establishment of a bank.
The baron has preference in establishing gas, road,
telegraph, mill, manufacturing, forge, pavement, and
all such enterprises. The Shah is to have 20 per
cent of the profits arising from the railways.
Finally, the baron may sell out whenever he
wants to.

It is a good "concession" in its way. It seems to

make the Shah say: "Run Persia at my expense and give me a fifth of the profits."

One's first impulse is to envy the baron; but, after all, I do not know. Some day, if things do not go to suit the Shah, he may say, "There is no head I admire so much as this baron's; bring it to me on a plate."

### DEPARTURE OF THE IMPERIAL CIRCUS.

We are all sorry to see the Shah leave us, and yet are glad on his account. We have had all the fun and he all the fatigue. He would not have lasted much longer here. I am just here reminded that the only way whereby you may pronounce the Shah's title correctly is by taking a pinch of snuff. The result will be "t-Shah!"

# A WONDERFUL PAIR OF SLIPPERS

## (WITH LETTERS CONCERNING THEM FROM MARK TWAIN AND ELSIE LESLIE LYDE)

### MARK TWAIN'S LETTER

HARTFORD, *Oct. 5, '89.*

DEAR ELSIE: The way of it was this. Away last spring, Gillette[1] and I pooled intellects on this proposition: to get up a pleasant surprise of some kind for you against your next visit—the surprise to take the form of a tasteful and beautiful testimonial of some sort or other, which should express somewhat of the love we felt for you. Together we hit upon just the right thing—a pair of slippers. Either one of us could have thought of a single slipper, but it took both of us to think of two slippers. In fact, one of us did think of one slipper, and then, quick as a flash, the other thought of the other one. It shows how wonderful the human mind is. It is really paleontological; you give one mind a bone, and the other one instantly divines the rest of the animal.

Gillette embroidered his slipper with astonishing facility and splendor, but I have been a long time pulling through with mine. You see, it was my very first attempt at art, and I couldn't rightly get the hang of it along at first. And then I was so busy that I couldn't get a chance to work at it at

---

[1] William Gillette, the distinguished actor and playwright.

87

home, and they wouldn't let me embroider on the cars; they said it made the other passengers afraid. They didn't like the light that flared into my eye when I had an inspiration. And even the most fair-minded people doubted me when I explained what it was I was making—especially brakemen. Brakemen always swore at it, and carried on, the way ignorant people do, about art. They wouldn't take my word that it was a slipper; they said they believed it was a snowshoe that had some kind of a disease.

But I have pulled through, and within twenty-four hours of the time I told you I would—day before yesterday. There ought to be a key to the designs, but I haven't had time to get one up. However, if you will lay the work before you with the forecastle pointing north, I will begin at that end and explain the whole thing, layer by layer, so that you can understand it.

I began with that first red bar, and without ulterior design, or plan of any sort—just as I would begin a Prince and Pauper, or any other tale. And mind you it is the easiest and surest way; because if you invent two or three people and turn them loose in your manuscript, something is bound to happen to them—you can't help it; and then it will take you the rest of the book to get them out of the natural consequences of that occurrence, and so, first thing you know, there's your book all finished up and never cost you an idea. Well, the red stripe, with a bias stitch, naturally suggested a blue one with a perpendicular stitch, and I slammed it in, though when it came daylight I saw it was green—which didn't make any difference, because green and blue are much the same, anyway, and in fact from a purely moral point of view are regarded by the best authorities as identical. Well, if you will notice, a blue perpendicular stitch always suggests a ropy red involved stitch, like a family of angle-worms trying to climb in under each other to keep warm—it would suggest that, every time, without the author of the slipper ever having to think about it at all.

Now at that point, young Dr. Root came in, and, of course, he was interested in the slipper right away, because he has always had a passion for art himself, but has never had a chance to try, because his folks are opposed to it and superstitious about it, and have done all they could to keep him back; and so he was eager to take a hand and see what he could do. And it was beautiful to see him sit there and tell Mrs. Clemens what had been happening while we were off on summer vacation, and hold the slipper up toward the end of his nose, and forget the sordid world, and imagine the canvas was a "subject" with a scalp wound, and nimbly whirl in that lovely surgical stitch which you see there—and never hesitating a moment in his talk except to say "Ouch" when he stuck himself, and then going right on again as smooth and easy as nothing. Yes, it was a charming spectacle. And it was real art, too—realistic, just native untaught genius; you can see the very scalp itself, showing through between the stitches.

Well, next I threw in that sheaf of green rods which the lictors used to carry before the Roman consuls to lick them with when they didn't behave—they turned blue in the morning, but that is the way green always acts.

The next week, after a good rest, I snowed in that sea of frothy waves, and set that yellow thing afloat in it and those two things that are skewered through it. It isn't a home plate, and it isn't a papal tiara with the keys of St. Peter; no, it is a heart—my heart—with two arrows stuck through it—arrows that go in blue and come out crimson—crimson with the best drops in that heart, and gladly shed for love of you, dear.

Now then, as you strike to the south'ard and drift along down the starboard side, abaft the main-to'-gallant scuppers, you come to that blue quarter-deck which runs the rest of the way aft to the jumping-off place. In the midst of that blue you will see some big red letters—M. T.; and west'ard, over on the port side, you will see some more red letters—TO E. L. Aggregated, these several groups of letters signify, Mark Twain to Elsie Leslie. And you will notice that you have a gift for art yourself, for the southern half of the L, embroidered by yourself, is as good as anything I can do, after all my experience.

There, now you understand the whole work. From a professional point of view I consider the Heart and Arrows by all odds the greatest triumph of the whole thing; in fact, one of the ablest examples of civil engineering in a beginner I ever saw—for it was all inspiration, just the lightninglike inspiration of the moment. I couldn't do it again in a hundred years—even if I recover this time and get just as well and strong as I was before. You notice what fire there is in it—what rapture, enthusiasm, frenzy —what blinding explosions of color. It is just a "Turner"—that is what it is. It is just like his "Slave Ship," that immortal work. What you see in the "Slave Ship" is a terrific explosion of radiating rags and fragments of flaming crimson flying from a common center of intense yellow which is in violent commotion—insomuch that a Boston reporter said it reminded him of a yellow cat dying in a platter of tomatoes.

Take the slippers and wear them next your heart, Elsie dear; for every stitch in them is a testimony of the affection which two of your loyalest friends bear you. Every single stitch cost us blood. I've got twice as many pores in me now as I used to have; and you would never believe how many places you can stick a needle into yourself until you go into the embroidery line and devote yourself to art.

Do not wear these slippers in public, dear; it would only excite envy; and, as like as not, somebody would try to shoot you.

Merely use them to assist you in remembering that among the many, many people who think all the world of you is your friend,

MARK TWAIN.


ELSIE'S REPLY.

NEW YORK, *October 9, 1889.*
MY DEAR MR. CLEMENS: The slipper the long letter and all the rest came this afternoon, I think

they are splendid and shall have them framed and keep them among my very most prechus things. I have had a great many nice things given to me and people often say very pleasant things but I am not quite shure they always mean it or that they are as trustable as you and "Leo" and I am very shure thay would not spend their prechus time and shed their blood for me so you see that is one reason why I will think so much of it and then it was all so funny to think of two great big men like you and "little Willie" (that is what "Leo" calls himself to me) imbroidering a pair of slippers for a little girl like me of corse you have a great many large words in your letter that I do not quite understand. One word comencing with P. has fifteen letters in it and I do not know what you mean by pooled unless you mean you and Leo put your two minds together to make the slippers which was very nice of you both I think you are just right about the angle worms thay did look like that this summer when I used to dig them for bate to fish with please tell Dr. Root I will think of him when I look at the part he did the Surgicle Stich I mean I hope you will be quite well and strong by the time you get this letter as you were before you made my slipper it would make me very sad if you were to be ill. Give my love to Mrs. Clemens Susie Clara Gene I-know and you-know and Vix and all of my Hartford friends tell Gene I wish I was with her and we would have a nice jump in the hay loft. When you come to New York you must call and see me then we will see about those big words my address is up in the top left corner of this letter.

>To my loyal friend
>Mark Twain
>From his little friend
>ELSIE LESLIE LYDE.

[Not Little Lord Fauntleroy now, but Tom Canty of Offal Court and Little Edward of Wales.][1]

[1] Elsie Leslie, then a little girl, played Little Lord Fauntleroy and the double part of Tom Canty and the Little Prince, with great success.

# AIX, THE PARADISE OF THE RHEUMATICS

(Contributed to the New York *Sun*, 1891)

AIX-LES-BAINS. Certainly this is an enchanting place. It is a strong word, but I think the
facts justify it. True, there is a rabble of nobilities,
big and little, here all the time, and often a king or
two; but as these behave quite nicely and also keep
mainly to themselves, they are little or no annoyance. And then a king makes the best advertisement there is, and the cheapest. All he costs is a
reception at the station by the mayor and the police
in their Sunday uniforms, shop-front decorations
along the route from station to hotel, brass band at
the hotel, fireworks in the evening, free bath in the
morning. This is the whole expense; and in return
for it he goes away from here with the broad of his
back metaphorically stenciled over with display ads.,
which shout to all nations of the world, assisted by
the telegraph:

> Rheumatism routed at Aix-les-Bains!
> Gout admonished, Nerves braced up!
> All diseases welcomed, and satisfaction given or the money
> returned at the door!

We leave nature's noble cliffs and crags undefiled
and uninsulted by the advertiser's paint brush. We
use the back of a king, which is better and properer

and more effective, too, for the cliffs stay still and few see it, but the king moves across the fields of the world and is visible from all points, like a constellation. We are out for kings this week, but one will be along soon—possibly His Satanic Majesty of Russia. There's a colossus for you! A mysterious and terrible form that towers up into unsearchable space and casts a shadow across the universe like a planet in eclipse. There will be but one absorbing spectacle in this world when we stencil him and start him out.

This is an old valley, this of Aix, both in the history of man and in the geological records of its rocks. Its little lake of Bourget carries the human history back to the lake dwellers, furnishing seven groups of their habitations, and Dr. William Wakefield says in his interesting local guide that the mountains round about furnish "Geographically, a veritable epitome of the globe." The stratified chapters of the earth's history are clearly and permanently written on the sides of the roaring bulk of the Dent du Chat, but many of the layers of race, religion, and government which in turn have flourished and perished here between the lake dweller of several thousand years ago and the French republican of to-day, are ill defined and uninforming by comparison. There are several varieties of pagans. They went their way, one after the other, down into night and oblivion, leaving no account of themselves, no memorials. The Romans arrived 2,300 years ago, other parts of France are rich with remembrances of their eight centuries of occupation, but not many are here. Other pagans followed the Romans. By and by Christianity arrived, some 400 years after the time of Christ. The long procession of races, languages, religions, and dynasties demolished one another's records—it is man's way always.

As a result, nothing is left of the handiwork of the remoter inhabitants of the region except the constructions of the lake dwellers and some Roman odds and ends. There is part of a small Roman temple, there is part of a Roman bath, there is a graceful and battered Roman arch. It stands on a turfy level over the way from the present great bath house, is surrounded by magnolia trees, and is both a picturesque and suggestive object. It has stood there some 1,600 years. Its nearest neighbor, not twenty steps away, is a Catholic church. They are symbols of the two chief eras in the history of Aix. Yes, and of the European world. I judge that the venerable arch is held in reverent esteem by everybody, and that this esteem is its sufficient protection from insult, for it is the only public structure I have yet seen in France which lacks the sign, "It is forbidden to post bills here." Its neighbor the church has that sign on more than one of its sides, and other signs, too, forbidding certain other sorts of desecration.

The arch's nearest neighbor—just at its elbow, like the church—is the telegraph office. So there you have the three great eras bunched together—the era of War, the era of Theology, the era of Business. You pass under the arch, and the buried Cæsars seem to rise from the dust of the centuries and flit before you; you pass by that old battered church, and are

in touch with the Middle Ages, and with another step
you can put down ten francs and shake hands with
Oshkosh under the Atlantic.

It is curious to think what changes the last of the
three symbols stand for; changes in men's ways and
thoughts, changes in material civilization, changes in
the Deity—or in men's conception of the Diety, if
that is an exacter way of putting it. The second of
the symbols arrived in the earth at a time when the
Deity's possessions consisted of a small sky freckled
with mustard-seed stars, and under it a patch of
landed estate not so big as the holdings of the Tsar
to-day, and all His time was taken up in trying to
keep a handful of Jews in some sort of order—exactly
the same number of them that the Tsar has lately
been dealing with in a more abrupt and far less loving and long-suffering way. At a later time—a time
within all old men's memories—the Deity was otherwise engaged. He was dreaming His eternities away
on His Great White Throne, steeped in the soft bliss
of hymns of praise wafted aloft without ceasing from
choirs of ransomed souls, Presbyterians and the rest.
This was a Deity proper enough to the size and conditions of things, no doubt a provincial Deity with
provincial tastes. The change since has been incon-
ceivably vast. His empire has been unimaginably
enlarged. To-day He is a Master of a universe made
up of myriads upon myriads of gigantic suns, and
among them, lost in that limitless sea of light, floats
that atom. His earth, which once seemed so good
and satisfactory and cost so many days of patient
labor to build, is a mere cork adrift in the waters of

a shoreless Atlantic. This is a business era, and no doubt he is governing His huge empire now, not by dreaming the time away in the buzz of hymning choirs, with occasional explosions of arbitrary power disproportioned to the size of the annoyance, but by applying laws of a sort proper and necessary to the sane and successful management of a complex and prodigious establishment, and by seeing to it that the exact and constant operation of these laws is not interfered with for the accommodation of any individual or political or religious faction or nation.

Mighty has been the advance of the nations and the liberalization of thought. A result of it is a changed Deity, a Deity of a dignity and sublimity proportioned to the majesty of His office and the magnitude of His empire, a Deity who has been freed from a hundred fretting chains and will in time be freed from the rest by the several ecclesiastical bodies who have these matters in charge. It was, without doubt, a mistake and a step backward when the Presbyterian Synods of America lately decided, by vote, to leave Him still embarrassed with the dogma of infant damnation. Situated as we are, we cannot at present know with how much of anxiety He watched the balloting, nor with how much of grieved disappointment He observed the result.

Well, all these eras above spoken of are modern, they are of last week, they are of yesterday, they are of this morning, so to speak. The springs, the healing waters that gush up from under this hillside village, indeed are ancient. They, indeed, are a genuine antiquity; they antedate all those fresh

human matters by processions of centuries; they
were born with the fossils of the Dent du Chat,
and they have been always abundant. They furnished a million gallons a day to wash the lake
dwellers with, the same to wash the Cæsars with,
no less to wash Balzac with, and have not diminished
on my account. A million gallons a day for how
many days? Figures cannot set forth the number.
The delivery, in the aggregate, has amounted to an
Atlantic. And there is still an Atlantic down in
there. By Doctor Wakefield's calculation the
Atlantic is three-quarters of a mile down in the
earth. The calculation is based upon the temperature of the water, which is 114 degrees to 117 degrees
Fahrenheit, the natural law being that below a certain depth heat augments at the rate of one degree
for every sixty feet of descent.

Aix is handsome, and is handsomely situated, too,
on its hill slope, with its stately prospect of mountain range and plain spread out before it and about
it. The streets are mainly narrow, and steep and
crooked and interesting, and offer considerable
variety in the way of names; on the corner of one
of them you read this: "Rue du Puits d'Enfer"
("Pit of Hell Street"). Some of the sidewalks are
only eighteen inches wide; they are for the cats,
probably. There is a pleasant park, and there are
spacious and beautiful grounds connected with the
two great pleasure resorts, the Cercle and the Villa
des Fleurs. The town consists of big hotels, little
hotels, and *pensions*. The season lasts about six
months, beginning with May. When it is at its

height there are thousands of visitors here, and in the course of the season as many as 20,000 in the aggregate come and go.

These are not all here for the baths; some come for the gambling facilities and some for the climate. It is a climate where the field strawberry flourishes through the spring, summer, and fall. It is hot in the summer, and hot in earnest; but this is only in the daytime; it is not hot at night. The English season is May and June; they get a good deal of rain then, and they like that. The Americans take July, and the French take August. By the 1st of July the open-air music and the evening concerts and operas and plays are fairly under way, and from that time onward the rush of pleasure has a steadily increasing boom. It is said that in August the great grounds and the gambling rooms are crowded all the time and no end of ostensible fun going on.

It is a good place for rest and sleep and general recuperation of forces. The book of Doctor Wakefield says there is something about this atmosphere which is the deadly enemy of insomnia, and I think this must be true, for if I am any judge, this town is at times the noisiest one in Europe, and yet a body gets more sleep here than he would at home, I don't care where his home is. Now, we are living at a most comfortable and satisfactory *pension*, with a garden of shade trees and flowers and shrubs, and a convincing air of quiet and repose. But just across the narrow street is the little market square, and at the corner of that is the church that is neighbor to the Roman arch, and that narrow street, and that billiard table of a market place, and that church are able, on a bet, to turn out more noise to a cubic yard at the wrong time than any other similar combination in the earth or out of it. In the street you have the skull-bursting thunder of the passing hack, a volume of sound not producible by six hacks anywhere else; on the hack is a lunatic with a whip which he cracks to notify the public to get out of his way. This crack is as keen and sharp and penetrating and ear-splitting as a pistol shot at close range, and the lunatic delivers it in volleys, not single shots. You think you will not be able to live till he gets by, and when he does get by he leaves only a vacancy for the bandit who sells *Le Petit Journal* to fill with his strange and awful yell. He arrives with the early morning and the market people, and there is a dog that arrives at about the same time and barks steadily at nothing till he dies, and they fetch another dog just like him. The bark of this breed is the twin of the whip volley, and stabs like a knife. By and by, what is left of you the church bell gets. There are many bells, and apparently six or seven thousand town clocks, and as they are all five minutes apart—probably by law—there are no intervals. Some of them are striking all the time—at least, after you go to bed they are. There is one clock that strikes the hour and then strikes it over again to see if it was right. Then for evenings and Sundays there is a chime—a chime that starts in pleasantly and musically, then suddenly breaks into a frantic roar, and boom, and crash of warring sounds that makes you think Paris is up and the Revolution come again. And yet, as I have said, one sleeps here—sleeps like the dead. Once he gets his grip on his sleep, neither hack, nor whip, nor news fiend, nor dog, nor bell cyclone, nor all of them together, can wrench it loose or mar its deep and tranquil continuity. Yes, there is indeed something in this air that is death to insomnia.

The buildings of the Cercle and the Villa des Fleurs are huge in size, and each has a theater in it, and a great restaurant, also conveniences for gambling and general and variegated entertainment. They stand in ornamental grounds of great extent and beauty. The multitudes of fashionable folk sit at refreshment tables in the open air, afternoons, and listen to the music, and it is there that they mainly go to break the Sabbath.

To get the privilege of entering these grounds and buildings you buy a ticket for a few francs, which is good for the whole season. You are then free to go and come at all hours, attend the plays and concerts free, except on special occasions, gamble, buy refreshments, and make yourself symmetrically comfortable.

Nothing could be handier than those two little theaters. The curtain doesn't rise until 8.30; then between the acts one can idle for half an hour in the other departments of the building, damaging his appetite in the restaurants or his pocketbook in the baccarat room. The singers and actors are from Paris, and their performance is beyond praise.

I was never in a fashionable gambling hell until I came here. I had read several millions of descriptions of such places, but the reality was new to me. I very much wanted to see this animal, especially the new historic game of baccarat, and this was a good place, for Aix ranks next to Monte Carlo for high play and plenty of it. But the result was what I might have expected—the interest of the looker-on perishes with the novelty of the spectacle; that is to say, in a few minutes. A permanent and intense interest is acquirable in baccarat, or in any other game, but you have to buy it. You don't get it by standing around and looking on.

The baccarat table is covered with green cloth and is marked off in divisions with chalk or something. The banker sits in the middle, the croupier opposite. The customers fill all the chairs at the table, and the rest of the crowd are massed at their back and leaning over them to deposit chips or gold coins. Constantly money and chips are flung upon the table, and the game seems to consist in the croupier's reaching for these things with a flexible sculling oar, and raking them home. It appeared to be a rational enough game for him, and if I could have borrowed his oar I would have stayed, but I didn't see where the entertainment of the others came in. This was because I saw without perceiving, and observed without understanding. For the widow and the orphan and the others do win money there. Once an old gray mother in Israel or elsewhere pulled out, and I heard her say to her daughter or her granddaughter as they passed me, "There, I've won six louis, and I'm going to quit while I'm ahead." Also there was this statistic. A friend pointed to a young man with the dead stub of a cigar in his mouth, which he kept munching nervously all the time and pitching hundred-dollar chips on the board while two sweet young girls reached down over his shoulders to deposit modest little gold pieces, and said: "He's only funning, now; wasting a few hundred to pass the time—waiting for the gold room to open, you know, which won't be till after midnight—then you'll see him bet! He won £14,000 there last night. They don't bet anything there but big money."

The thing I chiefly missed was the haggard people with the intense eye, the hunted look, the desperate mien, candidates for suicide and the pauper's grave. They are in the description, as a rule, but they were off duty that night. All the gamblers, male and female, old and young, looked abnormally cheerful and prosperous.

However, all the nations were there, clothed richly and speaking all the languages. Some of the women were painted, and were evidently shaky as to character. These items tallied with the descriptions well enough.

The etiquette of the place was difficult to master. In the brilliant and populous halls and corridors you don't smoke, and you wear your hat, no matter how many ladies are in the thick throng of drifting humanity, but the moment you cross the sacred threshold and enter the gambling hell, off the hat must come, and everybody lights his cigar and goes to suffocating the ladies.

But what I came here for five weeks ago was the baths. My right arm was disabled with rheumatism.

To sit at home in America and guess out the European bath best fitted for a particular ailment or combination of ailments, it is not possible, and it would not be a good idea to experiment in that way, anyhow. There are a great many curative baths on the Continent, and some are good for one disease and bad for another. So it is necessary to let your physician name a bath for you. As a rule, Americans go to Europe to get this advice, and South Americans go to Paris for it. Now and then an economist chooses his bath himself and does a thousand miles of railroading to get to it, and then the local physicians tell him he has come to the wrong place. He sees that he has lost time and money and strength, and almost the minute he realizes this he loses his temper. I had the rheumatism and was advised to go to Aix, not so much because I had that disease as because I had the promise of certain others. What they were was not explained to me, but they are either in the following menu or I have been sent to the wrong place. Doctor Wakefield's book says:

We know that the class of maladies benefited by the water and baths at Aix are those due to defect of nourishment, debility of the nervous system, or to a gouty, rheumatic, herpetic, or scrofulous diathesis—all diseases extremely debilitating, and requiring a tonic, and not depressing action of the remedy. This it seems to find here, as recorded experience and daily action can testify. According to the line of treatment followed particularly with due regard to the temperature, the action of the Aix waters can be made sedative, exciting, derivative, or alterative and tonic.

The "Establishment" is the property of France, and all the officers and servants are employees of the French government. The bathhouse is a huge and massive pile of white marble masonry, and looks more like a temple than anything else. It has several floors and each is full of bath cabinets. There is every kind of bath—for the nose, the ears, the throat, vapor baths, swimming baths, and all people's favorite, the douche. It is a good building to get lost in, when you are not familiar with it. From early morning until nearly noon people are streaming in and streaming out without halt. The majority come afoot, but great numbers are brought in sedan chairs, a sufficiently ugly contrivance whose cover is a steep little tent made of striped canvas. You see nothing of the patient in this diving bell as the bearers tramp along, except a glimpse of his ankles bound together and swathed around with blankets or towels to that generous degree that the result suggests a sore piano leg. By attention and practice the pallbearers have got so that they can keep out of step all the time—and they do it. As a consequence their veiled churn goes rocking, tilting, swaying along like a bell buoy in a ground swell. It makes the oldest sailor homesick to look at that spectacle.

The "course" is usually fifteen douche baths and five tub baths. You take the douche three days in succession, then knock off and take a tub. You keep up this distribution through the course. If one course does not cure you, you take another one after an interval. You seek a local physician and he examines your case and prescribes the kind of bath required for it, with various other particulars; then you buy your course tickets and pay for them in advance—nine dollars. With the tickets you get a memorandum book with your dates and hours all set down on it. The doctor takes you into the bath the first morning and gives some instructions to the two *doucheurs* who are to handle you through the course. The *pourboires* are about ten cents to each of the men for each bath, payable at the end of the course. Also at the end of the course you pay three or four francs to the superintendent of your department of the bathhouse. These are useful particulars to know, and are not to be found in the books. A servant of your hotel carries your towels and sheet to the bath daily and brings them away again. They are the property of the hotel; the French government doesn't furnish these things.

You meet all kinds of people at a place like this, and if you give them a chance they will submerge you under their circumstances, for they are either very glad or very sorry they came, and they want to spread their feelings out and enjoy them. One of these said to me:

"It's great, these baths. I didn't come here for my health; I only came to find out if there was anything the matter with me. The doctor told me if there was the symptoms would soon appear. After the first douche I had sharp pains in all my muscles. The doctor said it was different varieties of rheumatism, and the best varieties there were, too. After my second bath I had aches in my bones, and skull and around. The doctor said it was different varieties of neuralgia, and the best in the market, anybody would tell me so. I got many new kinds of pains out of my third douche. These were in my joints. The doctor said it was gout, complicated with heart disease, and encouraged me to go on. Then we had the fourth douche, and I came out on a stretcher that time, and fetched with me one vast, diversified undulating continental kind of pain, with horizons to it, and zones, and parallels of latitude, and meridians of longitude, and isothermal belts, and variations of the compass—oh, everything tidy, and right up to the latest developments, you know. The doctor said it was inflammation of the soul, and just the very thing. Well, I went right on gathering them in, toothache, liver complaint, softening of the brain, nostalgia, bronchitis, osteology, fits, Coleoptera, hydrangea, Cyclopædia Britannica, delirium tremens, and a lot of other things that I've got down on my list that I'll show you, and you can keep it if you like and tally off the bric-à-brac as you lay it in.

The doctor said I was a grand proof of what these baths could do; said I had come here as innocent of disease as a grindstone, and inside of three weeks these baths had sluiced out of me every important ailment known to medical science, along with considerable more that were entirely new and patentable. Why, he wanted to exhibit me in his bay window!

There seem to be a good many liars this year. I began to take the baths and found them most enjoyable; so enjoyable that if I hadn't had a disease I would have borrowed one, just to have a pretext for going on. They took me into a stone-floored basin about fourteen feet square, which had enough strange-looking pipes and things in it to make it look like a torture chamber. The two half-naked men seated me on a pine stool and kept a couple of warm-water jets as thick as one's wrist playing upon me while they kneaded me, stroked me, twisted me, and applied all the other details of the scientific massage to me for seven or eight minutes. Then they stood me up and played a powerful jet upon me all around for another minute. The cool shower bath came next, and the thing was over. I came out of the bathhouse a few minutes later feeling younger and fresher and finer than I have felt since I was a boy. The spring and cheer and delight of this exaltation lasted three hours, and the same uplifting effect has followed the twenty douches which I have taken since.

After my first douche I went to the chemist's on the corner, as per instructions, and asked for half a glass of Challe water. It comes from a spring sixteen miles from here. It was furnished to me, but, perceiving that there was something the matter with it, I offered to wait till they could get some that was fresh, but they said it always smelled that way. They said that the reason that this was so much ranker than the sulphur water of the bath was that this contained thirty-two times as much sulphur as that. It is true, but in my opinion that water comes from a cemetery, and not a fresh cemetery, either. History says that one of the early Roman generals lost an army down there somewhere. If he could come back now I think this water would help him find it again. However, I drank the Challe, and have drunk it once or twice every day since. I suppose it is all right, but I wish I knew what was the matter with those Romans.

My first baths developed plenty of pain, but the subsequent ones removed almost all of it. I have got back the use of my arm these last few days, and I am going away now.

There are many beautiful drives about Aix, many interesting places to visit, and much pleasure to be found in paddling around the little Lake Bourget on the small steamers, but the excursion which satisfied me best was a trip to Annecy and its neighborhood. You go to Annecy in an hour by rail, through a garden land that has not had its equal for beauty perhaps since Eden; and certainly not Eden was cultivated as this garden is. The charm and loveliness of the whole region are bewildering. Picturesque rocks, forest-clothed hills, slopes richly bright in the cleanest and greenest grass, fields of grain without freck or flaw, dainty of color and as shiny and shimmery as silk, old gray mansions and towers, half buried in foliage and sunny eminences, deep chasms with precipitous walls, and a swift stream of pale-blue water between, with now and then a tumbling cascade, and always noble mountains in view, with vagrant white clouds curling about their summits.

Then at the end of an hour you come to Annecy and rattle through its old crooked lanes, built solidly up with curious old houses that are a dream of the Middle Ages, and presently you come to the main object of your trip—Lake Annecy. It is a revelation; it is a miracle. It brings the tears to a body's eyes, it affects you just as all things that you instantly recognize as perfect affect you—perfect music, perfect eloquence, perfect art, perfect joy, perfect grief. It stretches itself out there in a caressing sunlight, and away toward its border of majestic mountains, a crisped and radiant plain of water of the divinest blue that can be imagined. All the blues are there, from the faintest shoal-water suggestion of the color, detectable only in the shadow of some overhanging object, all the way through, a little blue and a little bluer still, and again a shade bluer, till you strike the deep, rich Mediterranean splendor which breaks the heart in your bosom, it is so beautiful.

And the mountains, as you skim along on the steamboat, how stately their forms, how noble their proportions, how green their velvet slopes, how soft the mottlings of the sun and shadow that play about the rocky ramparts that crown them, how opaline the vast upheavals of snow banked against the sky in the remotenesses beyond—Mont Blanc and the others—how shall anybody describe? Why, not even the painter can quite do it, and the most the pen can do is to suggest.

Up the lake there is an old abbey—Tallories—relic of the Middle Ages. We stopped there; stepped from the sparkling water and the rush and boom and fret and fever of the nineteenth century into the solemnity and the silence and the soft gloom and the brooding mystery of a remote antiquity. The stone step at the water's edge had the traces of a worn-out inscription on it; the wide flight of stone steps that led up to the front door was polished smooth by the passing feet of forgotten centuries, and there was not an unbroken stone among them all. Within the pile was the old square cloister with covered arcade all around it where the monks of the ancient times used to sit and meditate, and now and then welcome to their hospitalities the wandering knight with his tin breeches on, and in the middle of the square court (open to the sky) was a stone well curb, cracked and slick with age and use, and all about it were weeds, and among the weeds moldy brickbats that the Crusaders used to throw at one another. A passage at the further side of the cloister led to another weedy and roofless little inclosure beyond where there was a ruined wall clothed to the top with masses of ivy, and flanking it was a battered and picturesque arch. All over the building there were comfortable rooms and comfortable beds and clean plank floors with no carpets on them. In one room upstairs were half a dozen portraits, dimming relics of the vanished centuries—portraits of abbots who used to be as grand as princes in their old day, and very rich, and much worshiped and very bold; and in the next room there were a howling chromo and an electric bell. Downstairs there was an ancient wood carving with a Latin word commanding silence, and there was a spang-new piano close by. Two elderly French women, with the kindest and honestest and sincerest faces, have the abbey now, and they board and lodge people who are tired of the roar of cities and want to be where the dead silence and serenity and peace of this old nest will heal their blistered spirits and patch up their ragged minds. They fed us well, they slept us well, and I wish I could have stayed there a few years and got a solid rest.

# MARIENBAD—A HEALTH FACTORY

THE SIMPLE BUT SUFFICIENT REGIMEN IMPOSED ON
PATIENTS IN AN AUSTRIAN RESORT—OBSERVATIONS
ON DIGESTION.

(Contributed to the New York *Sun*, 1891)

THIS place is the village of Marienbad, Bohemia.
It seems no very great distance from Annecy,
in Haute-Savoie, to this place—you make it in less
than thirty hours by these continental express
trains—but the changes in the scenery are great; they
are quite out of proportion to the distance covered.
From Annecy by Aix to Geneva, you have blue lakes,
with bold mountains springing from their borders,
and far glimpses of snowy wastes lifted against the
horizon beyond, while all about you is a garden
cultivated to the last possibility of grace and beauty
—a cultivation which doesn't stop with the handy
lower levels, but is carried right up the sheer steeps
and propped there with ribs of masonry, and made
to stay there in spite of Newton's law.    Beyond
Geneva—beyond Lausanne, at any rate—you have
for a while a country which noticeably resembles
New England, and seems out of place and like an
intruder—an intruder who is wearing his every-day
clothes at a fancy-dress ball.    But presently on your

right, huge green mountain ramparts rise up, and after that for hours you are absorbed in watching the rich shadow effects which they furnish, and are only dully aware that New England is gone and that you are flying past quaint and unspeakable old towns and towers. Next day you have the lake of Zurich, and presently the Rhine is swinging by you. How clean it is! How clear it is! How blue it is! How green it is! How swift and rollicking and insolent are its gait and style! How vivid and splendid its colors—beautiful wreck and chaos of all the soap bubbles in the universe! A person born on the Rhine must worship it.

I saw the blue Rhine sweep along; I heard, or seemed to hear,
The German songs we used to sing in chorus sweet and clear.

Yes, that is where his heart would be, that is where his last thoughts would be, the "soldier of the legion" who "lay dying in Algiers."

And by and by you are in a German region, which you discover to be quite different from the recent Swiss lands behind you. You have a sea before you, that is to say; the green land goes rolling away, in ocean swells, to the horizon. And there is another new feature. Here and there at wide intervals you have islands, hills two hundred and three hundred feet high, of a haystack form, that rise abruptly out of the green plain, and are wooded solidly to the top. On the top there is just room for a ruined castle, and there it is, every time; above the summit you see the crumbling arches and broken towers projecting.

Beyond Stuttgart, next day, you find other changes still. By and by, approaching and leaving Nuremberg and down by Newhaus, your landscape is humped everywhere with scattered knobs of rock, unsociable crags of a rude, towerlike look, and thatched with grass and vines and bushes. And now and then you have gorges, too, of a modest pattern as to size, with precipice walls curiously carved and honeycombed by—I don't know what —but water, no doubt.

The changes are not done yet, for the instant the country finds it is out of Württemberg and into Bavaria it discards one more thickness of soil to go with previous disrobings, and then nothing remains over the bones but the shift. There may be a poorer soil somewhere, but it is not likely.

A couple of hours from Bayreuth you cross into Bohemia, and before long you reach this Marienbad, and recognize another sharp change, the change from the long ago to to-day; that is to say from the very old to the spick and span new; from an architecture totally without shapeliness or ornament to an architecture attractively equipped with both; from universal dismalness as to color to universal brightness and beauty as to tint; from a town which seems made up of prisons to a town which is made up of gracious and graceful mansions proper to the light of heart and crimeless. It is like jumping out of Jerusalem into Chicago.

The more I think of these many changes, the more surprising the thing seems. I have never made so picturesque a journey before, and there cannot be another trip of like length in the world that can furnish so much variety and of so charming and interesting a sort.

There are only two or three streets here in this snug pocket in the hemlock hills, but they are handsome. When you stand at the foot of a street and look up at the slant of it you see only block fronts of graceful pattern, with happily broken lines and the pleasant accent of bay projections and balconies in orderly disorder and harmonious confusion, and always the color is fresh and cheery, various shades of cream, with softly contrasting trimmings of white, and now and then a touch of dim red. These blocks are all thick walled, solid, massive, tall for this Europe; but it is the brightest and newest looking town on the Continent, and as pretty as anybody could require. The steep hills spring high aloft from their very back doors and are clothed densely to their tops with hemlocks.

In Bavaria everybody is in uniform, and you wonder where the private citizens are, but here in Bohemia the uniforms are very rare. Occasionally one catches a glimpse of an Austrian officer, but it is only occasionally. Uniforms are so scarce that we seem to be in a republic. Almost the only striking figure is the Polish Jew. He is very frequent. He is tall and of grave countenance and wears a coat that reaches to his ankle bones, and he has a little wee curl or two in front of each ear. He has a prosperous look, and seems to be as much respected as anybody.

The crowds that drift along the promenade at

music time twice a day are fashionably dressed after the Parisian pattern, and they look a good deal alike, but they speak a lot of languages which you have not encountered before, and no ignorant person can spell their names, and they can't pronounce them themselves.

Marienbad—Mary's Bath. The Mary is the Virgin. She is the patroness of these curative springs. They try to cure everything—gout, rheumatism, leanness, fatness, dyspepsia, and all the rest. The whole thing is the property of a convent, and has been for six or seven hundred years. However, there was never a boom here until a quarter of a century ago.

If a person has the gout, this is what they do with him: they have him out at 5.30 in the morning, and give him an egg and let him look at a cup of tea. At six he must be at his particular spring, with his tumbler hanging at his belt—and he will have plenty of company there. At the first note of the orchestra he must lift his tumbler and begin to sip his dreadful water with the rest. He must sip slowly and be a long time at it. Then he must tramp about the hills for an hour or so, and get all the exercise and fresh air possible. Then he takes his tub or wallows in his mud, if mud baths are his sort. By noon he has a fine appetite, and the rules allow him to turn himself loose and satisfy it, so long as he is careful and eats only such things as he doesn't want. He puts in the afternoon walking the hills and filling up with fresh air. At night he is allowed to take three ounces of any kind of food he doesn't

like and drink one glass of any kind of liquor that
he has a prejudice against; he may also smoke one
pipe if he isn't used to it. At half past nine sharp
he must be in bed and his candle out. Repeat the
whole thing the next day. I don't see any advantage
in this over having the gout.

In the case of most diseases that is about what
one is required to undergo, and if you have any
pleasant habit that you value, they want that. They
want that the first thing. They make you drop
everything that gives an interest to life. Their idea
is to reverse your whole system of existence and
make a regenerating revolution. If you are a Republican, they make you talk free trade. If you are a
Democrat they make you talk protection; if you
are a Prohibitionist, you have got to go to bed
drunk every night till you get well. They spare
nothing, they spare nobody. Reform, reform, that
is the whole song. If a person is an orator, they gag
him; if he likes to read, they won't let him; if he
wants to sing, they make him whistle. They say
they can cure any ailment, and they do seem to do
it; but why should a patient come all the way here?
Why shouldn't he do these things at home and save
the money? No disease would stay with a person
who treated it like that.

I didn't come here to take baths, I only came to
look around. But first one person, then another
began to throw out hints, and pretty soon I was a
good deal concerned about myself. One of these
goutees here said I had a gouty look about the eye;
next a person who has catarrh of the intestines asked

me if I didn't notice a dim sort of stomach ache
when I sneezed. I hadn't before, but I did seem to
notice it then. A man that's here for heart disease
said he wouldn't come downstairs so fast if he had
my build and aspect. A person with an old-gold
complexion said a man died here in the mud bath
last week that had a petrified liver—good deal such
a looking man as I am, and the same initials, and
so on, and so on.

Of course, there was nothing to be uneasy about,
and I wasn't what you may call really uneasy; but
I was not feeling very well—that is, not brisk—and
I went to bed. I suppose that that was not a good
idea, because then they had me. I started in at the
supper end of the mill and went through. I am said
to be all right now, and free from disease, but this
does not surprise me. What I have been through
in these two weeks would free a person of pretty
much everything in him that wasn't nailed there—
any loose thing, any unattached fragment of bone,
or meat or morals, or disease or propensities or
accomplishments, or what not. And I don't say
but that I feel well enough, I feel better than I would
if I was dead, I reckon. And, besides, they say I
am going to build up now and come right along and
be all right. I am not saying anything, but I wish
I had enough of my diseases back to make me aware
of myself, and enough of my habits to make it
worth while to live. To have nothing the matter
with you and no habits is pretty tame, pretty colorless. It is just the way a saint feels, I reckon; it is
at least the way he looks. I never could stand a

saint. That reminds me that you see very few priests around here, and yet, as I have already said, this whole big enterprise is owned and managed by a convent. The few priests one does see here are dressed like human beings, and so there may be more of them than I imagine. Fifteen priests dressed like these could not attract as much of your attention as would one priest at Aix-les-Bains. You cannot pull your eye loose from the French priest as long as he is in sight, his dress is so fascinatingly ugly. I seem to be wandering from the subject, but I am not. This is about the coldest place I ever saw, and the wettest, too. This August seems like an English November to me. Rain? Why, it seems to like to rain here. It seems to rain every time there is a chance. You are strictly required to be out airing and exercising whenever the sun is shining, so I hate to see the sun shining because I hate air and exercise—duty air and duty exercise taken for medicine. It seems ungenuine, out of season, degraded to sordid utilities, a subtle spiritual something gone from it which one can't describe in words, but—don't you understand? With that gone what is left but canned air, canned exercise, and you don't want it.

When the sun does shine for a few moments or a few hours these people swarm out and flock through the streets and over the hills and through the pine woods, and make the most of the chance, and I have flocked out, too, on some of these occasions, but as a rule I stay in and try to get warm.

And what is there for means, besides heavy clothing and rugs, and the polished white tomb that stands lofty and heartless in the corner and thinks it is a stove? Of all the creations of human insanity this thing is the most forbidding. Whether it is heating the room or isn't, the impression is the same—cold indifference. You can't tell which it is doing without going and putting your hand on it. They burn little handfuls of kindlings in it, no substantial wood, and no coal.

The fire burns out every fifteen minutes, and there is no way to tell when this has happened. On these dismal days, with the rain steadily falling, it is no better company than a corpse. A roaring hickory fire, with the cordial flames leaping up the chimney— But I must not think of such things, they make a person homesick. This is a most strange place to come to get rid of disease.

That is what you think most of the time. But in the intervals, when the sun shines and you are tramping the hills and are comparatively warm, you get to be neutral, maybe even friendly. I went up to the Aussichtthurm the other day. This is a tower which stands on the summit of a steep hemlock mountain here; a tower which there isn't the least use for, because the view is as good at the base of it as it is at the top of it. But Germanic people are just mad for views—they never get enough of a view—if they owned Mount Blanc, they would build a tower on top of it.

The roads up that mountain through that hemlock forest are hard packed and smooth, and the grades are easy and comfortable. They are for walkers, not for carriages. You move through steep silence and twilight, and you seem to be in a million-columned temple; whether you look up the hill or down it you catch glimpses of distant figures flitting without sound, appearing and disappearing in the dim distances, among the stems of the trees, and it is all very spectral, and solemn and impressive. Now and then the gloom is accented and sized up to your comprehension in a striking way; a ray of sunshine finds its way down through and suddenly calls your attention, for where it falls, far up the hillslope in the brown duskiness, it lays a stripe that has a glare like lightning. The utter stillness of the forest depths, the soundless hush, the total absence of stir or motion of any kind in leaf or branch, are things which we have no experience of at home, and consequently no name for in our language. At home there would be the plaint of insects and the twittering of birds and vagrant breezes would quiver the foilage. Here it is the stillness of death. This is what the Germans are forever talking about, dreaming about, and despairingly trying to catch and imprison in a poem, or a picture, or a song—they adored Waldeinsamkeit, loneliness of the woods. But how catch it? It has not a body; it is a spirit. We don't talk about it in America, or dream of it, or sing about it, because we haven't it. Certainly there is something wonderfully alluring about it, beguiling, dreamy, unworldly. Where the gloom is softest and richest, and the peace and stillness deepest, far up on the side of that hemlock mountain, a spot where Goethe used to sit and dream, is marked by a granite obelisk, and on its side is carved this famous poem, which is the master's idea of Waldeinsamkeit:

> Ueber allen Wipfeln ist Ruh,
> In allen Wipfeln spürest du
> Kaum einen Hauch:
> Die Vogel in schweigen in Walde.
> Warte nur—Balde
> Ruhest du auch.

It is raining again now. However, it was doing that before. I have been over to the establishment and had a tub bath with two kinds of pine juice in it. These fill the room with a pungent and most pleasant perfume; they also turn the water to a color of ink and cover it with a snowy suds, two or three inches deep. The bath is cool—about 75° or 80° F., and there is a cooler shower bath after it. While waiting in the reception room all by myself two men came in and began to talk. Politics, literature, religion? No, their ailments. There is no other subject here, apparently. Wherever two or three of these people are gathered together, there you have it, every time. The first that can get his mouth open contributes his disease and the condition of it, and the others follow with theirs. The two men just referred to were acquaintances, and they followed the custom. One of them was built like a gasometer and is here to reduce his girth; the other was built like a derrick and is here to fat up, as they express it, at this resort. They were well satisfied with the progress they were making. The gasometer had lost a quarter of a ton in ten days, and showed the record on his belt with pride, and he walked briskly across the room, smiling in a vast and luminous way, like a harvest moon, and said he couldn't have done that when he arrived here. He buttoned his coat around his equator and showed how loose it was. It was pretty to see his happiness, it was so childlike and honest. He set his feet together and leaned out over his person and proved that he could see them. He said he hadn't seen them from that point before for fifteen years. He had a hand like a boxing glove. And on one of his fingers he had just found a diamond ring which he had missed eleven years ago.

The minute the derrick got a chance he broke in and began to tell how he was piling on blubber right along—three-quarters of an ounce every four days; and he was still piping away when I was sent for. I left the fat man standing there panting and blowing, and swelling and collapsing like a balloon, his next speech all ready and urgent for delivery.

The patients are always at that sort of thing, trying to talk one another to death. The fat ones and the lean ones are nearly the worse at it, but not quite; the dyspeptics are the worst. They are at it all day and all night, and all along. They have more symptoms than all the others put together and so there is more variety of experience, more change of condition, more adventure, and consequently more play for the imagination, more scope for lying, and in every way a bigger field to talk. Go where you will, hide where you may, you cannot escape that word liver; you overhear it constantly—in the street, in the shop, in the theater, in the music grounds. Wherever you see two or a dozen people of ordinary bulk talking together, you know they are talking about their livers. When you first arrive here your new acquaintances seem sad and hard to talk to, but pretty soon you get the lay of the land and the hand of things, and after that you haven't any more trouble. You look into the dreary dull eye and softly say:

"Well, how's your liver?"

You will see that dim eye flash up with a grateful flame, and you will see that jaw begin to work, and you will recognize that nothing is required of you from this out but to listen as long as you remain conscious. After a few days you will begin to notice that out of these people's talk a gospel is framing itself and next you will find yourself believing it. It is this—that a man is not what his rearing, his schooling, his beliefs, his principles make him, he is what his liver makes him; that with a healthy liver he will have the clear-seeing eye, the honest heart, the sincere mind, the loving spirit, the loyal soul, the truth and trust and faith that are based as Gibraltar is based, and that with an unhealthy liver he must and will have the opposite of all these, he will see nothing as it really is, he cannot trust anybody, or believe in anything, his moral foundations are gone from under him. Now, isn't that interesting? I think it is.

One of the most curious things in these countries is the street manners of the men and women. In meeting you they come straight on without swerving a hair's breadth from the direct line and wholly ignoring your right to any part of the road. At the last moment you must yield up your share of it and step aside, or there will be a collision. I noticed this strange barbarism first in Geneva twelve years ago.

In Aix-les-Bains, where sidewalks are scarce and everybody walks in the streets, there is plenty of room, but that is no matter; you are always escaping collisions by mere quarter inches. A man or woman who is headed in such a way as to cross your course presently without a collision will actually alter his direction shade by shade and compel a collision unless at the last instant you jump out of the way. Those folks are not dressed as ladies and gentlemen. And they do not seem to be consciously crowding you out of the road; they seem to be innocently and stupidly unaware that they are doing it. But not so in Geneva. There this class, especially the men, crowd out men, women, and girls of all rank and raiment consciously and intentionally—crowd them off the sidewalk and into the gutter.

There was nothing of this sort in Bayreuth. But here—well, here the thing is astonishing. Collisions are unavoidable unless you do all the yielding yourself. Another odd thing—here this savagery is confined to the folk who wear the fine clothes; the others are courteous and considerate. A big burly Comanche, with all the signs about him of wealth and education, will tranquilly force young ladies to step off into the gutter to avoid being run down by him. It is a mistake that there is no bath that will cure people's manners. But drowning would help.

However, perhaps one can't look for any real showy amount of delicacy of feeling in a country where a person is brought up to contemplate without a shudder the spectacle of women harnessed up with dogs and hauling carts. The woman is on one side of the pole, the dog on the other, and they bend to the work and tug and pant and strain—and the man tramps leisurely alongside and smokes his pipe. Often the woman is old and gray, and the man is her grandson. The Austrian national ornithological device ought to be replaced by a grandmother harnessed to a slush cart with a dog. This merely in the interest of fact. Heraldic fancy has been a little too much overworked in these countries, anyway.

Lately one of those curious things happened here which justify the felicitous extravagances of the stage and help us to accept them. A despondent man, bankrupt, friendless, and desperate, dropped a dose of strychnia into a bottle of whisky and went out in the dusk to find a handy place for his purpose, which was suicide. In a lonely spot he was stopped by a tramp, who said he would kill him if he didn't give up his money. Instead of jumping at the chance of getting himself killed and thus saving himself the impropriety and annoyance of suicide, he forgot all about his late project and attacked the tramp in a most sturdy and valiant fashion. He made a good fight, but failed to win. The night passed, the morning came, and he woke out of unconsciousness to find that he had been clubbed half to death and left to perish at his leisure. Then he reached for his bottle to add the finishing touch, but it was gone. He pulled himself together and went limping away, and presently came upon the tramp stretched out stone dead with the empty bottle beside him. He had drunk the whisky and committed suicide innocently. Now, while the man who had been cheated out of his suicide stood there bemoaning his hard luck and wondering how he might manage to raise money enough to buy some more whisky and poison, some people of the neighborhood came by and he told them about his curious adventure. They said that this tramp had been the scourge of the neighborhood and the dread of the constabulary. The inquest passed off quietly and to everybody's satisfaction, and then the people, to testify their gratitude to the hero of the occasion, put him on the police, on a good-enough salary, and he is all right now and is not meditating suicide any more. Here are all the elements of the naïvest Arabian tale; a man who resists robbery when he hasn't anything to be robbed of does the very best to save his life when he has come out purposely to throw it away; and finally is victorious in defeat, killing his adversary in an effectual and poetic fashion after being already *hors du combat* himself. Now if you let him rise in the service and marry the chief of police's daughter it has the requisite elements of the Oriental romance, lacking not a detail so far as I can see.

# DOWN THE RHÔNE

## (1891)

IN old times a summer sail down the Rhône was a favorite trip with travelers. But that day is long gone by. The conveniences for the sail disappeared many years ago—driven out of existence by the railway.

In August, 1891, I made this long-neglected voyage with a boatman and a courier. The following account of it is part diary and part comment. The main idea of the voyage was, not to see sights, but to rest up from sight-seeing. There was little or nothing on the Rhône to examine or study or write didactically about; consequently, to glide down the stream in an open boat, moved by the current only, would afford many days of lazy repose, with opportunity to smoke, read, doze, talk, accumulate comfort, get fat, and all the while be out of reach of the news and remote from the world and its concerns.

Our point of departure was to be the Castle of Châtillon on Lake Bourget, not very far from Aix-les-Bains. I went down from Geneva by rail on a Saturday afternoon, and reached the station nearest the castle during the evening. I found the courier waiting for me. He had been down in the lake region several days, hunting for a boat, engaging the boatman, etc.

*From my log.*—The luggage was given to the porters—a couple of peasant girls of seventeen or eighteen years, and a couple of younger ones— children, one might say, of twelve or thirteen. It consisted of heavy satchels and holdalls, but they gathered it up and trudged away, not seeming to mind the weight. The road was through woods and uphill—dark and steep and long. I tried to take the heavy valise from the smallest one, telling her I would carry it myself. She did not understand, of course, and resisted. I tried, then, to take the bag by gentle force. This alarmed her. The courier came and explained that she was afraid she was going to lose the trifle of money she was earning.

The courier told her this was not the case, but she looked doubtful and concluded to hang on to a sure thing.

"How much is it she's going to get?"

"She will charge about half a franc."

"Then pay her *now*, and she'll give up the bag."

But that scheme failed, too. The child hung to the bag and seemed distressed. No explanation could be got out of her, but one of the other girls said the child was afraid that if she gave it up, the fact would be used against her with tourists as proof that she was not strong enough to carry their luggage for them, and so she would lose chances to get work.

By and by the winding road carried us by an open space where we could see very well—see the ruins of a burned-out little hamlet of the humblest sort— stone walls with empty window holes, narrow alleys cluttered with wreckage and fallen thatch, etc. Our girls were eager to have us stop and view this wonder, the result of the only conflagration they had ever seen, the only large event that had ever accented their monotonous lives. It had happened a couple of months before, and the villagers had lost everything, even to their stockings of savings, and were too poor to rebuild their houses. A young woman, an old one, and all the horses had been burned to death; the young girls said they could take us among the ruins and show us the very spot.

We finally came out on the top of the hill, and there stood the castle, a rather picturesque old stack of masonry with a walled yard about it and an odd old stumpy tower in a corner of the yard handsomely clothed in vines. The castle is a private residence, whose owner leaves it in charge of his housekeeper and some menservants, and lives in Lyons except when he wants to fish or shoot.

The courier had engaged rooms, but the fact had probably been forgotten, for we had trouble in rousing the garrison. It was getting late and they were asleep. Eventually a man unlocked and unbarred the door and led us up a winding stair of heavy and very plain stonework. My bed was higher from the floor than necessary. This is apparently the rule in old French houses of the interior. But there is a stepladder.

In the morning I looked out of my window and saw the tops of trees below me, thick and beautiful foliage, and below the trees was the bright blue water of the lake shining in the sun. The window seemed to be about two hundred feet above the water. An airy and inspiring situation, indeed. A pope was born in that room a couple of centuries ago. I forget his name.

In that old day they built for utility, this was evident. Everything—floors, sashes, shutters, beams, joists—were cheap, coarse, ornamentless, but everlastingly solid and substantial. On the wall hung an indication of the politics of the present owner. This was a small photograph with "Philippe Comte de Paris" written under it.

The castle was ancient, in its way, but over the door of one of its rooms there was a picture set in a frame whose profound antiquity made all its surroundings seem modern and fresh. This frame was of good firm oak, as black as a coal, and had once been part of a lake-dweller's house. It was already a thing of antiquity when the Romans were planting colonies in France before the time of Christ. The remains of a number of lake villages have been dug out of the mud of Lake Bourget.

Breakfast was served in the open air on a precipice in a little arbor sheltered by vines, with glimpses through the tree tops of the blue water far below, and with also a wide prospect of mountain scenery. The coffee was the best I ever drank in Europe.

Presently there was a bugle blast from somewhere about the battlements—a fine Middle Age effect—and after a moment it was answered from the further shore of the lake, and we saw a boat put out from that shore. It was ours. We were soon on board and away.

It was a roomy, long flatboat, very light and easy to manage—easy to manage because its sides tapered a little toward both ends, and both ends curved up free from the water and made the steering prompt and easy. The rear half was sheltered from sun and rain by a temporary (and removable) canopy stretched over hoop-pole arches, after the fashion of the old-time wagon covers of the emigrants to California. We at once rolled the sides of the canopy high up, so that we might have the breeze and a free view on every hand.

On the other side of the lake we entered a narrow canal, and here we had our last glimpse of that picturesque Châtillon perched on its high promontory. The sides of the canal were walled with vines heavily laden with black grapes. The vine leaves were white with the stuff which is squirted on them from a thing like a fire extinguisher to kill the calamitous phylloxera. We saw only one living creature for the first lonely mile—a man with his extinguisher strapped on his back and hard at his deadly work. I asked our admiral, Joseph Rougier, of the village of Chanaz, if it would be a good idea to offer to sell this Sabbath breaker a few choice samples of foreign phylloxera, and he said yes, if one wanted to play the star part in an inquest.

At last two women and a man strolling churchward in their Sunday best gave us a courteous hail and walked briskly along abreast of us, plying the courier and the sailor with eager questions about our curious and unaccountable project, and by the time they had got their fill and dropped astern to digest the matter and finish wondering over it, we were serene again and busy discussing the scenery; for now there was really some scenery to look at, of a mild but pleasant type—low precipices, a country road shaded by large trees, a few cozy thatched cabins scattered along, and now and then an irruption of joyous children who flocked to inspect us and admire, followed by friendly dogs who stood and barked at us, but wagged their tails to say no offense was intended.

Soon the precipice grew bolder, and presently Chanaz came in sight and the canal bore us along its front—along its street, for it had only one. We stepped ashore. There was a roll of distant drums, and soon a company or two of French infantry came marching by. All the citizens were out, and every male took off his hat politely as the soldiers moved past him, and this salute was always returned by the officers.

I wanted envelopes, wine, grapes, and postage stamps, and was directed to a stone stairway and told to go up one flight. Up there I found a small well-smoked kitchen paved with worn-out bricks, with pots and pans hanging about the walls, and a bent and humped woman of seventy cooking a very frugal dinner. The tiredest dog I have seen this year lay asleep under the stove, in a roasting heat, an incredible heat, a heat that would have pulled a remark of the Hebrew children; but the dog slept along with perfect serenity and did not seem to know that there was anything the matter with the weather. The old woman set off her coffee pot.

Next she removed her pork chop to the table; it seemed to me that this was premature—the dog was better done.

We asked for the envelopes and things; she motioned us to the left with her ladle. We passed through a door and found ourselves in the smallest wholesale and retail commercial house in the world, I suppose. The place was not more than nine feet square. The proprietor was polite and cheerful enough for a place five or six times as large. He was weighing out two ounces of parched coffee for a little girl, and when the balances came level at last he took off a light bean and put on a heavier one in the handsomest way and then tied up the purchase in a piece of paper and handed it to the child with as nice a bow as one would see anywhere. In that shop he had a couple of bushels of wooden shoes—a dollar's worth, altogether, perhaps—but he had no other articles in such lavish profusion. Yet he had a pound or so or a dipperful of any kind of thing a person might want. You couldn't buy two things of a kind there, but you could buy one of any and every kind. It was a useful shop, and a sufficient one, no doubt, yet its contents could not have cost more than ten dollars. Here was home on a small scale, but everything comfortable, no haggard looks visible, no financial distress apparent. I got all the things I came for except double-postage stamps for foreign service; I had to take domestic stamps instead. The merchant said he kept a double-stamp in stock a couple of years, but there was no market for it, so he sent it back to Paris, because it was eating up its insurance. A careful man and thrifty; and of such is the commonwealth of France.

We got some hot fried fish in Chanaz and took them aboard and cleared out. With grapes and claret and bread they made a satisfactory luncheon. We paddled a hundred yards, turned a rock corner, and here was the furious gray current of the Rhône just a-whistling by! We crept into it from the narrow canal, and laid in the oars. The floating was begun. One needs no oar-help in a current like that. The shore seemed to fairly spin past. Where the current assaults the heavy stone barriers thrown out from the shores to protect the banks, it makes a break like the break of a steamboat, and you can hear the roar a couple of hundred yards off.

The river where we entered it was about a hundred yards wide, and very deep. The water was at medium stage. The Rhône is not a very long river— six hundred miles—but it carries a bigger mass of water to the sea than any other French stream.

For the first few miles we had lonely shores— hardly ever a house. On the left bank we had high precipices and domed hills; right bank low and wooded.

At one point in the face of a precipice we saw a great cross (carved out of the living rock, the Admiral said) forty feet above the carriage road, where a doctor has had his tomb scooped in the rock and lies in there safe from his surviving patients—if any.

At 1.25 P.M. we passed the slumbrous village of Massigneux de Rive on the right and the ditto village of Huissier on the left (in Savoie). We had to take all names by sound from the Admiral; he said nobody could spell them. There was a ferry at the former village. A wire is stretched across the river high overhead; along this runs a wheel which has ropes leading down and made fast to the ferry-boat in such a way that the boat's head is held farther upstream than its stern. This angle enables the current to drive the boat across, and no other motive force is needed. This would be a good thing on minor rivers in America.

2.10 P.M.—It is delightfully cool, breezy, shady (under the canopy), and still. Much smoking and lazy reflecting. There is no sound but the rippling of the current and the moaning of far-off breaks, except that now and then the Admiral dips a screechy oar to change the course half a point. In the distance one catches the faint singing and laughter of playing children or the softened note of a church bell or town clock. But the reposeful stillness—that is the charm —and the smooth swift gliding—and the fresh, clear, lively, gray-green water. There was such a rush, and boom, and life, and confusion, and activity in Geneva yesterday—how remote all that seems now, how wholly vanished away and gone out of this world!

2.15.—Village of Yenne. Iron suspension bridge. On the heights back of the town a chapel with a tower like a thimble, and a very tall white Virgin standing on it.

2.25.—Precipices on both sides now. River narrow —sixty yards.

2.30.—Immense precipice on right bank, with groups of buildings (Pierre Châtel) planted on the very edge of it. In its near neighborhood a massive and picturesque fortification.

All this narrow gut from the bridge down to the next bridge—a mile or two—is picturesque with its frowning high walls of rock.

In the face of the precipice above the second bridge sits a painted house on a rock bench—a chapel, *we* think, but the Admiral says it is for the storage of wine.

More fortifications at the corner where the river turns—no cannon, but narrow slits for musketry commanding the river. Also narrow slits in the solid (hollowed-out) precipice. Perhaps there is no need of cannon here where you can throw a biscuit across from precipice to precipice.

2.45.—Below that second bridge. On top of the bluffs more fortifications. Low banks on both sides here.

2.50.—Now both sets of fortifications show up, look huge and formidable, and are finely grouped. Through the glass they seem deserted and falling to ruin. Out of date, perhaps.

One will observe, by these paragraphs, that the Rhône is swift enough to keep one's view changing with a very pleasant alacrity.

At midafternoon we passed a steep and lofty bluff—right bank—which was crowned with the moldering ruins of a castle overgrown with trees. A relic of Roman times, the Admiral said. Name? No, he didn't know any name for it. Had it a history? Perhaps; he didn't know. Wasn't there even a legend connected with it? He didn't know of any.

Not even a legend. One's first impulse was to be irritated; whereas one should be merely thankful; for if there is one sort of invention in this world that is flatter than another, it is the average folklore legend. It could probably be proven that even the adventures of the saints in the Roman calendar are not of a lower grade as works of the inventor's art.

The dreamy repose, the infinite peace of these tranquil shores, this Sabbath stillness, this noiseless motion, this strange absence of the sense of sin, and the stranger absence of the desire to commit it— this was the perfectest day the year had brought! Now and then we slipped past low shores with grassy banks. A solitary thatched cottage close to the edge, one or two big trees with dense foliage sheltering the cottage, and the family in their Sunday clothes grouped in the deep shade, chatting, smoking, knitting, the dogs asleep about their feet, the kittens helping with the knitting, and all hands content and praising God without knowing it. We always got a friendly word of greeting and returned it. One of these families contained eighteen sons, and all were present. The Admiral was acquainted with everybody along the banks, and with all the domestic histories, notwithstanding he was so ineffectual on old Roman matters.

4.20.—Bronze statue of the Virgin on a sterile hill slope.

4.45.—Ruined Roman tower on a bluff. Belongs to the no-name series.

5.—Some more Roman ruins in the distance.

At 6 o'clock we rounded to. We stepped ashore

in a woodsy and lonely place and walked a short
mile through a country lane to the sizable and rather
modern-looking village of St.-Genix. Part of the way
we followed another pleasure party—six or eight
little children riding aloft on a mountain of fragrant
hay. This is the earliest form of the human pleasure
excursion, and for utter joy and perfect contentment
it stands alone in a man's threescore years and ten;
all that come after it have flaws, but this has
none.

We put up at the Hôtel Labully, in the little
square where the church stands. Satisfactory dinner. Later I took a twilight tramp along the high
banks of a moist ditch called the Guires River. If
it was my river I wouldn't leave it outdoors nights,
in this careless way, where any dog can come along
and lap it up. It is a tributary of the Rhône when
it is in better health.

It became dark while we were on our way back,
and then the bicyclers gave us many a sudden chill.
They never furnished us an early warning, but
delivered the paralyzing shock of their rubber-horn
hoot right at our shoulder blades and then flashed
spectrally by on their soundless wheels and floated
into the depths of the darkness and vanished from
sight before a body could collect his remark and
get it out. Sometimes they get shot. This is right.

I went to my room, No. 16. The floor was bare,
which is the rule down the Rhône. Its planks were
light colored, and had been smoothed by use rather
than art; they had conspicuous black knots in them.
The usual high and narrow bed was there, with the

usual little marble-topped commode by the head of it and the usual strip of foot carpet alongside, where you climb in. The wall paper was dark—which is usual on the Continent; even in the northern regions of Germany, where the daylight in winter is of such poor quality that they don't even tax it now.

When I woke in the morning it was eight o'clock and raining hard, so I stayed in bed and had my breakfast and a ripe old Paris paper of last week brought up. It was a good breakfast—one often gets that; and a liberal one—one seldom gets that. There was a big bowl for the coffee instead of a stingy cup which has to be refilled just as you are getting interested in it; there was a quart of coffee in the pot instead of a scant half pint; instead of the usual hollow curl of brittle butter which evades you when you try to scoop it on to the knife and crumbles when you try to carve it, there was a solid cream-colored lump as big as a brick; there was abundance of hot milk, and there was also the usual ostensible cream of Europe. There *must* be cream in Europe somewhere, but it is not in the cows; they have been examined.

The rain continued to pour until noon, then the sun burst out and we were soon up and filing through the village. By the time we had tramped our mile and pushed out into the stream, the watches marked 1.10 and the day was brilliant and perfect.

Over on the right were ruins of two castles, one of them of some size.

We passed under a suspension bridge; alongside of it was an iron bridge of a later pattern. Near by was a little steamer lying at the bank with no signs of life about her—the first boat, except ferryboats, encountered since we had entered the Rhône. A lonely river, truly.

We drifted past lofty highlands, but there was nothing inspiring about them. In Switzerland the velvet heights are sprinkled with homes clear to the clouds, but these hills were sterile, desolate, gray, melancholy, and so thin was the skin on them that the rocky bones showed through in places.

1.30.—We seem lost in the intricate channels of an archipelago of flat islands covered with bushes.

1.50.—We whirl around a corner into open river again, and observe that a vast bank of leaden clouds is piling itself up on the horizon; the tint thrown upon the distant stretches of water is rich and fine.

The river is wide now—a hundred and fifty yards —and without islands. Suddenly it has become nearly currentless and is like a lake. The Admiral explains that from this point for nine miles it is called L'Eau Morte—Dead Water.

The region is not entirely barren of life, it seems— solitary woman paddling a punt across the wide still pool.

The boat moved, but that is about all one could say. It was indolent progress; still, it was comfortable. There were flaming sunshine behind and that rich thunder gloom ahead, and now and then the fitful fanning of a pleasant breeze.

A woman paddled across—a rather young woman with a face like the "Mona Lisa." I had seen the "Mona Lisa" only a little while before, and stood two hours in front of that painting, repeating to myself: "People come from around the globe to stand here and worship. What is it they find in it?" To me it was merely a serene and subdued face, and there an end. There might be more in it, but I could not find it. The complexion was bad; in fact, it was not even human; there are no people of that color. I finally concluded that maybe others still saw in the picture faded and vanished marvels which *had* been there once and were now forever vanished.

Then I remembered something told me once by Noel Flagg,[1] the artist. There was a time, he said, when he wasn't yet an artist but thought he was. His pictures sold, and gave satisfaction, and that seemed a good-enough verdict. One day he was daubing away in his studio and feeling good and inspired, when Dr. Horace Bushnell, that noble old Roman, straggled in there without an invitation and fastened that deep eye of his on the canvas. The youth was proud enough of such a call, and glad there was something on the easel that was worthy of it. After a long look the great divine said:

"You have talent, boy." (That sounded good.) "What you want is teaching."

Teaching—he, an accepted and competent artist! He didn't like that. After another long look:

"Do you know the higher mathematics?"

"I? No, sir."

"You must acquire them."

"As a proper part of an artist's training?" This with veiled irony.

[1] Of Hartford, Connecticut.

"As an *essential* part of it. Do you know anatomy?"

"No, sir."

"You must learn how to dissect a body. What are you studying, now—principally?"

"Nothing, I believe."

"And the time flying, the time flying! Where are your books? What do you read?"

"There they are, on the shelves."

"I see. Poetry and romance. They must wait. Get to your mathematics and your anatomy right away. Another point: you must train your eye— you must teach yourself to see."

"Teach myself to see? I believe I was born with that ability."

"But nobody is born with a *trained* ability— nobody. A cow sees—she sees all the outsides of things, no doubt, but it is only the trained eye that sees deeper, sees the soul of them, the meaning of them, the spiritual essence. Are you sure that you see more than the cow sees? You must go to Paris. You will never learn to see here. There they'll teach you; there they'll train you; there they'll work you like a slave; there they'll bring out the talent that's in you. Be off! Don't twaddle here any longer!"

Flagg thought it over and resolved that the advice was worth taking. He and his brother cleared for Paris. They put in their first afternoon there scoffing at the works of the old masters in the Louvre. They laughed at themselves for crossing a wide ocean to learn what masterly painting might be by staring at these odious things. As for the "Mona Lisa," they exhausted their treasure of wit in making fun of it.

Next day they put themselves into the hands of the Beaux Arts people, and that was the end of play. They had to start at the very bottom of their trade and learn it over again, detail by detail, and learn it *right*, this time. They slaved away, night and day for three months, and wore themselves to shadows. Then they had a day off, and drifted into the Louvre. Neither said a word for some time; each disliked to begin; but at last, in front of the "Mona Lisa," after standing mute awhile one of them said:

"Speak out. Say it."

"Say it yourself."

"Well, then, we *were* cows before!"

"Yes—it's the right name for it. That is what we were. It is unbelievable, the change that has come over these pictures in three months. It is the difference between a landscape in the twilight and the same landscape in the daytime." Then they fell into each other's arms.

This all came back to me, now, as I saw this living "Mona Lisa" punting across L'Eau Morte.

2.40 P.M.—Made for a village on the right bank with all speed—Port de Groslee. Remains of Roman aqueduct on hilltop back of village. Rain!— Deluges of it. Took refuge in an inn on the bank —Hôtel des Voyageurs. The public room was full of voyageurs and tobacco smoke. The voyageurs may have been river folk in the old times when the

inn was built, but this present crowd was made up
of teamsters. They sat at bare tables, under their
feet was the bare floor, about them were the four
bare walls—a dreary place at any time, a heart-
breaking place now in the dark of the downpour.
However, it was manifestly not dreary to the teamsters. They were sipping red wine and smoking;
they all talked at once, and with great energy and
spirit, and every now and then they gave their
thighs a sounding slap and burst into a general
horse laugh. The courier said that this was in
response to rude wit and coarse anecdotes. The
brace of modest-looking girls who were waiting on
the teamsters did not seem troubled. The courier
said that they were used to all kinds of language
and were not defiled by it; that they had probably
seldom heard a spade called anything but a spade,
therefore the foulest words came innocent to their
ears.

This inn was built of stone—of course; everybody's house on the Continent, from palace to
hovel, is built of that dismal material, and as a
rule it is as square as a box and odiously plain and
destitute of ornament; it is formal, forbidding, and
breeds melancholy thoughts in people used to friend-
lier and more perishable materials of construction.
The frame house and the log house molder and pass
away, even in the builder's time, and this makes a
proper bond of sympathy and fellowship between
the man and his home; but the stone house remains
always the same to the person born in it; in his old
age it is still as hard, and indifferent, and unaffected

by time as it was in the long-vanished days of his childhood. The other kind of house shows by many touching signs that it has noted his griefs and misfortunes and has felt for them, but the stone house doesn't—it is not of his evanescent race, it has no kinship with him, nor any interest in him.

A professional letter writer happened along presently, and one of the young girls got him to write a letter for her. It seemed strange that she could not write it herself. The courier said that the peasant women of the Rhône do not care for education, but only for religion; that they are all good Catholics, and that their main ambition in life is to see the Rhône's long procession of stone and bronze Virgins added to, until the river shall be staked out with them from end to end; and that their main pleasure in life is to contribute from their scant centimes to this gracious and elevating work. He says it is a quite new caprice; that ten years ago there was not a Virgin in this part of France at all, and never had been. This may be true, and, of course, there is nothing unreasonable about it, but I have already found out that the courier's statements are not always exact.

I had a hot fried fish and coffee in a garden shed roofed with a mat of vines, but the rain came through in streams and I got drenched in spite of our umbrellas, for one cannot manage table implements and umbrellas all at the same time with anything like good success.

*Mem.*—Last evening, for economy's sake, proposed to be a Frenchman because Americans and English are always overcharged. Courier said it wouldn't deceive unless I played myself for a deaf-and-dumb Frenchman—which I did, and so the rooms were only a franc and a half each. But the Admiral must have let it out that I was only deaf and dumb in French, for prices were raised in the bill this morning.

4.10 P.M.—Left Port de Groslee.

4.50 P.M.—Château of the Count Cassiloa—or something like that—the Admiral's pronunciation is elusive. Courier guesses the spelling at "Quintionat." I don't quite see the resemblance. This courier's confidence in himself is a valuable talent. He must be descended from the idiot who taught our forefathers to spell tizzik with a *ph* and a *th*.

The river here is as still and smooth and nearly as dead as a lake. The water is swirly, though, and consequently makes uneasy steering.

River seems to draw together and greatly narrow itself below the count's house. No doubt the current will smarten up there.

Three new quarries along here. Dear me! how little there is in the way of sight-seeing, when a quarry is an event! Remarked upon with contentment.

Swept through the narrow canallike place with a good current.

On the left-hand point below, bush-grown ruins of an ancient convent (St. Alban's), picturesquely situated on a low bluff. There is a higher and handsomer bluff a trifle lower down. How did they overlook it? Those people generally went for the

best, not second best.  Shapely hole in latter bluff
one hundred feet above the water—anchorite's nest?
Interesting-looking hole, and would have cost but
little time and trouble to examine it, but it was not
done.  It is no matter; one can find other holes.

At last, below bluffs, we find some greensward—
not extensive, but a pleasant novelty.

5.30.—Lovely sunset.  Mottled clouds richly
painted by sinking sun, and fleecy shreds of clouds
drifting along the fronts of neighboring blue mountains.  Harrow in a field.  Apparently harrow, but
was distant and could not tell; could have been a
horse.

5.35—Very large gray broken-arched and unus-
ually picturesque ruin crowning a hilltop on right.
Name unknown.  This is a liberal mile above village
of Briord (my spelling—the Admiral's pronunciation), on same side.  Passed the village swiftly, and
left it behind.  The villagers came out and made fun
of our strange tub.  The dogs chased us and were
more noisy than necessary.

6 P.M.—Another suspension bridge—this is the
sixth one.  They have ceased to interest.  There
was nothing exciting about them, from the start.
Presently landed on left bank and shored the boat
for the night.  Hôtel du Rhône Moine.  Isolated.
Situated right on the bank.  Sort of a village—
villagette, to be exact—a little back.  Hôtel is two
stories high and not pretentious—family dwelling
and cow stable all under one roof.

I had been longing to have personal experience
of peasant life—be "on the inside" and see it for

myself, instead of at second hand in books. This was an opportunity and I was excited about it and glad. The kitchen was not clean, but it was a sociable place, and the family were kind and full of good will. There were three little children, a young girl, father, mother, grandparents, some dogs, and a plurality of cats. There was no discord; perfect harmony prevailed.

Our table was placed on the lawn on the river bank. One had no right to expect any finer style here than he would find in the cheapest and shabbiest little tavern in America, for the Hôtel du Rhône Moine was for foot wanderers and laborers on the flatboats that convey stone and sand and wood to Lyons, yet the style *was* superior—very much so. The tablecloth was white, and it and the table furniture were perfectly clean. We had a fish of a pretty coarse grain, but it was fresh from the river and hot from the pan; the bread was good, there was abundance of excellent butter, the milk was rich and pure, the sugar was white, the coffee was considerably better than that which is furnished by the choice hotels of the capitals of the Continent. Thus far, peasant life was a disappointment, it was so much better than anything we were used to at home in some respects. Two of the dogs came out, presently, and sat down by the table and rested their chins on it, and so remained. It was not to beg, for they showed no interest in the supper; they were merely there to be friendly, it was the only idea they had. A squadron of cats came out by and by and sat down in the neighborhood and looked me over languidly, then wandered away without passion, in fact with what looked like studied indifference. Even the cats and the dogs are well and sufficiently fed at the Hôtel du Rhône Moine—their dumb testimony was as good as speech.

I went to bed early. It is inside the house, not outside, that one really finds the peasant life. Our rooms were over the stable, and this was not an advantage. The cows and horses were not very quiet, the smell was extraordinary, the fleas were a disorderly lot, and these things helped the coffee to keep one awake. The family went to bed at nine and got up at two. The beds were very high; one could not climb into them without the help of a chair; and as they were narrow and arched, there was danger of rolling out in case one drifted into dreams of an imprudent sort. These lofty bedsteads were not high from caprice, but for a purpose—they contained chests of drawers, and the drawers were full of clothing and other family property. On the table in my room were some bright-colored, even gorgeous little waxen saints and a Virgin under bell-glasses; also the treasures of the house—jewelry and a silver watch. It was not costly jewelry, but it was jewelry, at any rate, and without doubt the family valued it. I judged that this household were accustomed to having honest guests and neighbors or they would have removed these things from the room when I entered it, for I do not look honester than others.

Not that I have always thought in this way about myself, for I haven't. I thought the reverse until the time I lost my overcoat, once, when I was going down to New York to see the Water Color exhibition, and had a sort of adventure in consequence. The house had been robbed in the night, and when I came downstairs to rush for the early train there was no overcoat. It was a raw day, and when I got to New York at noon I grew colder and colder as I walked along down the Avenue. When I reached East Thirty-fourth street I stopped on the corner and began to consider. It seemed to me that it must have been just about there that Smith,[1] the artist, took me one winter's night, with others, five years before, and caroused us with roasted oysters and Southern stories and hilarity in his fourth story until three or four in the morning; and now if I could only call to mind which of those houses over the way was his, I could borrow an overcoat. All the time that I was thinking and standing there and trying to recollect, I was dimly conscious of a figure near me, but only dimly, very dimly; but now as I came out of my reverie and found myself gazing, rapt but totally unconscious, at one of the houses over there, that figure solidified itself and became at once the most conspicuous thing in the landscape. It was a policeman. He was standing not six feet away, and was gazing as intently at my face as I had been gazing at the house. I was embarrassed—it is always embarrassing to come to yourself and find a stranger staring at you. You blush, even when you have not been doing any

[1] *Note, 1904.* Hopkinson Smith, now a distinguished man in literature, art, and architecture. S. L. C.

harm. So I blushed—a thing that does not commend
a person to a policeman; also I tried to smile a
placating smile, but it did not get any response, so
then I tried to make it a kind of friendly smile,
which was a mistake, because that only hardens a
policeman, and I saw at once that this smile had
hardened this one and made my situation more
difficult than ever; and so, naturally, my judgment being greatly impaired by now, I spoke—
which was an error, because in these circumstances
one cannot arrange without reflection a remark
which will not seem to have a kind of suspicious
something about it to a policeman, and that was
what happened this time; for I had fanned up that
haggard smile again, which had been dying out
when I wasn't noticing, and said:

"Could you tell me, please, if there's a Mr. Smith
lives over there in——"

"*What* Smith?"

That rude abruptness drove his other name out
of my mind; and as I saw I never should be able
to think of it with the policeman standing there
cowing me with his eye, that way, it seemed to me
best to get out a name of some kind, so as to avert
further suspicion, therefore I brought out the first
one which came into my mind, which was John—
another error. The policeman turned purple—apparently with a sense of injury and insult—and said
there were a million John Smiths in New York, and
*which* one was this? Also what did I want with
Smith? I could not remember—the overcoat was
gone out of my mind. So I told him he was a pupil

of mine and that I was giving him lessons in morals; moral culture—a new system.

That was a lucky hit, anyway. I was merely despicable, now, to the policeman, but harmless—I could see it in his eye. He looked me over a moment then said:

"You give him lessons, do you?"

"Yes, sir."

"How long have you been giving him lessons?"

"Two years, next month." I was getting my wind again, and confidence.

"Which house does he live in?"

"That one—the middle one in the block."

"Then what did you ask *me* for, a minute ago?"

I did not see my way out. He waited for an answer, but got tired before I could think of one that would fit the case and said:

"How is it that you haven't an overcoat on, such a day as this?"

"I—well, I never wear them. It doesn't seem cold to me."

He thought awhile, with his eye on me, then said, with a sort of sigh:

"Well, maybe you are all right—I don't know—but you want to walk pretty straight while you are on my beat; for, morals or no morals, blamed if I take much stock in you. Move on, now."

Then he turned away, swinging his club by its string. But his eye was over his shoulder, my way; so I had to cross to that house, though I didn't want to, any more. I did not expect it to be Smith's house, now that I was so out of luck, but I thought

I would ring and ask, and if it proved to be some one else's house, then I would explain that I had come to examine the gas meter and thus get out the back way and be all right again. The door was opened by a middle-aged matron with a gentle and friendly face, and she had a sweet serenity about her that was a notable contrast to my nervous flurry. I asked after Smith and if he lived there, and to my surprise and gratitude she said that this was his home.

"Can I see him? Can I see him right away—immediately?"

No; he was gone downtown. My rising hopes fell to ruin.

"Then can I see Mrs. Smith?"

But alas and alas! she was gone downtown with him. In my distress I was suddenly smitten by one of those ghastly hysterical inspirations, you know, when you want to do an insane thing just to astonish and petrify somebody; so I said, with a rather over-done pretense of playful ease and assurance:

"Ah, this is a very handsome overcoat on the hat rack—be so good as to lend it to me for a day or two!"

"With pleasure," she said—and she had the coat on me before I knew what had happened. It had been my idea to astonish and petrify her, but I was the person astonished and petrified, myself. So astonished and so petrified, in fact, that I was out of the house and gone, without a thank-you or a question, before I came to my senses again. Then I drifted slowly along, reflecting—reflecting pleasantly. I said to myself, "She simply divined my character by my face—what a far clearer intuition she had than that policeman." The thought sent a glow of self-satisfaction through me.

Then a hand was laid on my shoulder and I shrank together with a crash. It was the policeman. He scanned me austerely and said:

"Where did you get that overcoat?"

Although I had not been doing any harm, I had all the sense of being caught—caught in something disreputable. The officer's accusing eye and unbelieving aspect heightened this effect. I told what had befallen me at the house in as straightforward a way as I could, but I was ashamed of the tale, and looked it, without doubt, for I knew and felt how improbable it must necessarily sound to anybody, particularly a policeman. Manifestly he did not believe me. He made me tell it all over again, then he questioned me:

"You don't know the woman?"

"No, I don't know her."

"Haven't the least idea who she is?"

"Not the least."

"You didn't tell her your name?"

"No."

"She didn't ask for it?"

"No."

"You just asked her to lend you the overcoat, and she let you take it?"

"She put it on me herself."

"And didn't look frightened?"

"Frightened? Of course not."

"Not even surprised?"

"Not in the slightest degree."

He paused. Presently he said:

"My friend, I don't believe a word of it. Don't you see, yourself, it's a tale that won't wash? Do *you* believe it?"

"Yes. I know it's true."

"Weren't you surprised?"

"Clear through to the marrow!"

He had been edging me along back to the house. He had a deep design; he sprung it on me now. Said he:

"Stop where you are. I'll mighty soon find out!"

He walked to the door and up the steps, keeping a furtive eye out toward me and ready to jump for me if I ran. Then he pretended to pull the bell, and instantly faced about to observe the effect on me. But there wasn't any; I walked toward him instead of running away. That unsettled him. He came down the steps, evidently perplexed, and said:

"Well, I can't make it out. It may be all right, but it's too many for me. I don't like your looks and I won't have such characters around. Go along, now, and look sharp. If I catch you prowling around here again I'll run you *in*."

I found Smith at the Water Color dinner that night, and asked him if it were merely my face that had enabled me to borrow the overcoat from a stranger, but he was surprised and said:

"No! What an idea—and what intolerable conceit! She is my housekeeper, and remembered your drawling voice from overhearing it a moment that night four or five years ago in my house; so she knew where to send the police if you didn't bring the coat back!"

After all those years I was sitting here, now, at midnight in the peasant hotel, in my night clothes, and honoring womankind in my thoughts; for here was another woman, with the noble and delicate intuitions of her sex, trusting me, a total stranger, with all her modest wealth. She entered the room, just then, and stood beaming upon me a moment with her sweet matronly eyes—then took away the jewelry.

*Tuesday, September 22d.*—Breakfast in open air. Extra canvas was now to be added to the boat's hood to keep the passengers and valises better protected during rainstorms. I passed through the villagette and started to walk over the wooded hill, the boat to find us on the river bank somewhere below, by and by. I soon got lost among the high bushes and turnip gardens. Plenty of paths, but none went to river. Reflection. Decision—that the path most traveled was the one leading in the right direction. It was a poor conclusion. I got lost again; this time worse than before. But a peasant of above eighty (as she said, and certainly she was very old and wrinkled and gray and bent) found me presently and undertook to guide me safely. She was vigorous, physically, prompt and decided of movement, and altogether soldierlike; and she had a hawk's eye and beak, and a gypsy's complexion. She said that from her girlhood up to not so very many years ago she had done a man's work on a woman's pay on the big keel boats that carry stone down the river, and was as good a man as the best, in the matter

of handling stone. Said she had seen the great
Napoleon when she was a little child. Her face was
so wrinkled and dark and so eaglelike that she reminded me of old Indians one sees out on the Great
Plains—the outside signs of age, but in the eye an
indestructible spirit. She had a couple of laden
baskets with her which I had found heavy after
three minutes' carrying, when she was finding the
way for me, but they seemed nothing to her. She
impressed one rather as a man than as a woman;
and so, when she spoke of her child that was drowned,
and her voice broke a little and her lip quivered, it
surprised me; I was not expecting it. "Grandchild?"
No—it was her own child. "Indeed? When?" So
then it came out that it was sixty years ago. It
seemed strange that she should mind it so long. But
that was the woman of it, no doubt. She had a fragment of newspaper—religious—with rude holy wood-
cuts in it and doubtful episodes in the lives of mediæval saints and anchorites—and she could read these
instructive matters in fine print without glasses; also,
her eyes were as good at long distances. She led
hither and thither among the paths and finally
brought me out overlooking the river. There was a
steep sandy frontage there, where there had recently
been a small landslide, and the faint new path ran
straight across it for forty feet, like a slight snow
track along the slant of a very steep roof. I halted
and declined. I had no mind to try the crumbly
path and creep and quake along it with the boiling
river—and maybe some rocks—under my elbow
thirty feet below. Such places turn my stomach.

The old woman took note of me, understood, and said what sounded like, "*Lass' ma allez au premier*" —then she tramped briskly and confidently across with her baskets, sending miniature avalanches of sand and gravel down into the river with each step. One of her feet plowed from under her, about midway, but she snatched it back and marched on, not seeming to mind it. My pride urged me to move along, and put me to shame. After a time the old woman came back and coaxed me to try, and did at last get me started in her wake and I got as far as midway all right; but then to hearten me still more and show me how easy and safe it was, she began to prance and dance her way along, with her knuckles in her hips, kicking a landslide loose with every skip. The exhibition struck a cold panic through me and made my brain swim. I leaned against the slope and said I would stay there until the boat came and testified as to whether there were rocks under me or not. For the third time in my life I was in that kind of a fix—in a place where I could not go backward or forward, and mustn't stay where I was. The boat was a good while coming, but it seemed longer than that. Where I was, the slope was like a roof; where the slope ended the wall was perpendicular thence to the water, and one could not see over and tell what the state of things might be down there. When the boat came along, the courier said there was nothing down there but deep water—no rocks. I did not mind the water; so my fears disappeared, now, and I finished my march without discomfort. I gave the old woman some money, which pleased her very much and she tried her grateful best to give us a partridge, newly killed, which she rummaged out of one of her baskets, and seemed disappointed when I would not take it. But I couldn't; it would have been a shabby act. Then she went her way with her heavy baskets and I got aboard and afloat once more, feeling a great respect for her and very friendly toward her. She waved a good-by every now and then till her figure faded out in the plain, joining that interminable procession of friends made and lost in an hour that drifts past a man's life from cradle to grave and returns on its course no more. The courier said she was probably a poacher and stole the partridge.

The courier was not able to understand why I had not nerve enough to walk along a crumbling slope with a precipice only thirty feet high below me; but I had no difficulty in understanding it. It is constitutional with me to get nervous and incapable under the probability of getting myself dropped thirty feet on to a pile of rocks; it does not come from culture. Some people are made in one way, and some in another—and the above is my way. Some people who can skirt precipices without a tremor have a strong dread of the dentist's chair, whereas I was born without any prejudices against the dentist's chair; when in it I am interested, am not in a hurry, and do not greatly mind the pain. Taken by and large, my style of make has advantages over the other, I think. Few of us are obliged to circumnavigate precipices, but we all have to take a chance at the dental chair.

People who early learn the right way to choose a dentist have their reward. Professional superiority is not everything; it is only part. All dentists talk while they work. They have inherited this from their professional ancestors, the barbers. The dentist who talks well—other things being equal—is the one to choose. He tells anecdotes all the while and keeps his man so interested and entertained that he hardly notices the flight of time. For he not only tells anecdotes that are good in themselves, but he adds nice shadings to them with his instruments as he goes along, and now and then brings out effects which could not be produced with any other kind of tools at all. All the time that such a dentist as this is plowing down into a cavity with that spinning gouge which he works with a treadle, it is observable that he has found out where he has uncovered a nerve down in there, and that he only visits it at intervals, according to the needs of his anecdote, touching it lightly, very lightly and swiftly, now and then, to brighten up some happy conceit in his tale and call a delicate electric attention to it; and all the while he is working gradually and steadily up toward his climax with veiled and consummate art —then at last the spindle stops whirling and thundering in the cavity, and you know that the grand surprise is imminent, now—is hanging in the very air. You can hear your heart beat as the dentist bends over you with his grip on the spindle and his voice diminished to a murmur. The suspense grows bigger—bigger—bigger—your breath stops—then your heart. Then with lightning suddenness the "nub" is sprung and the spindle drives into the raw nerve! The most brilliant surprises of the stage are pale and artificial compared with this.

It is believed by people generally—or at least by many—that the exquisitely sharp sensation which results from plunging the steel point into the raw nerve is pain, but I think that this is doubtful. It is so vivid and sudden that one has no time to examine properly into its character. It is probably impossible, with our human limitations, to determine with certainty whether a sensation of so high and perfect an order as that is pain or whether it is pleasure. Its location brings it under the disadvantage of a common prejudice; and so men mistake it for pain when they might perceive that it is the opposite of that if it were anywhere but in a tooth. I may be in error, but I have experimented with it a great deal and I am satisfied in my own mind that it is not pain. It is true that it always feels like pain, but that proves nothing—ice against a naked back always passes for fire. I have every confidence that I can eventually prove to everyone's satisfaction that a nerve-stab produces pleasure; and not only that, but the most exquisite pleasure, the most perfect felicity which we are capable of feeling. I would not ask more than to be remembered hereafter as the man who conferred this priceless benefaction upon his race.

11.30.—Approaching the Falls of the Rhône. Canal to the left, walled with compact and beautiful masonry. It is a cut-off. We could pass through it and avoid the Falls—are advised by the Admiral to do it, but all decline, preferring to have a dangerous adventure to talk about.

However . . .

The truth is, the current began to grow ominously swift—and presently pretty lumpy and perturbed; soon we seemed to be simply flying past the shores. Then all of a sudden three hundred yards of boiling and tossing river burst upon our sight through the veiling tempest of rain! I did not see how our flimsy ark could live through such a place. If we were wrecked, swimming could not save us; the packed multitude of tall humps of water meant a bristling chaos of big rocks underneath, and the first rock we hit would break our bones. If I had been fortified with ignorance I might have wanted to stay in the boat and see the fun; but I have had much professional familiarity with water, and I doubted if there was going to be any fun there. So I said I would get out and walk, and I did. I need not tell anybody at home; I could leave out the Falls of the Rhône; they are not on the map, anyhow. If an adventure worth recording resulted, the Admiral and the courier would have it, and that would answer. I could see it from the bank—nothing could be better; it seemed even providential.

I ran along the bank in the driving rain, and enjoyed the sight to the full. I never saw a finer show than the passage of that boat was, through the fierce turmoil of water. Alternately she rose high and plunged deep, throwing up sheets of foaming spray and shaking them off like a mane. Several times she seemed to fairly bury herself, and I thought she was gone for good, but always she sprang high aloft the next moment, a gallant and stirring spectacle to see. The Admiral's steering was great. I had not seen the equal of it before.

The boat waited for me down at the Villebois bridge, and I presently caught up and went aboard. There was a stretch of a hundred yards of offensively rough water below the bridge, but it had no dangerous features about it. Still, I was obliged to claim that it had, and that these perils were much greater than the others.

Noon.—A mile of perpendicular precipices—very handsome. On the left, at the termination of this stately wall, a darling little old tree-grown ruin abreast a wooded islet with a large white mansion on it. Near that ruin nature has gotten up a clever counterfeit of one, tree-grown and all that, and, as its most telling feature, has furnished it a battered monolith that stands up out of the underbrush by itself and looks as if men had shaped it and put it there and time had gnawed it and worn it.

This is the prettiest piece of river we have found. All its aspects are dainty and gracious and alluring.

1 P.M.—Château de la Salette. This is the port of the Grotte de la Balme, "one of the seven wonders of Dauphiny." It is across a plain in the face of a bluff a mile from the river. A grotto is out of the common order, and I should have liked to see this one, but the rains have made the mud very deep and it did not seem well to venture so long a trip through it.

2.15 P.M.—St.-Etienne. On a distant ridge inland a tall openwork structure commandingly situated, with a statue of the Virgin standing on it.

Immense empty freight barges being towed upstream by teams of two and four big horses—not on the bank, but under it; not on the land, but always in the water—sometimes breast deep—and around the big flat bars.

We reached a not very promising-looking village about four o'clock, and concluded to land; munching fruit and filling the hood with pipe smoke had grown monotonous. We could not have the hood furled, because the floods of rain fell unceasingly. The tavern was on the river bank, as is the custom. It was dull there, and melancholy—nothing to do but look out of the window into the drenching rain and shiver; one could do that, for it was bleak and cold and windy, and there was no fire. Winter overcoats were not sufficient; they had to be supplemented with rugs. The raindrops were so large and struck the river with such force that they knocked up the water like pebble splashes.

With the exception of a very occasional wooden-shod peasant, nobody was abroad in this bitter weather—I mean of our sex. But all weathers are alike to the women in these continental countries. To them and the other animals life is serious; nothing interrupts their slavery. Three of them were washing clothes in the river under the window when we arrived, and they continued at it as long as there was light to work by. One was apparently thirty; another—the mother?—above fifty; the third—grandmother?—so old and worn and gray

she could have passed for eighty. They had no
waterproofs or rubbers, of course; over their heads
and shoulders they wore gunny sacks—simply con-
ductors for rivers of water; some of the volume
reached ground, the rest soaked in on the way.

At last a vigorous fellow of thirty-five arrived,
dry and comfortable, smoking his pipe under his big
umbrella in an open donkey cart—husband, son, and
grandson of those women? He stood up in the cart,
sheltering himself, and began to superintend, issuing
his orders in a masterly tone of command, and showing temper when they were not obeyed swiftly
enough. Without complaint or murmur the drowned
women patiently carried out the orders, lifting the
immense baskets of soaked clothing into the cart and
stowing them to the man's satisfaction. The cart
being full now, he descended, with his umbrella,
entered the tavern, and the women went drooping
homeward in the wake of the cart, and soon were
blended with the deluge and lost to sight. We
would tar and feather that fellow in America, and
ride him on a rail.

When we came down into the public room he had
his bottle of wine and plate of food on a bare table
black with grease, and was chomping like a horse.
He had the little religious paper which is in everybody's hands on the Rhône borders, and was en-
lightening himself with the histories of French saints
who used to flee to the desert in the Middle Ages to
escape the contamination of women.

Wednesday.—After breakfast, got under way.
Still storming as hard as ever. The whole land looks

defeated and discouraged. And very lonely; here and there a woman in the fields. They merely accent the loneliness.

NOTE.—The record ends here. Luxurious enjoyment of the excursion rendered the traveler indifferent to his notes. The drift continued to Arles, whence Mark Twain returned to Geneva and Ouchy by rail. Ten years later he set down another picture of this happy journey—"The Lost Napoleon"—which follows.—A. B. P.

# THE LOST NAPOLEON

THE lost Napoleon is a part of a mountain range. Several miles of it—say six. When you stand at the right viewpoint and look across the plain, there, miles away, stretched out on his back under the sky, you see the great Napoleon, sleeping, with his arm folded upon his breast. You recognize him at once and you catch your breath and a thrill goes through you from head to foot—a most natural thing to happen, for you have never been so superbly astonished in your life before, and you realize, if you live a century, it is not likely that you will ever encounter the like of that tremendous surprise again. You see, it is unique. You have seen mountain ridges before that looked like men lying down, but there was always some one to pilot you to the right viewpoint, and prepare you for the show, and then tell you which is the head and which the feet and which the stomach, and at last you get the idea and say, "Yes, now I see it, now I make it out—it *is* a man, and wonderful, too." But all this has damaged the surprise and there is not much thrill; moreover, the man is only a third-rate celebrity or no celebrity at all—he is no Napoleon the Great. But I discovered this stupendous Napoleon myself and was caught wholly by surprise, hence the splendid emotion, the uplifting astonishment.

We have all seen mountains that looked like whales, elephants, recumbent lions—correctly figured, too, and a pleasure to look upon—but we did not discover them, somebody pointed them out to us, and in the same circumstances we have seen and enjoyed stately crags and summits known to the people thereabouts as "The Old Man's Head," "The Elephant's Head," "Anthony's Nose," "The Lady's Head," etc., and we have seen others that were named "Shakespeare's Head," and "Satan's Head," but still the fine element of surprise was in almost all cases wanting.

The Lost Napoleon is easily the most colossal and impressive statue in the world. It is several miles long; in form and proportions it is perfect. It represents Napoleon himself and not another; and there is something about the dignity and repose of the great figure that stirs the imagination and half persuades it that this is not an unsentient artifice of nature, but the master of the world sentient and dreaming—dreaming of battle, conquest, empire. I call it the Lost Napoleon because I cannot remember just where I was when I saw it. My hope, in writing this, is that I may move some wandering tourist or artist to go over my track and seek for it—seek for it, find it, locate it exactly, describe it, paint it, and so preserve it against loss again.

My track was down the Rhône; I made the excursion ten or eleven years ago in the pleasantest season of the year. I took a courier with me and went from Geneva a couple of hours by rail to the blue little Lake Bourget, and spent the night in a mediæval

castle on an island in that little lake. In the early
morning our boat came for us. It was a roomy open
boat fifteen or twenty feet long, with a single pair of
long oars, and with it came its former owner, a
sturdy big boatman. The boat was mine now; I
think I paid five dollars for it. I was to pay the boatman a trifling daily wage and his keep, and he was to
take us all the way down the Rhône to Marseilles.
It was warm weather and very sunny, but we built a
canvas arch, like a wagon cover, over the aftermost
third of the boat, with a curtain at its rear which
could be rolled up to let the breeze blow through,
and I occupied that tent and was always comfortable. The sailor sat amidships and manned the oars,
and the courier had the front third of the boat to
himself. We crossed the lake and went winding down
a narrow canal bordered by peasant houses and vine-
yards, and after about a league of this navigation we
came in sight of the Rhône, a troubled gray stream
which went tearing past the mouth of the peaceful
canal at a racing gait. We emerged into it and laid
in the oars. We could go fast enough in that current
without artificial aid. During the first days we
slipped along down the curving bends at a speed of
about five miles an hour, but it slackened later.

Our days were all about alike. About four in the
afternoon we tied up at a village and I dined on the
greensward in front of the inn by the water's edge,
on the choicest chickens, vegetables, fruit, butter,
and bread, prepared in French perfection and
served upon the whitest linen; and as a rule I had
the friendly house cat and dog for guests and com-

pany and willing and able helpers. I slept in the inn; often in clean and satisfactory quarters, sometimes in the same room with the cows and the fleas. I breakfasted on the lawn in the morning with cat and dog again; then laid in a stock of grapes and other fruits gathered fresh from the garden and some bottles of red wine made on the premises, and at eight or nine we went floating down the river again. At noon we went ashore at a village, bought a freshly caught fish or two, had them broiled, got some bread and vegetables, and set sail again at once. We always lunched on board as we floated along. I spent my days reading books, making notes, smoking, and in other lazy and enchanting ways, and had the delightfulest ten-day voyage I have ever experienced.

It took us ten days to float to Arles. There the current gave out and I closed the excursion and returned to Geneva by rail. It was twenty-eight miles to Marseilles, and we should have been obliged to row. That would not have been pleasure; it would have meant work for the sailor, and I do not like work even when another person does it.

I think it was about the eighth day that I discovered Napoleon. My notes cover four or five days; there they stop; the charm of the trip had taken possession of me, and I had no energy left. It was getting toward four in the afternoon—time to tie up for the day. Down ahead on the right bank I saw a compact jumble of yellowy-browny cubes stacked together, some on top of the others, and no visible cracks in the mass, and knew it for a village—

a village common to that region down there; a village jammed together without streets or alleys, substantially—where your progress is mainly *through* the houses, not *by* them, and where privacy is a thing practically unknown; a village which probably hadn't had a house added to the jumble for five hundred years. We were anywhere from half a mile to a mile above the village when I gave the order to proceed to that place and tie up. Just then I glanced to my left toward the distant mountain range, and got that soul-stirring shock which I have said so much about. I pointed out the grand figure to the courier, and said:

"Name it. Who is it?"

"Napoleon!"

"Yes, it is Napoleon. Show it to the sailor and ask him to name it."

The sailor said, "Napoleon." We watched the figure all the time then until we reached the village. We walked up the river bank in the morning to see how far one might have to go before the shape would materially change, but I do not now remember the result. We watched it afterward as we floated away from the village, but I cannot remember at what point the shape began to be marred. However, the mountains being some miles away, I think that the figure would be recognizable as Napoleon along a stretch of as much as a mile above and a mile below the village, though I think that the likeness would be strongest at the point where I first saw it—that is, half a mile or more above the village.

We talked the grand apparition over at great length

and with a strong interest. I said I believed that if its presence were known to the world such shoals of tourists would come flocking there to see it that all the spare ground would soon be covered with hotels; and I think so yet. I think it would soon be the most celebrated natural curiosity on the planet, that it would be more visited than Niagara or the Alps, and that all the other famous natural curiosities of the globe would fall to a rank away below it. I think so still.

There is a line of lumbering and thundering great freight steamers on the Rhône, and I think that if some man will board one of them at Arles and make a trip of some hours upstream—say from three to six—and keep an eye out to the right and watch that mountain range he will be certain to find the Lost Napoleon and have no difficulty in rediscovering the mighty statue when he comes to the right point. It will cost nothing to make the experiment, and I hope it will be done.

NOTE.—Mark Twain's biographer rediscovered it in 1913. It is some miles below Valence, opposite the village of Beauchastel.

# SOME NATIONAL STUPIDITIES

(1891-1892)

THE slowness of one section of the world about adopting the valuable ideas of another section of it is a curious thing and unaccountable. This form of stupidity is confined to no community, to no nation; it is universal. The fact is the human race is not only slow about borrowing valuable ideas—it sometimes persists in not borrowing them at all.

Take the German stove, for instance—the huge white porcelain monument that towers toward the ceiling in the corner of the room, solemn, unsympathetic, and suggestive of death and the grave— where can you find it outside of the German countries? I am sure I have never seen it where German was not the language of the region. Yet it is by long odds the best stove and the most convenient and economical that has yet been invented.[1]

To the uninstructed stranger it promises nothing; but he will soon find that it is a masterly performer, for all that. It has a little bit of a door which you couldn't get your head into—a door which seems foolishly out of proportion to the rest of the edifice; yet the door is right, for it is not necessary that bulky fuel shall enter it. Small-sized fuel is used, and mar-

[1] Compare with his remarks on the same subject, in "Marienbad —A Health Factory," written about a year earlier.

velously little of that. The door opens into a tiny cavern which would not hold more fuel than a baby could fetch in its arms. The process of firing is quick and simple. At half past seven on a cold morning the servant brings a small basketful of slender pine sticks—say a modified armful—and puts half of these in, lights them with a match, and closes the door. They burn out in ten or twelve minutes. He then puts in the rest and *locks* the door, and carries off the key. The work is done. He will not come again until next morning. All day long and until past midnight all parts of the room will be delightfully warm and comfortable, and there will be no headaches and no sense of closeness or oppression. In an American room, whether heated by steam, hot water, or open fires, the neighborhood of the register or the fireplace is warmest—the heat is not equally diffused through the room; but in a German room one is as comfortable in one part of it as in another. Nothing is gained or lost by being near the stove. Its surface is not hot; you can put your hand on it anywhere and not get burnt. Consider these things. One firing is enough for the day; the cost is next to nothing; the heat produced is the same all day, instead of too hot and too cold by turns; one may absorb himself in his business in peace; he does not need to feel any anxieties or solicitudes about his fire; his whole day is a realized dream of bodily comfort.

The German stove is not restricted to wood; peat is used in it, and coal bricks also. These coal bricks are made of waste coal dust pressed in a mold. In effect they are dirt and in fact are dirt cheap. The brick is about as big as your two fists; the stove will burn up twenty of them in half an hour, then it will need no more fuel for that day.

This noble stove is at its very best when its front has a big square opening in it for a *visible* wood fire. The real heating is done in the hidden regions of the great structure, of course—the open fire is merely to rejoice your eye and gladden your heart.

America could adopt this stove, but does America do it? No, she sticks placidly to her own fearful and wonderful inventions in the stove line. She has fifty kinds, and not a rational one in the lot. The American wood stove, of whatsoever breed, is a terror. There can be no tranquillity of mind where it is. It requires more attention than a baby. It has to be fed every little while, it has to be watched all the time; and for all reward you are roasted half your time and frozen the other half. It warms no part of the room but its own part; it breeds headaches and suffocation, and makes one's skin feel dry and feverish; and when your wood bill comes in you think you have been supporting a volcano.

We have in America many and many a breed of coal stoves, also—fiendish things, everyone of them. The base-burner sort are handy and require but little attention; but none of them, of whatsoever kind, distributes its heat uniformly through the room, or keeps it at an unvarying temperature, or fails to take the life out of the atmosphere and leave it stuffy and smothery and stupefying.

It seems to me that the ideal of comfort would be

a German stove to heat one's room, and an open
wood fire to make it cheerful; then have furnace-
heat in the halls. We could easily find some way
to make the German stove beautiful, and that is all
it needs at present. Still, even as it is to-day, it is
lovely, it is a darling, compared with any "radiator"
that has yet been intruded upon the world. That
odious gilded skeleton! It makes all places ugly that
it inhabits—just by contagion.

It is certainly strange that useful customs and
devices do not spread from country to country with
more facility and promptness than they do. You
step across the German border almost anywhere, and
suddenly the German stove has disappeared. In
Italy you find a foolish and ineffectual modification
of it, in Paris you find an unprepossessing "adaptation" of our base-burner on a reduced pattern.

Fifteen years ago Paris had a cheap and cunning
little fire kindler consisting of a pine shaving, curled
as it came from the carpenter's plane, and gummed
over with an inflammable substance which would
burn several minutes and set fire to the most ob-
durate wood. It was cheap and handy, but no
stranger carried the idea home with him. Paris has
another swift and victorious kindler, now, in the
form of a small black cake made of I don't know
what; but you shove it under the wood and touch a
match to it and your fire is made. No one will think
to carry that device to America, or elsewhere. In
America we prefer to kindle the fire with the kero-
sene can and chance the inquest. I have been in a
multitude of places where pine cones were abundant,

but only in the French Riviera and in one place in
Italy have I seen them in the wood box to kindle the
fires with.

For perfect adaptation to the service required,
look at the American gum shoe and the American
arctic. Their virtues ought to have carried them to
all wet and snowy lands; but they haven't done anything of the kind. There are few places on the continent of Europe where one can buy them.

And observe how slowly our typewriting machine
makes its way. In the great city of Florence I was
able to find only one place where I could get typewriting done; and then it was not done by a native,
but by an American girl. In the great city of Mu-
nich I found one typewriting establishment, but the
operator was sick and that suspended the business.
I was told that there was no opposition house. In
the prodigious city of Berlin I was not able to find
a typewriter at all. There was not even one in our
Embassy or its branches. Our representative there
sent to London for the best one to be had in that
capital, and got an incapable, who would have been
tarred and feathered in Mud Springs, Arizona. Four
years ago a typewritten page was a seldom sight in
Europe, and when you saw it it made you heart-
sick, it was so inartistic, and so blurred and shabby
and slovenly. It was because the Europeans made
the machines themselves, and the making of nice
machinery is not one of their gifts. England im-
ports ours, now. This is wise; she will have her
reward.

In all these years the American fountain pen has

hardly got a start in Europe. There is no market
for it. It is too handy, too inspiring, too capable,
too much of a time saver. The dismal steel pen and
the compass-jawed quill are preferred. And semi-
liquid mud is preferred to ink, apparently, everywhere in Europe. This in face of the fact that there
is ink to be had in America—and at club rates, too.

Then there is the elevator, lift, *ascenseur*. America
has had the benefit of this invaluable contrivance for
a generation and a half, and it is now used in all our
cities and villages, in all hotels, in all lofty business
buildings and factories, and in many private dwell-
ings. But we can't spread it, we can't beguile
Europe with it. In Europe an elevator is even to
this day a rarity and a curiosity. Especially a curiosity. As a rule it seats but three or four persons—
often only two—and it travels so slowly and cautiously and timorously and piously and solemnly
that it makes a person feel creepy and crawly and
scary and dismal and repentant. Anybody with
sound legs can give the continental elevator two
flights the start and beat it to the sixth floor. Every
time these nations merely import an American idea,
instead of importing the concreted thing itself, the
result is a failure. They tried to make the sewing
machine, and couldn't; they are trying to make
fountain pens and typewriters and can't; they are
making these dreary elevators, now—and patenting
them! Satire can no further go.

I think that as a rule we develop a borrowed
European idea forward, and that Europe develops
a borrowed American idea backward. We borrowed

gas lighting and the railroad from England, and the arc light from France, and these things have improved under our culture. We have lent Europe our tramway, telegraph, sewing machine, phonograph, telephone, and kodak, and while we may not claim that in these particular instances she has developed them backward, we are justified in claiming that she has added no notable improvements to them. We have added the improvements ourselves and she has accepted them. Why she has not accepted and universally adopted the improved elevator is a surprising and puzzling thing. Its rightful place is among the great ideas of our great age. It is an epoch maker. It is a concentrator of population, and economizer of room. It is going to build our cities skyward instead of out toward the horizons.[1] It is going to enable five millions of people to live comfortably on the same ground space that one million uncomfortably lives on now. It is going to make cheap quarters for Tom, Dick, and Harry near their work, in place of three miles from it, as is the rule to-day. It is going to save them the necessity of adding a six-flight climb to the already sufficient fatigue of their day's labor.

We imitate some of the good things which we find in Europe, and we ought to imitate more of them. At the same time Europe ought to imitate us somewhat more than she does. The crusty, ill-mannered and in every way detestable Parisian cabman ought to imitate our courteous and friendly Boston cab-

[1] This was good prophecy. There were no skyscrapers in New York City when it was written.

man—and stop there. He can't learn anything from the guild in New York. And it would morally help the Parisian shopkeeper if he would imitate the fair dealing of his American cousin. With us it is not necessary to ask the price of small articles before we buy them, but in Paris the person who fails to take that precaution will get scorched. In business we are prompt, fair, and trustworthy in all our small trade matters. It is the rule. In the friendliest spirit I would recommend France to imitate these humble virtues. Particularly in the kodak business. Pray get no kodak pictures developed in France—and especially in Nice. They will send you your bill to Rome or Jericho, or whithersoever you have gone, but that is all you will get. You will never see your negatives again, or the developed pictures, either. And by and by the head house in Paris will demand payment once more, and constructively threaten you with "proceedings." If you inquire if they mailed your package across the frontier without registering it, they are coldly silent. If you inquire how they expected to trace and recover a lost package without a post-office receipt, they are dumb again. A little intelligence inserted into the kodak business in those regions would be helpful, if it could be done without shock.

But the worst of all is, that Europe cannot be persuaded to imitate our railway methods. Two or three years ago I liked the European methods, but experience has dislodged that superstition. All over the Continent the system—to call it by an extravagant term—is sufficiently poor and slow and clumsy, or unintelligent; but in these regards Italy and France are entitled to the chromo. In Italy it takes more than half an hour to buy a through ticket to Paris at Cook & Sons' offices, there is such a formidable amount of red tape and recording connected with the vast transaction. Every little detail of the matter must be written down in a set of books—your name, condition, nationality, religion, date, hour, number of the train, and all that; and at last you get your ticket and think you are done, but you are not; it must be carried to the station and stamped; and even that is not the end, for if you stop over at any point it must be stamped again or it is forfeited. And yet you save time and trouble by going to Cook instead of to the station. Buying your ticket does not finish your job. Your trunks must be weighed, and paid for at about human-being rates. This takes another quarter of an hour of your time—perhaps half an hour if you are at the tail of the procession. You get paper checks, which are twice as easy to lose as brass ones. You cannot secure a seat beforehand, but must take your chances with the general rush to the train. If you have your family with you, you may have to distribute them among several cars. There is one annoying feature which is common all over the Continent, and that is, that if you want to make a short journey you cannot buy your ticket whenever you find the ticket office open, but must wait until it is doing business for your particular train; and that only begins, as a rule, a quarter of an hour before the train's time of starting. The cars are most ingeniously inconvenient, cramped, and uncomfortable, and in Italy they are phenomenally dirty. The European "system" was devised either by a maniac or by a person whose idea was to hamper, bother, and exasperate the traveler in all conceivable ways and sedulously and painstakingly discourage custom. In Italy, as far as my experience goes, it is the custom to use the sleeping cars on the day trains and take them off when the sun goes down. One thing is sure, anyway: if that is not the case, it will be, presently, when they think of it. They can be depended upon to snap up as darling an idea as that with joy.

No, we are bad enough about not importing valuable European ideas, but Europe is still slower about introducing ours. Europe has always—from away back—been neglectful in this regard. Take our admirable postal and express system, for instance. We had it perfectly developed and running smoothly and beautifully more than three hundred years ago; and Europe came over and admired it and eloquently praised it—but didn't adopt it. We Americans . . . But let Prescott tell about it. I quote from the *Conquest of Peru,* chapter 2, vol. 1:

As the distance each courier had to perform was small, they ran over the ground with great swiftness, and messages were carried through the whole extent of the long routes at the rate of a hundred and fifty miles a day. Their office was not limited to carrying dispatches. They brought various articles. Fish from the distant ocean, fruits, game, and different commodities from the hot regions of the coast were taken to the capital in good condition. It is remarkable that this important institution should have been found among two barbarian nations of the New World long before it was introduced among the civilized nations of Europe. By these wise contrivances of the Incas, the most distant parts of the long-extended empire of Peru were brought into intimate relations with each other. And while the capitals of Christendom, but a few hundred miles apart, remained as far asunder as if seas had rolled between them, the great capitals Cuzco and Quito were placed in immediate correspondence. Intelligence from the numerous provinces was transmitted on the wings of the wind to the Peruvian metropolis, the great focus to which all the lines of communication converged.

There—that is what we had, three hundred and twenty-five years before Europe had anything that could be called a businesslike and effective postal and express service. We are a great people. We have always been a great people, from the start: always alive, alert, up early in the morning, and ready to teach. But Europe has been a slow and discouraging pupil from the start; always, from the very start. It seems to me that something ought to be done about this.

# THE CHOLERA EPIDEMIC IN HAMBURG
(1892)

I BELIEVE I have never been so badly situated
before as I have been during these last four weeks.
To begin with, the time-hallowed and business-
worn thunderbolt out of the clear sky fell about the
18th of August—people in Hamburg dying like flies
of something resembling cholera! A normal death
rate of forty a day suddenly transformed into a
terrific daily slaughter without notice to anybody
to prepare for such a surprise! Certainly that was
recognizable as that kind of a thunderbolt.

It was at this point that the oddity of the situation
above referred to began. For you will grant that it
is odd to live four weeks a twelve-hour journey from
a devastating plague nest and remain baffled and
defeated all that time in all your efforts to get at the
state of the case there. Naturally one flies to the
newspapers when a pestilence breaks out in his
neighborhood. He feels sure of one thing, at any
rate: that the paper will cast all other interests into
the background and devote itself to the one supreme interest of the day; that it will throw wide its
columns and cram them with information, valuable
and otherwise, concerning that great event; and that
it will even leave out the idle jaunts of little dukes and
kinglets to make room for the latest plague item. I

sought the newspapers, and was disappointed. I know now that nothing that can happen in this world can stir the German daily journal out of its eternal lethargy. When the Last Day comes it will note the destruction of the world in a three-line paragraph and turn over and go to sleep again.

This sort of journalism furnishes plenty of wonders. I have seen ostensible telegrams from Hamburg four days old, gravely put forth as news, and no apology offered. I have tracked a news item from one paper to another day after day until it died of old age and fatigue—and yet everybody treated it with respect, nobody laughed. Is it believable that these antiquities are forwarded by telegraph? It would be more rational to send them by slow freight, because less expensive and more speedy.

Then, the meagerness of the news meal is another marvel. That department of the paper is not headed "Poverty Column," nobody knows why. We know that multitudes of people are being swept away daily in Hamburg, yet the daily telegrams from there could be copied on a half page of note paper, as a rule. If any newspaper has sent a special reporter thither he has not arrived yet.

The final miracle of all is the character of this daily dribble of so-called news. The wisest man in the world can get no information out of it. It is an Irish stew made up of unrelated odds and ends, a mere chaotic confusion and worthless. What can one make out of statistics like these:

Up to noon, 655 cases, 333 deaths. Of these 189 were previously reported.

The report that 650 bodies are lying unburied is not true. There are only 340, and the most of these will be buried to-night.

There are 2,062 cases in the hospitals, 215 deaths.

The figures are never given in such a way as to afford one an opportunity to compare the death list of one day with that of another; consequently there is no way of finding out whether the pest abates or increases. Sometimes a report uses the expression "to-day" and does not say when the day began or ended; sometimes the deaths for several days are bunched together in a divisionless lump; sometimes the figures make you think the deaths are five or six hundred a day, while other figures in the same paragraph seem to indicate that the rate is below two hundred.

A day or two ago the word cholera was not discoverable at all in that day's issue of one of our principal dailies; in to-day's issue of the same paper there is no cholera report from Hamburg. Yet a private letter from there says the raging pestilence is actually increasing.

One might imagine that the papers are forbidden to publish cholera news. I had that impression myself. It seemed the only explanation of the absence of special Hamburg correspondence. But it appears now, that the Hamburg papers are crammed with matter pertaining to the cholera, therefore that idea was an error. How does one find this out? In this amazing way: that a daily newspaper located ten or twelve hours from Hamburg describes with owl-eyed wonder the stirring contents of a Hamburg daily journal *six days old*, and yet gets from it the only informing matter, the only matter worth reading, which it has yet published from that smitten city concerning the pestilence.

You see, it did not even occur to that petrified editor to bail his columns dry of their customary chloroform and copy that Hamburg journal entire. He is so used to shoveling gravel that he doesn't know a diamond when he sees it. I would trust that man with untold bushels of precious news, and nobody to watch him. Among other things which he notes in the Hamburg paper is the fact that its supplements contained one hundred of the customary elaborate and formal German death notices. That means—what nobody has had reason to suppose before—that the slaughter is not confined to the poor and friendless. I think so, because that sort of death notice occupies a formidable amount of space in an advertising page, and must cost a good deal of money.

I wander from my proper subject to observe that one hundred of these notices in a single journal must make that journal a sorrow to the eye and a shock to the taste, even among the Germans themselves, who are bred to endure and perhaps enjoy a style of "display ads" which far surpasses even the vilest American attempts, for insane and outrageous ugliness. Sometimes a death notice is as large as a foolscap page, has big black display lines, and is bordered all around with a coarse mourning border as thick as your finger. The notices are of all sizes from foolscap down to a humble two-inch square, and they suggest lamentation of all degrees, from the

hundred-dollar hurricane of grief to the two-shilling
sigh of a composed and modest regret. A newspaper
page blocked out with mourning compartments of
fifty different sizes flung together without regard
to order or system or size must be a spectacle to see.

# Todes-Anzeige.

Theilnehmenden Freunden und Bekannten hier-
durch die schmerzliche Nachricht, daß mein lieber
Freund und langjähriger, treuer Mitarbeiter

## Rudolf Beck

gestern Abend an einem Herzschlag plötzlich ver-
schieden ist.

Langen, den 5. September 1892.

### Otto Steingoetter
Firma Beck & Steingoetter.

Die Beerdigung findet Dienstag, den 6. Sept.,
Nachmittags 3½ Uhr, statt.

25958

The notice copied above is modest and straightforward. The advertiser informs sympathizing
friends and acquaintances that his dear friend and
old and faithful fellow laborer has been suddenly
smitten with death; then signs his name and adds
"of the firm of Beck & Steingoetter," which is
perhaps another way of saying that the business
will be continued as usual at the old stand. The

average notice is often refreshed with a whiff of business at the end.

The 100 formal notices in the Hamburg paper did not mean merely 100 deaths; each told of one death, but many of them told of more—in some cases they told of four and five. In the same issue there were 132 one-line death notices. If the dates of these deaths were all stated, the 232 notices together could be made the basis of a better guess at the current mortality in Hamburg than the "official" reports furnished, perhaps. You would know that a certain number died on a certain day who left behind them people able to publish the fact and pay for it. Then you could correctly assume that the vast bulk of that day's harvest were people who were penniless and left penniless friends behind. You could add your facts to your assumption and get *some* sort of idea of the death rate, and this would be strikingly better than the official reports, since they give you no idea at all.

To-day a physician was speaking of a private letter received here yesterday from a physician in Hamburg which stated that every day numbers of poor people are snatched from their homes to the pest houses, and that that is the last that is heard of a good many of them. No intelligible record is kept; they die unknown and are buried so. That no intelligible record is kept seems proven by the fact that the public cannot get hold of a burial list for one day that is not made impossible by the record of the day preceding and the one following it.

What I am trying to make the reader understand is, the strangeness of the situation here—a mighty tragedy being played upon a stage that is close to us, and yet we are as ignorant of its details as we should be if the stage were in China. We sit "in front," and the audience is in fact the world; but the curtain is down and from behind it we hear only an inarticulate murmur. The Hamburg disaster must go into history as the disaster without a history. And yet a well-trained newspaper staff would find a way to secure an accurate list of the new hospital cases and the burials daily, and would do it, and not take it out in complaining of the foolishness and futility of the official reports. Every day we know exactly what is going on in the two cholera-stricken ships in the harbor of New York. That is all the cholera news we get that is worth printing or believing.

All along we have heard rumors that the force of workers at Hamburg was too small to cope with the pestilence; that more help was impossible to get; and we have seen statements which confirmed these sorrowful facts; statements which furnished the pitiful spectacle of brave workers dying at their posts from exhaustion; of corpses lying in the halls of the hospitals, waiting there because there was no worker idle; and now comes another confirmatory item; it is in the physician's letter above referred to—an item which shows you how hard pressed the authorities are by their colossal burden—an item which gives you a sudden and terrific sense of the situation there; for in a line it flashes before you this ghastly picture, a thing seen by the physician: a wagon going along the street with five sick people in it, and with them four corpses!

# QUEEN VICTORIA'S JUBILEE

(1897)

SO far as I can see, a procession has value in but
two ways—as a show and as a symbol; its minor
function being to delight the eye, its major one to
compel thought, exalt the spirit, stir the heart, and
inflame the imagination. As a mere show, and meaningless—like a Mardi-Gras march—a magnificent
procession is a sight worth a long journey to see; as
a symbol, the most colorless and unpicturesque procession, if it have a moving history back of it, is
worth a thousand of it.

After the Civil War ten regiments of bronzed New
York veterans marched up Broadway in faded uniforms and bearing faded battle flags that were mere
shot-riddled rags—and in each battalion as it swung
by, one noted a great gap, an eloquent vacancy where
had marched the comrades who had fallen and would
march no more! Always, as this procession advanced
between the massed multitudes, its approach was
welcomed by each block of people with a burst of
proud and grateful enthusiasm—then the head of it
passed, and suddenly revealed those pathetic gaps,
and silence fell upon that block; for every man in it
had choked up, and could not get command of his
voice and add it to the storm again for many minutes.
That was the most moving and tremendous effect

that I have ever witnessed—those affecting silences falling between those hurricanes of worshiping enthusiasm.

There was no costumery in that procession, no color, no tinsel, no brilliancy, yet it was the greatest spectacle and the most gracious and exalting and beautiful that has come within my experience. It was because it had history back of it, and because it was a symbol, and stood for something, and because one viewed it with the spiritual vision, not the physical. There was not much for the physical eye to see, but it revealed continental areas, limitless horizons, to the eye of the imagination and the spirit.

A procession, to be valuable, must do one thing or the other—clothe itself in splendors and charm the eye, or symbolize something sublime and uplifting, and so appeal to the imagination. As a mere spectacle to look at, I suppose that the Queen's procession will not be as showy as the Tsar's late pageant; it will probably fall much short of the one in Tannhäuser in the matter of rich and adorable costumery; in the number of renowned personages on view in it, it will probably fall short of some that have been seen in England before this. And yet in its major function, its symbolic function, I think that if all the people in it wore their everyday clothes and marched without flags or music, it would still be incomparably the most memorable and most important procession that ever moved through the streets of London.

For it will stand for English history, English growth, English achievement, the accumulated power and renown and dignity of twenty centuries of strenuous effort. Many things about it will set one to reflecting upon what a large feature of this world England is to-day, and this will in turn move one, even the least imaginative, to cast a glance down her long perspective and note the steps of her progress and the insignificance of her first estate. In this matter London is itself a suggestive object lesson.

I suppose that London has always existed. One cannot easily imagine an England that had no London. No doubt there was a village here 5,000 years ago. It was on the river somewhere west of where the Tower is now; it was built of thatched mud huts close to a couple of limpid brooks, and on every hand for miles and miles stretched rolling plains of fresh green grass, and here and there were groups and groves of trees. The tribes wore skins—sometimes merely their own, sometimes those of other animals. The chief was monarch, and helped out his complexion with blue paint. His industry was the chase; his relaxation was war. Some of the Englishmen who will view the procession to-day are carrying his ancient blood in their veins.

It may be that that village remained about as it began, away down to the Roman occupation, a couple of thousand years ago. It was still not much of a town when Alfred burned the cakes. Even when the Conqueror first saw it, it did not amount to much. I think it must have been short of distinguished architecture or he would not have traveled down into the country to the village of Westminster to get crowned. If you skip down 350 years further you will find a London of some little consequence, but I believe that

that is as much as you can say for it. Still, I am
interested in that London, for it saw the first two
processions which will live longer than any other in
English history, I think; the date of the one is 1415,
that of the other is 1897.

The compactly built part of the London of 1415
was a narrow strip not a mile long, which stretched
east and west through the middle of what is now
called "the City." The houses were densest in the
region of Cheapside. South of the strip were scattering residences which stood in turfy lawns which
sloped to the river. North of the strip, fields and
country homes extended to the walls. Let us represent that London by three checker-board squares
placed in a row; then open out a New York
newspaper like a book, and the space which it covers
will properly represent the London of to-day by comparison. It is the difference between your hand and
a blanket. It is possible that that ancient London
had 100,000 inhabitants, and that 100,000 outsiders
came to town to see the procession. The present
London contains five or six million inhabitants, and
it has been calculated that the population has jumped
to 10,000,000 to-day.

The pageant of 1415 was to celebrate the gigantic
victory of Agincourt, then and still the most colossal
in England's history.

From that day to this there has been nothing that
even approached it but Plassey. It was the third
and greatest in the series of monster victories won by
the English over the French in the Hundred Years'
War—Crecy, Poitiers, Agincourt. At Agincourt,

according to history, 15,000 English, under Henry V, defeated and routed an army of 100,000 French. Sometimes history makes it 8,000 English and 60,000 French; but no matter, in both cases the proportions are preserved. Eight thousand of the French nobility were slain and the rest of the order taken prisoners —1,500 in number—among them the Dukes of Orléans and Bourbon and Marshal Boucicaut; and the victory left the whole northern half of France an English possession. This wholesale depletion of the aristocracy made such a stringent scarcity in its ranks that when the young peasant girl, Joan of Arc, came to undo Henry's mighty work fourteen years later she could hardly gather together nobles enough to man her staff.

The battle of Agincourt was fought on the 25th of October, and a few days later the tremendous news was percolating through England. Presently it was sweeping the country like a tidal wave, like a cyclone, like a conflagration. Choose your own figure, there is no metaphor known to the language that can exaggerate the tempest of joy and pride and exultation that burst everywhere along the progress of that great news.

The king came home and brought his soldiers with him—he and they the idols of the nation, now. He brought his 1,500 captive knights and nobles, too— we shall not see any such output of blue blood as that to-day, bond or free. The king rested three weeks in his palace, the Tower of London, while the people made preparations and prepared the welcome due him. On the 22d of December all was ready.

There were no cables, no correspondents, no newspapers then—a regrettable defect, but not irremediable. A young man who would have been a correspondent if he had been born 500 years later was in London at the time, and he remembers the details. He has communicated them to me through a competent spirit medium, phrased in a troublesome mixture of obsolete English and moldy French, and I have thoroughly modernized his story and put it into straight English, and will here record it. I will explain that his Sir John Oldcastle is a person whom we do not know very well by that name, nor much care for; but we know him well and adore him, too, under his other name—Sir John Falstaff. Also, I will remark that two miles of the Queen's progress to-day will be over ground traversed by the procession of Henry V; all solid bricks and mortar, now, but open country in Henry's day, and clothed in that unapproachable beauty which has been the monopoly of sylvan England since the creation. Ah, where now are those long-vanished forms, those unreturning feet! Let us not inquire too closely. Translated, this is the narrative of the spirit-correspondent, who is looking down upon me at this moment from his high home, and admiring to see how the art and mystery of spelling has improved since his time!

### NARRATIVE OF THE SPIRIT CORRESPONDENT

I was commanded by my lord the Lord Mayor to make a report for the archives, and was furnished with a fleet horse, and with a paper permitting me to go anywhere at my will, without let or hindrance, even up and down the processional route, though no other person not of the procession itself was allowed this unique privilege during the whole of the 21st and the 22d.

On the morning of the 22d, toward noon, I rode from the Tower into the city, and through it as far as St. Paul's. All the way, on both sides, all the windows, balconies, and roofs were crowded with people, and wherever there was a vacancy it had been built up in high tiers of seats covered with red cloth, and these seats were also filled with people—in all cases in bright holiday attire—the woman of fashion barring the view from all in the rear with those tiresome extinguisher hats, which of late have grown to be a cloth-yard high. From every balcony depended silken stuffs of splendid and various colors, and figured and pictured rich tapestries. It was brisk, sharp weather, but a rare one for sun, and when one looked down this swinging double wall of beautiful fabrics, glowing and flashing and changing color like prisms in the flooding light, it was a most fair sight to see. And there were frequent May poles, garlanded to their tops, and from the tops swung sheaves of silken long ribbons of all bright colors, which in the light breeze writhed and twisted and prettily mingled themselves together.

I rode solitary—in state, as it might be—and was envied, as I could see, and did not escape comment, but had a plenty of it; for the conduits were running gratis wine, and the results were accumulating. I got many ribald compliments on my riding, on my clothes, on my office. Everybody was happy, so it was best to seem so myself, which I did—for those people's aim was better than their eggs.

A place had been reserved for me on a fine and fanciful erection in St. Paul's Churchyard, and there I waited for the procession. It seemed a long time, but at last a dull booming sound arose in the distance, and after a while we saw the banners and the head of the procession come into view, and heard the muffled roar of voices that welcomed it. The roar moved continuously toward us, growing steadily louder and louder, and stronger and stronger, and with it the bray and crash of music; and presently it was right with us, and seemed to roll over us and submerge us, and stun us, and deafen us—and behold, there was the hero of Agincourt passing by!

All the multitude was standing up, red-faced, frantic, bellowing, shouting, the tears running down their faces; and through the storm of waving hats and handkerchiefs one glimpsed the battle banners and the drifting host of marching men as through a dimming flurry of snow.

The king, tall, slender, handsome, rode with his visor up, that all might see his face. He was clad in his silver armor from head to heel, and had his great two-handed sword at his side, his battle-ax at his pommel, his shield upon his arm, and about his helmet waved and tossed a white mass of fluffy plumes. On either side of him rode the captive dukes, plumed like himself, but wearing long crimson satin gowns over their armor; after these came the French marshal similarly habited; after him followed the fifteen

hundred French knights, with robes of various colors
over their armor, and with each two rode two English
knights, sometimes robed in various colors, sometimes in white with a red cross on the shoulder, these
white-clad ones being Knights Templars. Every man
of the three thousand bore his shield upon his left
arm, newly polished and burnished, and on it was
his device.

As the king passed the church he bowed his head
and lifted his shield, and by one impulse all the
knights did the same; and so as far down the line as
the eye could reach one saw the lifted shields simultaneously catch the sun, and it was like a sudden
mile-long shaft of flashing light; and, Lord! it lit up
that dappled sea of color with a glory like "the
golden vortex in the west over the foundered sun"!
(The introduction of this quotation is very interesting,
for it shows that our literature of to-day has a circu-
lation in heaven—pirated editions, no doubt.—M.T.)

The knights were a long time in passing; then
came 5,000 Agincourt men-at-arms, and they were
a long time; and at the very end, last of all, came
that intolerable old tun of sack and godless ruffler,
Sir John Oldcastle (now risen from the dead for the
third time), fat-faced, purple with the spirit of bygone
and lamented drink, smiling his hospitable, wide
smile upon all the world, leering at the women,
wallowing about in his saddle, proclaiming his
valorous deeds as fast as he could lie, taking the
whole glory of Agincourt to his single self, measuring
off the miles of his slain and then multiplying them
by 5, 7, 10, 15, as inspiration after inspiration came

to his help—the most inhuman spectacle in England, a living, breathing outrage, a slander upon the human race; and after him came, mumming and blethering, his infamous lieutenants; and after them his "paladins," as he calls them, the mangiest lot of starvelings and cowards that was ever littered, the disgrace of the noblest pageant that England has ever seen. God rest their souls in the place appointed for all such!

There was a moment of prayer at the Temple, the procession moved down the country road, its way walled on both sides by welcoming multitudes, and so, by Charing Cross, and at last to the Abbey for the great ceremonies. It was a grand day, and will remain in men's memories.

That was as much of it as the spirit correspondent could let me have; he was obliged to stop there because he had an engagement to sing in the choir, and was already late.

The contrast between that old England and the present England is one of the things which will make the pageant of the present day impressive and thought-breeding. The contrast between the England of the Queen's reign and the England of any previous British reign is also an impressive thing. British history is two thousand years old, and yet in a good many ways the world has moved further ahead since the Queen was born than it moved in all the rest of the two thousand put together. A large part of this progress has been moral, but naturally the material part of it is the most striking and the easiest to measure. Since the Queen first saw the light she has seen invented and brought into use (with the exception of the cotton gin, the spinning frames, and the steamboat) every one of the myriad of strictly modern inventions which, by their united powers, have created the bulk of the modern civilization and made life under it easy and difficult, convenient and awkward, happy and horrible, soothing and irritating, grand and trivial, an indispensable blessing and an unimaginable curse—she has seen all these miracles, these wonders, these marvels piled up in her time, and yet she is but seventy-eight years old. That is to say, she has seen more things invented than any other monarch that ever lived; and more than the oldest old-time English commoner that ever lived, including Old Parr; and more than Methuselah himself—five times over.

Some of the details of the moral advancement which she has seen are also very striking and easily graspable.

She has seen the English criminal laws prodigiously modified, and 200 capital crimes swept from the statute book.

She has seen English liberty greatly broadened— the governing and lawmaking powers, formerly the possession of the few, extended to the body of the people, and purchase in the army abolished.

She has seen the public educator—the newspaper —created, and its teachings placed within the reach of the leanest purse. There was nothing properly describable as a newspaper until long after she was born.

She has seen the world's literature set free, through the institution of international copyright.

She has seen America invent arbitration, the eventual substitute for that enslaver of nations, the standing army; and she has seen England pay the first bill under it, and America shirk the second—but only temporarily; of this we may be sure.

She has seen a Hartford American (Doctor Wells) apply anæsthetics in surgery for the first time in history, and for all time banish the terrors of the surgeon's knife; and she has seen the rest of the world ignore the discoverer and a Boston doctor steal the credit of his work.

She has seen medical science and scientific sanitation cut down the death rate of civilized cities by more than half, and she has seen these agencies set bounds to the European march of the cholera and imprison the Black Death in its own home.

She has seen woman freed from the oppression of many burdensome and unjust laws; colleges established for her; privileged to earn degrees in men's colleges—but not get them; in some regions rights accorded to her which lifted her near to political equality with man, and a hundred bread-winning occupations found for her where hardly one existed before—among them medicine, the law, and professional nursing. The Queen has herself recognized merit in her sex; of the 501 lordships which she has conferred in sixty years, one was upon a woman.

The Queen has seen the right to organize trade unions extended to the workman, after that right had

been the monopoly of guilds of masters for six
hundred years.

She has seen the workman rise into political notice,
then into political force, then (in some parts of the
world) into the chief and commanding political force;
she has seen the day's labor of twelve, fourteen, and
eighteen hours reduced to eight, a reform which has
made labor a means of extending life instead of a
means of committing salaried suicide.

But it is useless to continue the list—it has no
end.

There will be complexions in the procession to-day
which will suggest the vast distances to which the
British dominion has extended itself around the fat
rotundity of the globe since Britain was a remote
unknown back settlement of savages with tin for
sale, two or three thousand years ago; and also
how great a part of this extension is comparatively
recent; also, how surprisingly speakers of the English
tongue have increased within the Queen's time.

When the Queen was born there were not more
than 25,000,000 English-speaking people in the world;
there are about 120,000,000 now. The other long-
reign queen, Elizabeth, ruled over a short 100,000
square miles of territory and perhaps 5,000,000 subjects; Victoria reigns over more territory than any
other sovereign in the world's history ever reigned
over; her estate covers a fourth part of the habitable
area of the globe, and her subjects number about
400,000,000.

It is indeed a mighty estate, and I perceive now
that the English are mentioned in the Bible:

"Blessed are the meek, for they shall inherit the earth."

The Long-Reign Pageant will be a memorable thing to see, for it stands for the grandeur of England, and is full of suggestion as to how it had its beginning and what have been the forces that have built it up.

I got to my seat in the Strand just in time—five minutes past ten—for a glance around before the show began. The houses opposite, as far as the eye could reach in both directions, suggested boxes in a theater snugly packed. The gentleman next to me likened the groups to beds of flowers, and said he had never seen such a massed and multitudinous array of bright colors and fine clothes.

These displays rose up and up, story by story, all balconies and windows being packed, and also the battlements stretching along the roofs. The sidewalks were filled with standing people, but were not uncomfortably crowded. They were fenced from the roadway by red-coated soldiers, a double stripe of vivid color which extended throughout the six miles which the procession would traverse.

Five minutes later the head of the column came into view and was presently filing by, led by Captain Ames, the tallest man in the British army. And then the cheering began. It took me but a little while to determine that this procession could not be described. There was going to be too much of it, and too much variety in it, so I gave up the idea. It was to be a spectacle for the kodak, not the pen.

Presently the procession was without visible beginning or end, but stretched to the limit of sight in both directions—bodies of soldiery in blue, followed by a block of soldiers in buff, then a block of red, a block of buff, a block of yellow, and so on, an interminable drift of swaying and swinging splotches of strong color sparkling and flashing with shifty light reflected from bayonets, lance heads, brazen helmets, and burnished breastplates. For varied and beautiful uniforms and unceasing surprises in the way of new and unexpected splendors, it much surpassed any pageant that I have ever seen.

I was not dreaming of so stunning a show. All the nations seemed to be filing by. They all seemed to be represented. It was a sort of allegorical suggestion of the Last Day, and some who live to see that day will probably recall this one if they are not too much disturbed in mind at the time.

There were five bodies of Oriental soldiers of five different nationalities, with complexions differentiated by five distinct shades of yellow. There were about a dozen bodies of black soldiers from various parts of Africa, whose complexions covered as many shades of black, and some of these were the very blackest people I have ever seen yet.

Then there was an exhaustive exhibition of the hundred separate brown races of India, the most beautiful and satisfying of all the complexions that have been vouchsafed to man, and the one which best sets off colored clothes and best harmonizes with all tints.

The Chinese, the Japanese, the Koreans, the Africans, the Indians, the Pacific Islanders—they were all there, and with them samples of all the whites that inhabit the wide reach of the Queen's dominions.

The procession was the human race on exhibition, a spectacle curious and interesting and worth traveling far to see. The most splendid of the costumes were those worn by the Indian princes, and they were also the most beautiful and richest. They were men of stately build and princely carriage, and wherever they passed the applause burst forth.

Soldiers, soldiers, soldiers, and still more and more soldiers and cannon and muskets and lances—there seemed to be no end to this feature. There are 50,000 soldiers in London, and they all seemed to be on hand. I have not seen so many except in the theater, when thirty-five privates and a general march across the stage and behind the scenes and across the front again and keep it up till they have represented 300,000.

In the early part of the procession the colonial premiers drove by, and by and by after a long time there was a grand output of foreign princes, thirty-one in the invoice.

The feature of high romance was not wanting, for among them rode Prince Rupert of Bavaria, who would be Prince of Wales now and future king of England and emperor of India if his Stuart ancestors had conducted their royal affairs more wisely than they did. He came as a peaceful guest to represent his mother, Princess Ludwig, heiress of the house of Stuart, to whom English Jacobites still pay unavailing homage as the rightful queen of England.

The house of Stuart was formally and officially

shelved nearly two centuries ago, but the microbe of Jacobite loyalty is a thing which is not exterminable by time, force, or argument.

At last, when the procession had been on view an hour and a half, carriages began to appear. In the first came a detachment of two-horse ones containing ambassadors extraordinary, in one of them Whitelaw Reid, representing the United States; then six containing minor foreign and domestic princes and princesses; then five four-horse carriages freighted with offshoots of the family.

The excitement was growing now; interest was rising toward the boiling point. Finally a landau driven by eight cream-colored horses, most lavishly unholstered in gold stuffs, with postilions and no drivers, and preceded by Lord Wolseley, came bowling along, followed by the Prince of Wales, and all the world rose to its feet and uncovered.

The Queen Empress was come. She was received with great enthusiasm. It was realizable that she was the procession herself; that all the rest of it was mere embroidery; that in her the public saw the British Empire itself. She was a symbol, an allegory of England's grandeur and the might of the British name.

It is over now; the British Empire has marched past under review and inspection. The procession stood for sixty years of progress and accumulation, moral, material, and political. It was made up rather of the beneficiaries of these prosperities than of the creators of them.

As far as mere glory goes, the foreign trade of Great Britain has grown in a wonderful way since the Queen ascended the throne. Last year it reached the enormous figure of £620,000,000, but the capitalist, the manufacturer, the merchant, and the workingmen were not officially in the procession to get their large share of the resulting glory.

Great Britain has added to her real estate an average of 165 miles of territory per day for the past sixty years, which is to say she has added more than the bulk of an England proper per year, or an aggregate of seventy Englands in the sixty years.

But Cecil Rhodes was not in the procession; the Chartered Company was absent from it. Nobody was there to collect his share of the glory due for his formidable contributions to the imperial estate. Even Doctor Jameson was out, and yet he had tried so hard to accumulate territory.

Eleven colonial premiers were in the procession, but the dean of the order, the imperial Premier, was not, nor the Lord Chief Justice of England, nor the Speaker of the House. The bulk of the religious strength of England dissent was not officially represented in the religious ceremonials. At the Cathedral that immense new industry, speculative expansion, was not represented unless the pathetic shade of Barnato rode invisible in the pageant.

It was a memorable display and must live in history. It suggested the material glories of the reign finely and adequately. The absence of the chief creators of them was perhaps not a serious disadvantage. One could supply the vacancies by imagination, and thus fill out the procession very effectively. One can enjoy a rainbow without necessarily forgetting the forces that made it.

# LETTERS TO SATAN

## (1897)

### SWISS GLIMPSES

### I

IF Your Grace would prepay your postage it would be a pleasant change. I am not meaning to speak harshly, but only sorrowfully. My remark applies to all my outland correspondents, and to everybody's. None of them puts on the full postage, and that is just the same as putting on none at all: the foreign governments ignore the half postage, and we who are abroad have to pay full postage on those half-paid letters. And as for writing on thin paper, none of my friends ever think of it; they all use pasteboard, or sole leather, or things like that. But enough of that subject; it is painful.

I believe you have set me a hard task; for if it is true that you have not been in the world for three hundred years, and have not received into your establishment an educated person in all that time, I shall be obliged to talk to you as if you had just been born and knew nothing at all about the things I speak of. However, I will do the best I can, and will faithfully try to put in all the particulars, trivial ones as well as the other sorts. If my report shall induce Your Grace to come out of your age-

long seclusion and make a pleasure tour through the
world in person, instead of doing it by proxy through
me, I shall feel that I have labored to good purpose.
You have many friends in the world; more than
you think. You would have a vast welcome in
Paris, London, New York, Chicago, Washington,
and the other capitals of the world; if you would
go on the lecture platform you could charge what
you pleased. You would be the most formidable
attraction on the planet. The curiosity to see you
would be so great that no place of amusement would
contain the multitude that would come. In London
many devoted people who have seen the Prince of
Wales only fifteen hundred or two thousand times
would be willing to miss one chance of seeing him
again for the sake of seeing you. In Paris, even
with the Tsar on view, you could do a fairly good
business; and in Chicago— Oh, but you ought to
go to Chicago, you know. But further of this anon.
I will to my report, now, and tell you about Lucerne,
and how I journeyed hither; for doubtless you will
travel by the same route when you come.

I kept house a few months in London, with my
family, while I arranged the matters which you were
good enough to intrust me with. There were no
adventures, except that we saw the Jubilee. Afterward I was invited to one of the Queen's functions,
which was a royal garden party. A garden is a
green and bloomy countrified stretch of land which
— But you remember the Garden of Eden; well,
it is like that. The invitation prescribed the costume
that must be worn: "Morning dress with trousers."

I was intending to wear mine, for I always wear something at garden parties where ladies are to be present; but I was hurt by this arbitrary note of compulsion, and did not go. All the European courts are particular about dress, and you are not allowed to choose for yourself in any case; you are always told exactly what you must wear; and whether it is going to become you or not, you are not allowed to make any changes. Yet the court taste is often bad, and sometimes even indelicate. I was once invited to dine with an emperor when I was living awhile in Germany, and the invitation card named the dress I must wear: "Frock coat and black cravat." To put it in English, that meant swallow-tail and black cravat. It was cold weather, too, the middle of winter; and not only that, but ladies were to be present. That was five years ago. By this time the coat has gone out, I suppose, and you would feel at home there if you still remember the old Eden styles.

As soon as the Jubilee was fairly over we broke up housekeeping and went for a few days to what is called in England "an hotel." If we could have afforded an horse and an hackney cab we could have had an heavenly good time flitting around on our preparation errands, and could have finished them up briskly; but the buses are slow and they wasted many precious hours for us. A bus is a sort of great cage on four wheels, and is six times as strong and eleven times as heavy as the service required of it demands—but that is the English of it. The bus aptly symbolizes the national character. The

Englishman requires that everything about him shall be stable, strong, and permanent, except the house which he builds to rent. His own private house is as strong as a fort. The rod which holds up the lace curtains could hold up an hippopotamus. The three-foot flagstaff on his bus, which supports a Union Jack the size of a handkerchief, would still support it if it were one of the gates of Gaza. Everything he constructs is a deal heavier and stronger than it needs to be. He built ten miles of terraced benches to view the Jubilee procession from, and put timber enough in them to make them a permanent contribution to the solidities of the world—yet they were intended for only two days' service.

When they were being removed an American said, "Don't do it—save them for the Resurrection." If anything gets in the way of the Englishman's bus it must get out of it or be bowled down—and that is English. It is the serene self-sufficient spirit which has carried his flag so far. He ought to put his aggressive bus in his coat of arms, and take the gentle unicorn out.

We made our preparations for Switzerland as fast as we could; then bought the tickets. Bought them of Thomas Cook & Sons, of course—nowadays shortened to "Cook's," to save time and words. Things have changed in thirty years. I can remember when to be a "Cook's tourist" was a thing to be ashamed of, and when everybody felt privileged to make fun of Cook's "personally conducted" gangs of economical provincials. But that has all gone by, now. All sorts and conditions of men fly to

Cook in our days. In the bygone times travel in Europe was made hateful and humiliating by the wanton difficulties, hindrances, annoyances, and vexations put upon it by ignorant, stupid, and disobliging transportation officials, and one had to travel with a courier or risk going mad. You could not buy a railway ticket on one day which you purposed to use next day—it was not permitted. You could not buy a ticket for *any* train until fifteen minutes before that train was due to leave. Though you had twenty trunks, you must manage somehow to get them weighed and the extra weight paid for within that fifteen minutes; if the time was not sufficient you would have to leave behind such trunks as failed to pass the scales. If you missed your train, your ticket was no longer good. As a rule, you could make neither head nor tail of the railway guide, and if your intended journey was a long one you would find that the officials could tell you little about which way to go; consequently you often bought the wrong ticket and got yourself lost. But Cook has remedied all these things and made travel simple, easy, and a pleasure. He will sell you a ticket to any place on the globe, or all the places, and give you all the time you need, and as much more besides; and it is good for all trains of its class, and its baggage is weighable at all hours. It provides hotels for you everywhere, if you so desire; and you cannot be overcharged, for the coupons show just how much you must pay. Cook's servants at the great stations will attend to your baggage, get you a cab, tell you how much to pay cabmen and porters, procure guides for you, or horses, donkeys, camels, bicycles, or anything else you want, and make life a comfort and a satisfaction to you. And if you get tired of traveling and want to stop, Cook will take back the remains of your ticket, with 10 per cent off. Cook is your banker everywhere, and his establishment your shelter when you get caught out in the rain. His clerks will answer all the questions you ask, and do it courteously. I recommend Your Grace to travel on Cook's tickets when you come; and I do this without embarrassment, for I get no commission. I do not know Cook. (But if you would rather travel with a courier, let me recommend Joseph Very. I employed him twenty years ago, and spoke of him very highly in a book, for he was an excellent courier—then. I employed him again, six or seven years ago—for a while. Try him. And when you go home, take him with you.)

That London hotel was a disappointment. It was up a back alley, and we supposed it would be cheap. But, no, it was built for the moneyed races. It was all costliness and show. It had a brass band for dinner—and little else—and it even had a telephone and a lift. A telephone is a wire stretched on poles or underground, and has a thing at each end of it. These things are to speak into and to listen at. The wire carries the words; it can carry them several hundred miles. It is a time-saving, profanity-breeding, useful invention, and in America is to be found in all houses except parsonages. It is dear in America, but cheap in England; yet in England telephones are as rare as are icebergs in your place.

I know of no way to account for this; I only know that it is extraordinary. The English take kindly to the other modern conveniences, but for some puzzling reason or other they will not use the telephone. There are 44,000,000 people there who have never even seen one.

The lift is an elevator. Like the telephone, it also is an American invention. Its office is to hoist people to the upper stories and save them the fatigue and delay of climbing. That London hotel could accommodate several hundred people, and it had just one lift—a lift which would hold four persons. In America such an hotel would have from two to six lifts. When I was last in Paris, three years ago, they were using there what they thought was a lift. It held two persons, and traveled at such a slow gait that a spectator could not tell which way it was going. If the passengers were going to the sixth floor, they took along something to eat; and at night, bedding. Old people did not use it; except such as were on their way to the good place, anyhow. Often people that had been lost for days were found in those lifts, jogging along, jogging along, frequently still alive. The French took great pride in their ostensible lift, and called it by a grand name— *ascenseur*. An hotel that had a lift did not keep it secret, but advertised it in immense letters, *Il y a une ascenseur,*" with three exclamation points after it.

In that London hotel— But never mind that hotel; it was a cruelly expensive and tawdry and ill-conditioned place, and I wish I could do it a damage. I will think up a way some time. We went to Queenboro by the railroad. A railroad is a—well, a railroad is a railroad. I will describe it more explicitly another time.

Then we went by steamer to Flushing—eight hours. If you sit at home you can make the trip in less time, because then you can travel by the steamer company's advertisement, and that will take you across the Channel five hours quicker than their boats can do it. Almost everywhere in Europe the advertisements can give the facts several hours' odd in the twenty-four and get in first.

## II

We tarried overnight at a summer hotel on the seashore near Flushing—the Grand Hôtel des Bains. The word Grand means nothing in this connection; it has no descriptive value. On the Continent, all hotels, inns, taverns, hash houses and slop troughs employ it. It is tiresome. This one was a good-enough hotel, and comfortable, but there was nothing grand about it but the bill, and even that was not extravagant enough to make the title entirely justifiable. Except in the case of one item—Scotch whisky. I ordered a sup of that, for I always take it at night as a preventive of toothache. I have never had the toothache; and what is more, I never intend to have it. They charged me a dollar and a half for it. A dollar and a half for half a pint; a dollar and a half for that wee little mite—really hardly enough to break a pledge with. It will be a kindness to me if Your Grace will show the landlord some special attentions when he arrives. Not merely on account of that piece of extortion, but because he got us back to town and the station next day, more than an hour before train time.

There were no books or newspapers for sale there, and nothing to look at but a map. Fortunately it was an interesting one. It was a railway map of the Low Countries, and was of a new sort to me, for it was made of tiles—the ground white, the lines black. It could be washed if it got soiled, and if no accident happens to it it will last ten thousand years and still be as bright and fine and new and beautiful then as it is to-day. It occupied a great area of the wall, and one could study it in comfort halfway across the house. It would be a valuable thing if our own railway companies would adorn their waiting rooms with maps like that.

We left at five in the afternoon. The Dutch road was admirably rough; we went bumping and bouncing and swaying and sprawling along in a most vindictive and disorderly way; then passed the frontier into Germany, and straightway quieted down and went gliding as smoothly through the landscape as if we had been on runners. We reached Cologne after midnight.

But this letter is already too long. I will close it by saying that I was charmed with England and sorry to leave it. It is easy to do business there. I carried out all of Your Grace's instructions, and did it without difficulty. I doubted if it was needful to grease Mr. Cecil Rhodes's palm any further, for I think he would serve you just for the love of it;

still, I obeyed your orders in the matter. I made him Permanent General Agent for South Africa, got him and his South Africa Company whitewashed by the Committee of Inquiry, and promised him a dukedom. I also continued the European Concert in office, without making any change in its material. In my opinion this is the best material for the purpose that exists outside of Your Grace's own personal Cabinet. It coddles the Sultan, it has defiled and degraded Greece, it has massacred a hundred thousand Christians in Armenia and a splendid multitude of them in Turkey, and has covered civilization and the Christian name with imperishable shame. If Your Grace would instruct me to add the Concert to the list of your publicly acknowledged servants, I think it would have a good effect. The Foreign Offices of the whole European world are now under your sovereignty, and little attentions like this would keep them so.

# A WORD OF ENCOURAGEMENT FOR OUR BLUSHING EXILES

## (1898)

*. . . Well, what do you think of our country now? And what do you think of the figure she is cutting before the eyes of the world? For one, I am ashamed—(Extract from a long and heated letter from a Voluntary Exile, Member of the American Colony, Paris.)*

AND so you are ashamed. I am trying to think out what it can have been that has produced this large attitude of mind and this fine flow of sarcasm. Apparently you are ashamed to look Europe in the face; ashamed of the American name; temporarily ashamed of your nationality. By the light of remarks made to me by an American here in Vienna, I judge that you are ashamed because:

1. We are meddling where we have no business and no right; meddling with the private family matters of a sister nation; intruding upon her sacred right to do as she pleases with her own, unquestioned by anybody.

2. We are doing this under a sham humanitarian pretext.

3. Doing it in order to filch Cuba, the formal and distinct disclaimer in the ultimatum being very, very thin humbug, and easily detectable as such by you and virtuous Europe.

4. And finally you are ashamed of all this because

it is new, and base, and brutal, and dishonest; and because Europe, having had no previous experience of such things, is horrified by it and can never respect us nor associate with us any more.

Brutal, base, dishonest? We? Land thieves? Shedders of innocent blood? We? Traitors to our official word? We? Are we going to lose Europe's respect because of this new and dreadful conduct? Russia's, for instance? Is she lying stretched out on her back in Manchuria, with her head among her Siberian prisons and her feet in Port Arthur, trying to read over the fairy tales she told Lord Salisbury, and not able to do it for crying because we are maneuvering to treacherously smouch Cuba from feeble Spain, and because we are ungently shedding innocent Spanish blood?

Is it France's respect that we are going to lose? Is our unchivalric conduct troubling a nation which exists to-day because a brave young girl saved it when its poltroons had lost it—a nation which deserted her as one man when her day of peril came? Is our treacherous assault upon a weak people distressing a nation which contributed Bartholomew's Day to human history? Is our ruthless spirit offending the sensibilities of the nation which gave us the Reign of Terror to read about? Is our unmanly intrusion into the private affairs of a sister nation shocking the feelings of the people who sent Maximilian to Mexico? Are our shabby and pusillanimous ways outraging the fastidious people who have sent an innocent man (Dreyfus) to a living hell, taken to their embraces the slimy guilty one, and

# A WORD FOR OUR BLUSHING EXILES

submitted to a thousand indignities Emile Zola—the manliest man in France?

Is it Spain's respect that we are going to lose? Is she sitting sadly conning her great history and contrasting it with our meddling, cruel, perfidious one—our shameful history of foreign robberies, humanitarian shams, and annihilations of weak and unoffending nations? Is she remembering with pride how she sent Columbus home in chains; how she sent half of the harmless West Indians into slavery and the rest to the grave, leaving not one alive; how she robbed and slaughtered the Inca's gentle race, then beguiled the Inca into her power with fair promises and burned him at the stake; how she drenched the New World in blood, and earned and got the name of The Nation with the Bloody Footprint; how she drove all the Jews out of Spain in a day, allowing them to sell their property, but forbidding them to carry any money out of the country; how she roasted heretics by the thousands and thousands in her public squares, generation after generation, her kings and her priests looking on as at a holiday show; how her Holy Inquisition imported hell into the earth; how she was the first to institute it and the last to give it up—and then only under compulsion; how, with a spirit unmodified by time, she still tortures her prisoners to-day; how, with her ancient passion for pain and blood unchanged, she still crowds the arena with ladies and gentlemen and priests to see with delight a bull harried and persecuted and a gored horse dragging his entrails on the ground; and how, with this incredible character sur-

223

viving all attempts to civilize it, her Duke of Alva rises again in the person of General Weyler—to-day the most idolized personage in Spain—and we see a hundred thousand women and children shut up in pens and pitilessly starved to death?

Are we indeed going to lose Spain's respect? Is there no way to avoid this calamity—or this compliment? Are we going to lose her respect because we have made a promise in our ultimatum which she thinks we shall break? And meantime is she trying to recall some promise of her own which she has kept?

Is the Professional Official Fibber of Europe really troubled with our morals? Dear Parisian friend, are you taking seriously the daily remark of the newspaper and the orator about "this noble nation with an illustrious history"? That is mere kindness, mere charity for a people in temporary hard luck. The newspaper and the orator do not mean it. They wink when they say it.

And so you are ashamed. Do not be ashamed; there is no occasion for it.

# DUELING

(Vienna, Austria, 1898)

THIS pastime is as common in Austria to-day as it is in France. But with this difference—that here in the Austrian states the duel is dangerous, while in France it is not. Here it is tragedy, in France it is comedy; here it is a solemnity, there it is monkeyshines; here the duelist risks his life, there he does not even risk his shirt. Here he fights with pistol or saber, in France with a hairpin—a blunt one. Here the desperately wounded man tries to walk to the hospital; there they paint the scratch so that they can find it again, lay the sufferer on a stretcher, and conduct him off the field with a band of music.

At the end of a French duel the pair hug and kiss and cry, and praise each other's valor; then the surgeons make an examination and pick out the scratched one, and the other one helps him on to the litter and pays his fare; and in return the scratched one treats to champagne and oysters in the evening, and then "the incident is closed," as the French say. It is all polite, and gracious, and pretty, and impressive. At the end of an Austrian duel the antagonist that is alive gravely offers his hand to the other man, utters some phrases of courteous regret, then bids him good-by and goes his way, and that incident also is closed. The French duelist is painstakingly protected from danger, by the rules of the game. His antagonist's weapon cannot reach so far as his body; if he gets a scratch it will not be above his elbow. But in Austria the rules of the game do not provide against danger, they carefully provide *for* it, usually. Commonly the combat must be kept up until one of the men is disabled; a nondisabling slash or stab does not retire him.

For a matter of three months I watched the Viennese journals, and whenever a duel was reported in their telegraphic columns I scrap-booked it. By this record I find that dueling in Austria is not confined to journalists and old maids, as in France, but is indulged in by military men, journalists, students, physicians, lawyers, members of the legislature, and even the Cabinet, the bench, and the police. Dueling is forbidden by law; and so it seems odd to see the makers and administrators of the laws dancing on their work in this way. Some months ago Count Badeni, at that time chief of the government, fought a pistol duel here in the capital city of the Empire with Representative Wolf, and both of those distinguished Christians came near getting turned out of the Church—for the Church as well as the state forbids dueling.

In one case, lately, in Hungary, the police interfered and stopped a duel after the first innings. This was a saber duel between the chief of police and the city attorney. Unkind things were said about it by the newspapers. They said the police remembered their duty uncommonly well when their own officials were the parties concerned in duels. But I think the underlings showed bread-and-butter judgment. If their superiors had carved each other well, the public would have asked, "Where were the police?" and their place would have been endangered; but custom does not require them to be around where mere unofficial citizens are explaining a thing with sabers.

There was another duel—a double duel—going on in the immediate neighborhood at the time, and in this case the police obeyed custom and did not disturb it. Their bread and butter was not at stake there. In this duel a physician fought a couple of surgeons, and wounded both—one of them lightly, the other seriously. An undertaker wanted to keep people from interfering, but that was quite natural again.

Selecting at random from my record, I next find a duel at Tranopol between military men. An officer of the Tenth Dragoons charged an officer of the Ninth Dragoons with an offense against the laws of the card table. There was a defect or a doubt somewhere in the matter, and this had to be examined and passed upon by a court of honor. So the case was sent up to Lemberg for this purpose. One would like to know what the defect was, but the newspaper does not say. A man here who has fought many duels and has a graveyard says that probably the matter in question was as to whether the accusation was true or not; that if the charge was a very grave one—cheating, for instance—proof of its truth would rule the guilty officer out of the field of honor; the court would not allow a gentleman to fight with such a person. You see what a solemn thing it is;

you see how particular they are; any little careless speech can lose you your privilege of getting yourself shot, here. The court seems to have gone into the matter in a searching and careful fashion, for several months elapsed before it reached a decision. It then sanctioned a duel and the accused killed his accuser.

Next I find a duel between a prince and a major; first with pistols—no result satisfactory to either party; then with sabers, and the major badly hurt.

Next, a saber duel between journalists—the one a strong man, the other feeble and in poor health. It was brief; the strong one drove his sword through the weak one, and death was immediate.

Next, a duel between a lieutenant and a student of medicine. According to the newspaper report, these are the details: The student was in a restaurant one evening; passing along, he halted at a table to speak with some friends; near by sat a dozen military men; the student conceived that one of these was "staring" at him; he asked the officer to step outside and explain. This officer and another one gathered up their capes and sabers and went out with the student. Outside—this is the student's account—the student introduced himself to the offending officer and said, "You seemed to stare at me"; for answer, the officer struck the student with his fist; the student parried the blow; both officers drew their sabers and attacked the young fellow, and one of them gave him a wound on the left arm; then they withdrew. This was Saturday night. The duel followed on Monday, in the military riding school— the customary dueling ground all over Austria, apparently. The weapons were pistols. The dueling terms were somewhat beyond custom in the matter of severity, if I may gather that from the statement that the combat was fought "unter sehr schweren Bedingungen"—to wit, "distance, 15 steps—with 3 steps advance." There was but one exchange of shots. The student was hit. "He put his hand on his breast, his body began to bend slowly forward, then collapsed in death and sank to the ground."

It is pathetic. There are other duels in my list, but I find in each and all of them one and the same ever-recurring defect—the *principals* are never present, but only by their sham representatives. The *real* principals in any duel are not the duelists themselves, but their *families*. They do the mourning, the suffering; theirs is the loss and theirs the misery. They stake all that, the duelist stakes nothing but his life, and that is a trivial thing compared with what his death must cost those whom he leaves behind him. Challenges should not mention the duelist; he has nothing much at stake, and the real vengeance cannot reach him. The challenge should summon the offender's old gray mother and his young wife and his little children—these, or any of whom he is a dear and worshiped possession—and should say, "You have done me no harm, but I am the meek slave of a custom which requires me to crush the happiness out of your hearts and condemn you to years of pain and grief, in order that I may wash clean with your tears a stain which has been put upon me by another person."

The logic of it is admirable; a person has robbed

me of a penny; I must beggar ten innocent persons
to make good my loss. Surely nobody's "honor" is
worth all that.

Since the duelist's family are the real principals in
a duel, the state ought to compel them to be present
at it. Custom, also, ought to be so amended as to
require it; and without it no duel ought to be
allowed to go on. If that student's unoffending
mother had been present and watching the officer
through her tears as he raised his pistol, he—why,
he would have fired in the air! We know that. For
we know how we are all made. Laws ought to be
based upon the ascertained facts of our nature. It
would be a simple thing to make a dueling law which
would stop dueling.

As things are now, the mother is never invited.
She submits to this; and without outward complaint, for she, too, is the vassal of custom, and
custom requires her to conceal her pain when she
learns the disastrous news that her son must go to
the dueling field, and by the powerful force that is
lodged in habit and custom she is enabled to obey
this trying requirement—a requirement which exacts
a miracle of her, and gets it. In January a neighbor
of ours who has a young son in the army was awak-
ened by this youth at three o'clock one morning, and
she sat up in bed and listened to his message:

"I have come to tell you something, mother,
which will distress you, but you must be good and
brave and bear it. I have been affronted by a fellow
officer and we fight at three this afternoon. Lie
down and sleep, now, and think no more about it."

She kissed him good night and lay down paralyzed with grief and fear, but said nothing. But she did not sleep; she prayed and mourned till the first streak of dawn, then fled to the nearest church and implored the Virgin for help; and from that church she went to another and another; church after church, and still church after church, and so spent all the day until three o'clock on her knees in agony and tears; then dragged herself home and sat down, comfortless and desolate, to count the minutes, and wait, with an outward show of calm, for what had been ordained for her—happiness, or endless misery. Presently she heard the clank of a saber—she had not known before what music was in that sound—and her son put his head in and said:

"X was in the wrong and he apologized."

So that incident was closed; and for the rest of her life the mother will always find something pleasant about the clank of a saber, no doubt.

In one of my listed duels— However, let it go, there is nothing particularly striking about it except that the seconds interfered. And prematurely, too, for neither man was dead. This was certainly irregular. Neither of the men liked it. It was a duel with cavalry sabers, between an editor and a lieutenant. The editor walked to the hospital; the lieutenant was carried. In Austria an editor who can write well is valuable, but he is not likely to remain so unless he can handle a saber with charm.

The following very recent telegram shows that also in France duels are humanely stopped as soon as they approach the (French) danger point:

# EUROPE AND ELSEWHERE

(Reuter's Telegram)

PARIS, *March 5th.*

The duel between Colonels Henry and Picquart took place this morning in the riding school of the École Militaire, the doors of which were strictly guarded in order to prevent intrusion. The combatants, who fought with swords, were in position at ten o'clock.

At the first re-engagement Lieut.-Col. Henry was slightly scratched in the forearm, and just at the same moment his own blade appeared to touch his adversary's neck. Senator Ranc, who was Colonel Picquart's second, stopped the fight, but as it was found that his principal had not been touched, the combat continued. A very sharp encounter ensued, in which Colonel Henry was wounded in the elbow, and the duel then terminated.

After which the stretcher and the band. In lurid contrast with this delicate flirtation, we have an account of a deadly duel of day before yesterday in Italy, where the earnest Austrian duel is in vogue. I knew one of the principals, Cavalotti, slightly, and this gives me a sort of personal interest in his duel. I first saw him in Rome several years ago. He was sitting on a block of stone in the Forum, and was writing something in his notebook—a poem or a challenge, or something like that—and the friend who pointed him out to me said, "That is Cavalotti —he has fought thirty duels; do not disturb him." I did not disturb him.

# SKELETON PLAN OF A PROPOSED CASTING VOTE PARTY

## (1901)

NOTE.—Mark Twain's effort was always for clean politics. In 1901 he formulated what to him seemed a feasible plan to obtain this boon. It is here first published.—A. B. P.

### ITS MAIN OBJECT

TO compel the two Great Parties to nominate their *best man* always.

### FOUNDATION PRINCIPLES

With the offices all filled by the best men of either of the two Great Parties, we shall have good government. We hold that this is beyond dispute, and does not need to be argued.

### DETAILS

1. The C. V. Party should be *organized*. This, in order to secure its continuance and permanency.
2. Any of the following acts must sever the connection of a member with the Casting Vote party:

The seeking of any office, appointive or elective.

The acceptance of a nomination to any such office.

The acceptance of such an office.

3. The organization should never vote for *any but a nominee of one or the other of the two Great Parties*, and should then cast their *entire vote* for that nominee.

4. They should have no dealings with minor parties.

5. There should be ward organizations, township, town, city, congressional district, state and national organizations. The party should work wherever there is an elective office, from the lowest up to the Presidency.

6. As a rule, none of the organizations will need to be large. In most cases they will be able to control the action of the two Great Parties without that. In the matter of membership, quality will be the main thing, rather than quantity.

In small constituencies, where a town constable or a justice of the peace is to be elected it will often be the case that a Casting Vote lodge of fifty members can elect the nominee it prefers. In every such community the material for the fifty is present. It will be found among the men who are disgusted with the prevailing political methods, the low ambitions and ideals, of the politicians; dishonesty in office; corruption; the frank distribution of appointments among characterless and incompetent men as pay for party service; the evasion and sometimes straight-out violation of the civil-service laws. The fifty will be found among the men who are ashamed of this condition of things and who have despaired of seeing it bettered; *who stay away from the polls and do not vote;* who do not attend primaries, and would be insulted there if they did.

The fifty exist in every little community; they are not seen, not heard, not regarded—but they are there. There, and deeply and sincerely desirous of good and sound government, and ready to give the best help they can if any will place before them a competent way. They are reserved and quiet merchants and shopkeepers, middle-aged; they are young men making their way in the offices of doctors and lawyers and behind counters; they are journeyman high-class mechanics; they are organizers of, and workers for, the community's charities, art and other social-improvement clubs, university settlements, Young Men's Christian Association, circulating libraries; they are readers of books, frequenters of the library. They have never seen a primary, and they have an aversion for the polls.

7. Men proposing to create a Casting Vote lodge should not advertise their purpose; conspiracies for good, like conspiracies for evil, are best conducted privately until success is sure. The poll of the two Great Parties should be examined, and the winning party's majority noted. *It is this majority which the Casting Vote must overcome and nullify.* If the total vote cast was 1,000 and the majority vote fifty, the proposers of a lodge should canvass privately until they have secured 75 or 100 names; they can organize then, without solicitude; the balance of power is in their hands, and this fact by itself will add names to its membership. If the total vote is 10,000 and the majority vote 1,000, the procedure should be as before: the thousand-and-upward should be secured by private canvass before

public organization is instituted. Where a total vote is 1,000,000 the majority vote is not likely to exceed 30,000. Five or six canvassers can begin the listing; each man secured becomes a canvasser, ten know three apiece who will join; the thirty know three apiece who will join; the ninety know three hundred, the three hundred know a thousand, the thousand know three thousand—and so on; the required thirty or forty thousand can be secured in ten days, the lodge organized, and its casting vote be ready and self-pledged and competent to elect the best of the nominees the two Great Parties may put up at that date or later.

8. In every ward of every city there is enough of this material to hold the balance of power over the two Great Parties in a ward election; in every city there is enough of it to determine which of the two nominees shall be mayor; in every congressional district there is enough of it to elect the Governor; also to elect the legislature and choose the U. S. Senators; and in the United States there is enough of it to throw the Casting Vote for its choice between the nominees of the two Great Parties and seat him in the presidential chair.

9. From constable up to President there is no office for which the two Great Parties cannot furnish able, clean, and acceptable men. Whenever the balance of power shall be lodged in a permanent third party with no candidates of its own and no function but to cast its *whole vote* for the best man put forward by the Republicans and Democrats, these two parties *will select the best men they have in*

*their ranks.* Good and clean government will follow, let its party complexion be what it may; and the country will be quite content.

### THE LODGES

The primal lodge—call it A—should consist of 10 men only. It is enough and can meet in a dwelling house or a shop, and get well acquainted at once. It has before it the names of the nominees of the two Great Parties—Jones (Republican), Smith (Democrat). It fails of unanimity—both candidates perchance being good men and about equally acceptable—and casts seven votes, say, for Jones and three for Smith.

It elects one of its ten to meet similar delegates from any number of local A lodges and hand in its vote. This body—call it a B lodge—examines the aggregate vote; this time the majority may be with Smith. The members carry the result to the A lodges; and these, by the conditions of their membership, must vote for Smith.

In the case of a state election, bodies each consisting of a number of B lodges would elect a delegate to a state council, and the state council would examine the aggregate vote and give its decision in favor of the Republican or Democratic candidate receiving the majority of the Casting Vote's suffrages.

In the case of a presidential contest, the state council would appoint delegates to a national convention, and these would examine the aggregate Casting Vote vote and determine and announce the choice of the Casting Vote organizations of the whole country. At the presidential election the A lodges throughout the land would vote for presidential electors of the Party indicated.

If the reader thinks well of the project, let him begin a private canvass among his friends and give it a practical test, without waiting for other people to begin. If in the hands of men who regard their citizenship as a high trust this scheme shall fail upon trial, a better must be sought, a better must be invented; for it cannot be well or safe to let the present political conditions continue indefinitely. They can be improved, and American citizenship should rouse up from its disheartenment and see that it is done.

# THE UNITED STATES OF LYNCHERDOM

## (1901)

NOTE.—Mark Twain always felt strongly on the subject of lynch law, and when in 1901 a particularly barbarous incident occurred in his native state he was moved to express himself in print. The article was not offered for publication, perhaps because the moment of timeliness had passed. Its general timeliness, however, is perennial and a word from "America's foremost private citizen" on the subject is worthy of preservation.—A. B. P.

## I

AND so Missouri has fallen, that great state! Certain of her children have joined the lynchers, and the smirch is upon the rest of us. That handful of her children have given us a character and labeled us with a name, and to the dwellers in the four quarters of the earth we are "lynchers," now, and ever shall be. For the world will not stop and think —it never does, it is not its way; its way is to generalize from a single sample. It will not say, "Those Missourians have been busy eighty years in building an honorable good name for themselves; these hundred lynchers down in the corner of the state are not real Missourians, they are renegades." No, that truth will not enter its mind; it will generalize from the one or two misleading samples and say, "The Missourians are lynchers." It has no reflection, no logic, no sense of proportion. With it, figures go for nothing; to it, figures reveal nothing, it cannot reason upon them rationally; it would say, for instance, that China is being swiftly and surely Christianized, since nine Chinese Christians are being made every day; and it would fail, with him, to notice that the fact that 33,000 pagans are *born* there every day, damages the argument. It would say, "There are a hundred lynchers there, therefore the Missourians are lynchers"; the considerable fact that there are two and a half million Missourians who are *not* lynchers would not affect their verdict.

## II

Oh, Missouri!

The tragedy occurred near Pierce City, down in the southwestern corner of the state. On a Sunday afternoon a young white woman who had started alone from church was found murdered. For there are churches there; in my time religion was more general, more pervasive, in the South than it was in the North, and more virile and earnest, too, I think; I have some reason to believe that this is still the case. The young woman was found murdered. Although it was a region of churches and schools the people rose, lynched three negroes—two of them very aged ones—burned out five negro households, and drove thirty negro families into the woods.

I do not dwell upon the provocation which moved the people to these crimes, for that has nothing to do with the matter; the only question is, does the assassin *take the law into his own hands?* It is very simple, and very just. If the assassin be proved to have usurped the law's prerogative in righting his wrongs, that ends the matter; a thousand provocations are no defense. The Pierce City people had bitter provocation—indeed, as revealed by certain of the particulars, the bitterest of all provocations—but no matter, they took the law into their own hands, when by the terms of their statutes their victim would certainly hang if the law had been allowed to take its course, for there are but few negroes in that region and they are without authority and without influence in overawing juries.

Why has lynching, with various barbaric accompaniments, become a favorite regulator in cases of "the usual crime" in several parts of the country? Is it because men think a lurid and terrible punishment a more forcible object lesson and a more effective deterrent than a sober and colorless hanging done privately in a jail would be? Surely sane men do not think that. Even the average child should know better. It should know that any strange and much-talked-of event is always followed by imitations, the world being so well supplied with excitable people who only need a little stirring up to make them lose what is left of their heads and do mad things which they would not have thought of ordinarily. It should know that if a man jump off Brooklyn Bridge another will imitate him; that if a person venture down Niagara Whirlpool in a barrel another will imitate him; that if a Jack the Ripper make notoriety by slaughtering women in dark alleys he will be imitated; that if a man attempt a king's life and the newspapers carry the noise of it around the globe, regicides will crop up all around. The child should know that one much-talked-of outrage and murder committed by a negro will upset the disturbed intellects of several other negroes and produce a series of the very tragedies the community would so strenuously wish to prevent; that each of these crimes will produce another series, and year by year steadily increase the tale of these disasters instead of diminishing it; that, in a word, the lynchers are themselves the worst enemies of their women. The child should also know that by a law of our make, communities, as well as individuals, are imitators; and that a much-talked-of lynching will infallibly produce other lynchings here and there and yonder, and that in time these will breed a mania, a fashion; a fashion which will spread wide and wider, year by year, covering state after state, as with an advancing disease. Lynching has reached Colorado, it has reached California, it has reached Indiana—and now Missouri! I may live to see a negro burned in Union Square, New York, with fifty thousand people present, and not a sheriff visible, not a governor, not a constable, not a colonel, not a clergyman, not a law-and-order representative of any sort.

*Increase in Lynching.*—In 1900 there were eight more cases than in 1899, and probably this year there will be more than there were last year. The year is little more than half gone, and yet there are eighty-eight cases as compared with one hundred and fifteen for all of last year. The four Southern states, Alabama, Georgia, Louisiana, and Mississippi are the worst offenders. Last year there were eight cases in Alabama, sixteen in Georgia, twenty in Louisiana, and twenty in Mis-

sissippi—over one-half the total. This year to date there have
been nine in Alabama, twelve in Georgia, eleven in Louisiana,
and thirteen in Mississippi—again more than one-half the total
number in the whole United States.—Chicago *Tribune*.

It must be that the increase comes of the inborn
human instinct to imitate—that and man's com-
monest weakness, his aversion to being unpleasantly
conspicuous, pointed at, shunned, as being on the
unpopular side. Its other name is Moral Cowardice,
and is the commanding feature of the make-up of
9,999 men in the 10,000. I am not offering this as
a discovery; privately the dullest of us knows it
to be true. History will not allow us to forget or
ignore this supreme trait of our character. It persistently and sardonically reminds us that from the
beginning of the world no revolt against a public
infamy or oppression has ever been begun but by
the one daring man in the 10,000, the rest timidly
waiting, and slowly and reluctantly joining, under
the influence of that man and his fellows from the
other ten thousands. The abolitionists remember.
Privately the public feeling was with them early,
but each man was afraid to speak out until he got
some hint that his neighbor was privately feeling
as he privately felt himself. Then the boom followed. It always does. It will occur in New York,
some day; and even in Pennsylvania.

It has been supposed—and said—that the people
at a lynching enjoy the spectacle and are glad of a
chance to see it. It cannot be true; all experience
is against it. The people in the South are made like
the people in the North—the vast majority of whom

are right-hearted and compassionate, and would be cruelly pained by such a spectacle—and *would attend it*, and let on to be pleased with it, if the public approval seemed to require it. We are made like that, and we cannot help it. The other animals are not so, but we cannot help that, either. They lack the Moral Sense; we have no way of trading ours off, for a nickel or some other thing above its value. The Moral Sense teaches us what is right, and how to avoid it—when unpopular.

It is thought, as I have said, that a lynching crowd enjoys a lynching. It certainly is not true; it is impossible of belief. It is freely asserted—you have seen it in print many times of late—that the lynching impulse has been misinterpreted; that it is *not* the outcome of a spirit of revenge, but of a "mere atrocious hunger *to look upon human suffering*." If that were so, the crowds that saw the Windsor Hotel burn down would have enjoyed the horrors that fell under their eyes. Did they? No one will think that of them, no one will make that charge. Many risked their lives to save the men and women who were in peril. Why did they do that? Because *none would disapprove*. There was no restraint; they could follow their natural impulse. Why does a crowd of the same kind of people in Texas, Colorado, Indiana, stand by, smitten to the heart and miserable, and by ostentatious outward signs pretend to enjoy a lynching? Why does it lift no hand or voice in protest? Only because it would be unpopular to do it, I think; each man is afraid of his neighbor's disapproval—a thing which, to the general run of the race, is more dreaded than wounds and death. When there is to be a lynching the people hitch up and come miles to see it, bringing their wives and children. Really to see it? No— they come only because they are afraid to stay at home, lest it be noticed and offensively commented upon. We may believe this, for we all know how *we* feel about such spectacles—also, how we would act under the like pressure. We are not any better nor any braver than anybody else, and we must not try to creep out of it.

A Savonarola can quell and scatter a mob of lynchers with a mere glance of his eye: so can a Merrill[1] or a Beloat.[2] For no mob has any sand in the presence of a man known to be splendidly brave. Besides, a lynching mob would *like* to be scattered, for of a certainty there are never ten men in it who would not prefer to be somewhere else—and would be, if they but had the courage to go. When I was a boy I saw a brave gentleman deride and insult a mob and drive it away; and afterward, in Nevada, I saw a noted desperado make two hundred men sit still, with the house burning under them, until he gave them permission to retire. A plucky man can rob a whole passenger train by himself; and the half of a brave man can hold up a stagecoach and strip its occupants.

Then perhaps the remedy for lynchings comes to this: station a brave man in each affected community

[1] Sheriff of Carroll County, Georgia.
[2] Sheriff, Princeton, Indiana. By that formidable power which lies in an established reputation for cold pluck they faced lynching mobs and securely held the field against them.

to encourage, support, and bring to light the deep disapproval of lynching hidden in the secret places of its heart—for it is there, beyond question. Then those communities will find something better to imitate—of course, being human, they must imitate something. Where shall these brave men be found? That is indeed a difficulty; there are not three hundred of them in the earth. If merely *physically* brave men would do, then it were easy; they could be furnished by the cargo. When Hobson called for seven volunteers to go with him to what promised to be certain death, four thousand men responded—the whole fleet, in fact. Because *all the world would approve*. They knew that; but if Hobson's project had been charged with the scoffs and jeers of the friends and associates, whose good opinion and approval the sailors valued, he could not have got his seven.

No, upon reflection, the scheme will not work. There are not enough morally brave men in stock. We are out of moral-courage material; we are in a condition of profound poverty. We have those two sheriffs down South who—but never mind, it is not enough to go around; they have to stay and take care of their own communities.

But if we only *could* have three or four more sheriffs of that great breed! Would it help? I think so. For we are all imitators: other brave sheriffs would follow; to be a dauntless sheriff would come to be recognized as the correct and only thing, and the dreaded disapproval would fall to the share of the other kind; courage in this office would become custom, the absence of it a dishonor, just as courage presently replaces the timidity of the new soldier; then the mobs and the lynchings would disappear, and——

However. It can never be done without some starters, and where are we to get the starters? Advertise? Very well, then, let us advertise.

In the meantime, there is another plan. Let us import American missionaries from China, and send them into the lynching field. With 1,511 of them out there converting two Chinamen apiece per annum against an uphill birth rate of 33,000 pagans per day,[1] it will take upward of a million years to make the conversions balance the output and bring the Christianizing of the country in sight to the naked eye; therefore, if we can offer our missionaries as rich a field at home at lighter expense and quite satisfactory in the matter of danger, why shouldn't they find it fair and right to come back and give us a trial? The Chinese are universally conceded to be excellent people, honest, honorable, industrious, trustworthy, kind-hearted, and all that—leave them alone, they are plenty good enough just as they are; and besides, almost every convert runs a risk of catching our civilization. We ought to be careful. We ought to think twice before we encourage a risk like that; for, *once civilized, China can never be*

[1] These figures are not fanciful; all of them are genuine and authentic. They are from official missionary records in China. See Doctor Morrison's book on his pedestrian journey across China; he quotes them and gives his authorities. For several years he has been the London *Times's* representative in Peking, and was there through the siege.

*uncivilized again.* We have not been thinking of that. Very well, we ought to think of it now. Our missionaries will find that we have a field for them—and not only for the 1,511, but for 15,011. Let them look at the following telegram and see if they have anything in China that is more appetizing. It is from Texas:

> The negro was taken to a tree and swung in the air. Wood and fodder were piled beneath his body and a hot fire was made. *Then it was suggested that the man ought not to die too quickly, and he was let down to the ground while a party went to Dexter, about two miles distant, to procure coal oil.* This was thrown on the flames and the work completed.

We implore them to come back and help us in our need. Patriotism imposes this duty on them. Our country is worse off than China; they are our countrymen, their motherland supplicates their aid in this her hour of deep distress. They are competent; our people are not. They are used to scoffs, sneers, revilings, danger; our people are not. They have the martyr spirit; nothing but the martyr spirit can brave a lynching mob, and cow it and scatter it. They can save their country, we beseech them to come home and do it. We ask them to read that telegram again, and yet again, and picture the scene in their minds, and soberly ponder it; then multiply it by 115, add 88; place the 203 in a row, allowing 600 feet of space for each human torch, so that there may be viewing room around it for 5,000 Christian American men, women, and children, youths and maidens; make it night, for grim effect; have the show in a gradually rising plain, and let the course of the stakes be uphill; the eye can then take in the whole line of twenty-four miles of blood-and-flesh bonfires unbroken, whereas if it occupied level ground the ends of the line would bend down and be hidden from view by the curvature of the earth. All being ready, now, and the darkness opaque, the stillness impressive—for there should be no sound but the soft moaning of the night wind and the muffled sobbing of the sacrifices—let all the far stretch of kerosened pyres be touched off simultaneously and the glare and the shrieks and the agonies burst heavenward to the Throne.

There are more than a million persons present; the light from the fires flushes into vague outline against the night the spires of five thousand churches. O kind missionary, O compassionate missionary, leave China! come home and convert these Christians!

I believe that if anything can stop this epidemic of bloody insanities it is martial personalities that can face mobs without flinching; and as such personalities are developed only by familiarity with danger and by the training and seasoning which come of resisting it, the likeliest place to find them must be among the missionaries who have been under tuition in China during the past year or two. We have abundance of work for them, and for hundreds and thousands more, and the field is daily growing and spreading. Shall we find them? We can try. In 75,000,000 there must be other Merrills and Beloats; and it is the law of our make that each example shall wake up drowsing chevaliers of the same great knighthood and bring them to the front.

# TO THE PERSON SITTING IN DARKNESS

*(North American Review,* 1901)

See introduction to this volume for some account of this and the following article.

Christmas will dawn in the United States over a people full of hope and aspiration and good cheer. Such a condition means contentment and happiness. The carping grumbler who may here and there go forth will find few to listen to him. The majority will wonder what is the matter with him and pass on.—New York *Tribune,* on Christmas Eve.

## From the *Sun,* of New York:

The purpose of this article is not to describe the terrible offenses against humanity committed in the name of Politics in some of the most notorious East Side districts. *They could not be described, even verbally.* But it is the intention to let the great mass of more or less careless citizens of this beautiful metropolis of the New World get some conception of the havoc and ruin wrought to man, woman, and child in the most densely populated and least-known section of the city. Name, date, and place can be supplied to those of little faith—or to any man who feels himself aggrieved. It is a plain statement of record and observation, written without license and without garnish.

Imagine, if you can, a section of the city territory completely dominated by one man, without whose permission neither legitimate nor illegitimate business can be conducted; *where illegitimate business is encouraged and legitimate business discouraged;* where the respectable residents have to fasten their doors and windows summer nights and sit in their rooms with asphyxiating air and 100-degree temperature, rather than try to catch the faint whiff of breeze in their natural breathing places, the stoops of their homes; *where naked women dance by night in the streets, and unsexed men prowl like vultures through the darkness on* "*business*" not only permitted but encouraged by the police;

*where the education of infants begins with the knowledge of prostitution* and the training of little girls is training in the arts of Phryne; where *American* girls brought up with the refinements of *American* homes are imported from small towns up-state, Massachusetts, Connecticut, and New Jersey, and kept as virtually prisoners as if they were locked up behind jail bars until they have lost all semblance of womanhood; *where small boys are taught to solicit for the women of disorderly houses;* where there is an organized society of young men *whose sole business in life is to corrupt young girls and turn them over to bawdy houses;* where men walking with their wives along the street are openly insulted; *where children that have adult diseases are the chief patrons of the hospitals and dispensaries;* where it is the rule, rather than the exception, that *murder, rape, robbery, and theft go unpunished*—in short where the Premium of the most awful forms of Vice is the Profit of the politicians.

The following news from China appeared in the *Sun*, of New York, on Christmas Eve. The italics are mine:

The Rev. Mr. Ament, of the American Board of Foreign Missions, has returned from a trip which he made for the purpose of collecting indemnities for damages done by Boxers. *Everywhere he went he compelled the Chinese to pay.* He says that all his native Christians are now provided for. He had 700 of them under his charge, and 300 were killed. He has *collected 300 taels for each* of these murders, and has *compelled full payment for all the property belonging to Christians* that was destroyed. He also assessed *fines* amounting to THIRTEEN TIMES the amount of the indemnity. *This money will be used for the propagation of the Gospel.*

Mr. Ament declares that the compensation he has collected is *moderate* when compared with the amount secured by the Catholics, who demand, in addition to money, *head for head.* They collect 500 taels for each murder of a Catholic. In the Wenchiu country, 680 Catholics were killed, and for this the European Catholics here demand 750,000 strings of cash and 680 *heads.*

In the course of a conversation, Mr. Ament referred to the attitude of the missionaries toward the Chinese. He said:

"I deny emphatically that the missionaries are *vindictive*, that they *generally* looted, or that they have done anything *since* the siege that *the circumstances did not demand*. I criticize the Americans. *The soft hand of the Americans is not as good as the mailed fist of the Germans*. If you deal with the Chinese with a soft hand they will take advantage of it.

"The statement that the French government will return the loot taken by the French soldiers is the source of the greatest amusement here. The French soldiers were more systematic looters than the Germans, and it is a fact that to-day *Catholic Christians*, carrying French flags and armed with modern guns, *are looting villages* in the Province of Chili."

By happy luck, we get all these glad tidings on Christmas Eve—just in time enable us to celebrate the day with proper gayety and enthusiasm. Our spirits soar, and we find we can even make jokes: Taels, I win, Heads you lose.

Our Reverend Ament is the right man in the right place. What we want of our missionaries out there is, not that they shall merely represent in their acts and persons the grace and gentleness and charity and loving-kindness of our religion, but that they shall also represent the American spirit. The oldest Americans are the Pawnees. Macallum's History says:

When a white Boxer kills a Pawnee and destroys his property, the other Pawnees do not trouble to seek *him* out, they kill any white person that comes along; also, they make some white village pay deceased's heirs the full cash value of deceased, together with full cash value of the property destroyed; they also make the village pay, in addition, *thirteen times* the value of that property into a fund for the dissemination of the Pawnee religion, which they regard as the best of all religions for the softening and humanizing of the heart of man. It is their idea that it is only fair and right that the innocent should be made to suffer for the guilty, and that it is better that ninety and nine innocent should suffer than that one guilty person should escape.

Our Reverend Ament is justifiably jealous of those enterprising Catholics, who not only get big money for each lost convert, but get "head for head" besides. But he should soothe himself with the reflections that the entirety of their exactions are for their own pockets, whereas he, less selfishly, devotes only 300 taels per head to that service, and gives the whole vast thirteen repetitions of the property-indemnity to the service of propagating the Gospel. His magnanimity has won him the approval of his nation, and will get him a monument. Let him be content with these rewards. We all hold him dear for manfully defending his fellow missionaries from exaggerated charges which were beginning to distress us, but which his testimony has so considerably modified that we can now contemplate them without noticeable pain. For now we know that, even before the siege, the missionaries were not "generally" out looting, and that, "since the siege," they have acted quite handsomely, except when "circumstances" crowded them. I am arranging for the monument. Subscriptions for it can be sent to the American Board; designs for it can be sent to me. Designs must allegorically set forth the Thirteen Reduplications of the Indemnity, and the Object for which they were exacted; as Ornaments, the designs must exhibit 680 Heads, so disposed as to give a pleasing and pretty effect; for the Catholics have done nicely, and are entitled to notice in the monument. Mottoes may be suggested, if any shall be discovered that will satisfactorily cover the ground.

Mr. Ament's financial feat of squeezing a thirteen-fold indemnity out of the pauper peasants to square other people's offenses, thus condemning them and their women and innocent little children to inevitable starvation and lingering death, in order that the blood money so acquired might be *"used for the propagation of the Gospel,"* does not flutter my serenity; although the act and the words, taken together, concrete a blasphemy so hideous and so colossal that, without doubt, its mate is not findable in the history of this or of any other age. Yet, if a layman had done that thing and justified it with those words, I should have shuddered, I know. Or, if I had done the thing and said the words myself— However, the thought is unthinkable, irreverent as some imperfectly informed people think me. Sometimes an ordained minister sets out to be blasphemous. When this happens, the layman is out of the running; he stands no chance.

We have Mr. Ament's impassioned assurance that the missionaries are not "vindictive." Let us hope and pray that they will never become so, but will remain in the almost morbidly fair and just and gentle temper which is affording so much satisfaction to their brother and champion to-day.

The following is from the New York *Tribune* of Christmas Eve. It comes from that journal's Tokyo correspondent. It has a strange and impudent sound, but the Japanese are but partially civilized as yet. When they become wholly civilized they will not talk so:

# TO THE PERSON SITTING IN DARKNESS

The missionary question, of course, occupies a foremost place in the discussion. It is now felt as essential that the Western Powers take cognizance of the sentiment here, that religious invasions of Oriental countries by powerful Western organizations are tantamount to filibustering expeditions, and should not only be discountenanced, but that stern measures should be adopted for their suppression. The feeling here is that the missionary organizations constitute a constant menace to peaceful international relations.

*Shall we?* That is, shall we go on conferring our Civilization upon the peoples that sit in darkness, or shall we give those poor things a rest? Shall we bang right ahead in our old-time, loud, pious way, and commit the new century to the game; or shall we sober up and sit down and think it over first? Would it not be prudent to get our Civilization tools together, and see how much stock is left on hand in the way of Glass Beads and Theology, and Maxim Guns and Hymn Books, and Trade Gin and Torches of Progress and Enlightenment (patent adjustable ones, good to fire villages with, upon occasion), and balance the books, and arrive at the profit and loss, so that we may intelligently decide whether to continue the business or sell out the property and start a new Civilization Scheme on the proceeds?

Extending the Blessings of Civilization to our Brother who Sits in Darkness has been a good trade and has paid well, on the whole; and there is money in it yet, if carefully worked—but not enough, in my judgment, to make any considerable risk advisable. The People that Sit in Darkness are getting to be too scarce—too scarce and too shy. And such darkness as is now left is really of but an indifferent quality, and not dark enough for the game. The most of those People that Sit in Darkness have been furnished with more light than was good for them or profitable for us. We have been injudicious.

The Blessings-of-Civilization Trust, wisely and cautiously administered, is a Daisy. There is more money in it, more territory, more sovereignty, and other kinds of emolument, than there is in any other game that is played. But Christendom has been playing it badly of late years, and must certainly suffer by it, in my opinion. She has been so eager to get every stake that appeared on the green cloth, that the People who Sit in Darkness have noticed it—they have noticed it, and have begun to show alarm. They have become suspicious of the Blessings of Civilization. More—they have begun to examine them. This is not well. The Blessings of Civilization are all right, and a good commercial property; there could not be a better, in a dim light. In the right kind of a light, and at a proper distance, with the goods a little out of focus, they furnish this desirable exhibit to the Gentlemen who Sit in Darkness:

| | |
|---|---|
| LOVE, | LAW AND ORDER, |
| JUSTICE, | LIBERTY, |
| GENTLENESS, | EQUALITY, |
| CHRISTIANITY, | HONORABLE DEAL- |
| PROTECTION TO THE | ING, |
| WEAK, | MERCY, |
| TEMPERANCE, | EDUCATION, |

—and so on.

There. Is it good? Sir, it is pie. It will bring into camp any idiot that sits in darkness anywhere. But not if we adulterate it. It is proper to be emphatic upon that point. This brand is strictly for Export—apparently. *Apparently*. Privately and confidentially, it is nothing of the kind. Privately and confidentially, it is merely an outside cover, gay and pretty and attractive, displaying the special patterns of our Civilization which we reserve for Home Consumption, while *inside* the bale is the Actual Thing that the Customer Sitting in Darkness buys with his blood and tears and land and liberty. That Actual Thing is, indeed, Civilization, but it is only for Export. Is there a difference between the two brands? In some of the details, yes.

We all know that the Business is being ruined. The reason is not far to seek. It is because our Mr. McKinley, and Mr. Chamberlain, and the Kaiser, and the Tsar and the French have been exporting the Actual Thing *with the outside cover left off*. This is bad for the Game. It shows that these new players of it are not sufficiently acquainted with it.

It is a distress to look on and note the mismoves, they are so strange and so awkward. Mr. Chamberlain manufactures a war out of materials so inadequate and so fanciful that they make the boxes grieve and the gallery laugh, and he tries hard to persuade himself that it isn't purely a private raid for cash, but has a sort of dim, vague respectability about it somewhere, if he could only find the spot; and that, by and by, he can scour the flag clean again after he has finished dragging it through the

mud, and make it shine and flash in the vault of
heaven once more as it had shone and flashed there
a thousand years in the world's respect until he laid
his unfaithful hand upon it. It is bad play—bad.
For it exposes the Actual Thing to Them that Sit
in Darkness, and they say: "What! Christian
against Christian? And only for money? Is *this*
a case of magnanimity, forbearance, love, gentleness,
mercy, protection of the weak—this strange and
overshowy onslaught of an elephant upon a nest of
field mice, on the pretext that the mice had squeaked
an insolence at him—conduct which "no self-
respecting government could allow to pass un-
avenged"? as Mr. Chamberlain said. Was that a
good pretext in a small case, when it had not been
a good pretext in a large one?—for only recently
Russia had affronted the elephant three times and
survived alive and unsmitten. Is this Civilization
and Progress? Is it something better than we already
possess? These harryings and burnings and desert-
makings in the Transvaal—is this an improvement
on our darkness? Is it, perhaps, possible that there
are two kinds of Civilization—one for home consumption and one for the heathen market?"

Then They that Sit in Darkness are troubled, and
shake their heads; and they read this extract from
a letter of a British private, recounting his exploits
in one of Methuen's victories, some days before
the affair of Magersfontein, and they are troubled
again:

We tore up the hill and into the intrenchments, and the Boers
saw we had them; so they dropped their guns and went down

on their knees and put up their hands clasped, and begged for mercy. And we gave it them—*with the long spoon.*

The long spoon is the bayonet. See *Lloyd's Weekly*, London, of those days. The same number—and the same column—contained some quite unconscious satire in the form of shocked and bitter upbraidings of the Boers for their brutalities and inhumanities!

Next, to our heavy damage, the Kaiser went to playing the game without first mastering it. He lost a couple of missionaries in a riot in Shantung, and in his account he made an overcharge for them. China had to pay a hundred thousand dollars apiece for them, in money; twelve miles of territory, containing several millions of inhabitants and worth twenty million dollars; and to build a monument, and also a Christian church; whereas the people of China could have been depended upon to remember the missionaries without the help of these expensive memorials. This was all bad play. Bad, because it would not, and could not, and will not now or ever, deceive the Person Sitting in Darkness. He knows that it was an overcharge. He knows that a missionary is like any other man: he is worth merely what you can supply his place for, and no more. He is useful, but so is a doctor, so is a sheriff, so is an editor; but a just Emperor does not charge war prices for such. A diligent, intelligent, but obscure missionary, and a diligent, intelligent country editor are worth much, and we know it; but they are not worth the earth. We esteem such an editor, and we are sorry to see him go; but, when he goes, we should consider twelve miles of territory, and a church, and a fortune, overcompensation for his loss. I mean, if he was a Chinese editor, and we had to settle for him. It is no proper figure for an editor or a missionary; one can get shop-worn kings for less. It was bad play on the Kaiser's part. It got this property, true; but it *produced the Chinese revolt*, the indignant uprising of China's traduced patriots, the Boxers. The results have been expensive to Germany, and to the other Disseminators of Progress and the Blessings of Civilization.

The Kasier's claim was paid, yet it was bad play, for it could not fail to have an evil effect upon Persons Sitting in Darkness in China. They would muse upon the event, and be likely to say: "Civilization is gracious and beautiful, for such is its reputation; but can we afford it? There are rich Chinamen, perhaps they can afford it; but this tax is not laid upon them, it is laid upon the peasants of Shantung; it is they that must pay this mighty sum, and their wages are but four cents a day. Is this a better civilization than ours, and holier and higher and nobler? Is not this rapacity? Is not this extortion? Would Germany charge America two hundred thousand dollars for two missionaries, and shake the mailed fist in her face, and send warships, and send soldiers, and say: 'Seize twelve miles of territory, worth twenty millions of dollars, as additional pay for the missionaries; and make those peasants build a monument to the missionaries, and a costly Christian church to remember them by?' And later would Germany say to her soldiers: 'March through

America and slay, *giving no quarter;* make the German face there, as has been our Hun-face here, a terror for a thousand years; march through the Great Republic and slay, slay, slay, carving a road for our offended religion through its heart and bowels?' Would Germany do like this to America, to England, to France, to Russia? Or only to China, the helpless —imitating the elephant's assault upon the field mice? Had we better invest in this Civilization— this Civilization which called Napoleon a buccaneer for carrying off Venice's bronze horses, but which steals our ancient astronomical instruments from our walls, and goes looting like common bandits— that is, all the alien soldiers except America's; and (Americans again excepted) storms frightened villages and cables the result to glad journals at home every day: 'Chinese losses, 450 killed; ours, *one officer and two men wounded.* Shall proceed against neighboring village to-morrow, where a *massacre* is reported.' Can we afford Civilization?"

And next Russia must go and play the game injudiciously. She affronts England once or twice —with the Person Sitting in Darkness observing and noting; by moral assistance of France and Germany, she robs Japan of her hard-earned spoil, all swimming in Chinese blood—Port Arthur—with the Person again observing and noting; then she seizes Manchuria, raids its villages, and chokes its great river with the swollen corpses of countless massacred peasants—that astonished Person still observing and noting. And perhaps he is saying to himself: "It is yet *another* Civilized Power, with its banner of the

Prince of Peace in one hand and its loot basket and its butcher knife in the other. Is there no salvation for us but to adopt Civilization and lift ourselves down to its level?"

And by and by comes America, and our Master of the Game plays it badly—plays it as Mr. Chamberlain was playing it in South Africa. It was a mistake to do that; also, it was one which was quite unlooked for in a Master who was playing it so well in Cuba. In Cuba, he was playing the usual and regular *American* game, and it was winning, for there is no way to beat it. The Master, contemplating Cuba, said: "Here is an oppressed and friendless little nation which is willing to fight to be free; we go partners, and put up the strength of seventy million sympathizers and the resources of the United States: play!" Nothing but Europe combined could call that hand: and Europe cannot combine on anything. There, in Cuba, he was following our great traditions in a way which made us very proud of him, and proud of the deep dissatisfaction which his play was provoking in continental Europe. Moved by a high inspiration, he threw out those stirring words which proclaimed that forcible annexation would be "criminal aggression"; and in that utterance fired another "shot heard round the world." The memory of that fine saying will be outlived by the remembrance of no act of his but one—that he forgot it within the twelvemonth, and its honorable gospel along with it.

For, presently, came the Philippine temptation. It was strong; it was too strong, and he made that

bad mistake: he played the European game, the
Chamberlain game. It was a pity; it was a great
pity, that error; that one grievous error, that irrev-
ocable error. For it was the very place and time
to play the American game again. And at no cost.
Rich winnings to be gathered in, too; rich and
permanent; indestructible; a fortune transmissible
forever to the children of the flag. Not land, not
money, not dominion—no, something worth many
times more than that dross: our share, the spectacle
of a nation of long harassed and persecuted slaves
set free through our influence; our posterity's share,
the golden memory of that fair deed. The game
was in our hands. If it had been played according
to the American rules, Dewey would have sailed
away from Manila as soon as he had destroyed the
Spanish fleet—after putting up a sign on shore
guaranteeing foreign property and life against damage by the Filipinos, and warning the Powers that
interference with the emancipated patriots would be
regarded as an act unfriendly to the United States.
The Powers cannot combine, in even a bad cause,
and the sign would not have been molested.

Dewey could have gone about his affairs elsewhere,
and left the competent Filipino army to starve out
the little Spanish garrison and send it home, and the
Filipino citizens to set up the form of government
they might prefer, and deal with the friars and their
doubtful acquisitions according to Filipino ideas of
fairness and justice—ideas which have since been
tested and found to be of as high an order as any
that prevail in Europe or America.

But we played the Chamberlain game, and lost the chance to add another Cuba and another honorable deed to our good record.

The more we examine the mistake, the more clearly we perceive that it is going to be bad for the Business. The Person Sitting in Darkness is almost sure to say: "There is something curious about this—curious and unaccountable. There must be two Americas: one that sets the captive free, and one that takes a once-captive's new freedom away from him, and picks a quarrel with him with nothing to found it on; then kills him to get his land."

The truth is, the Person Sitting in Darkness *is* saying things like that; and for the sake of the Business we must persuade him to look at the Philippine matter in another and healthier way. We must arrange his opinions for him. I believe it can be done; for Mr. Chamberlain has arranged England's opinion of the South African matter, and done it most cleverly and successfully. He presented the facts—some of the facts—and showed those confiding people what the facts meant. He did it statistically, which is a good way. He used the formula: "Twice 2 are 14, and 2 from 9 leaves 35." Figures are effective; figures will convince the elect.

Now, my plan is a still bolder one than Mr. Chamberlain's, though apparently a copy of it. Let us be franker than Mr. Chamberlain; let us audaciously present the whole of the facts, shirking none, then explain them according to Mr. Chamberlain's formula. This daring truthfulness will astonish and dazzle the Person Sitting in Darkness, and he will

take the Explanation down before his mental vision
has had time to get back into focus.  Let us say
to him:

"Our case is simple.  On the 1st of May, Dewey
destroyed the Spanish fleet.  This left the Archipelago in the hands of its proper and rightful owners,
the Filipino nation.  Their army numbered 30,000
men, and they were competent to whip out or starve
out the little Spanish garrison; then the people
could set up a government of their own devising.
Our traditions required that Dewey should now set
up his warning sign, and go away.  But the Master
of the Game happened to think of another plan—
the European plan.  He acted upon it.  This was,
to send out an army—ostensibly to help the native
patriots put the finishing touch upon their long and
plucky struggle for independence, but really to take
their land away from them and keep it.  That is,
in the interest of Progress and Civilization.  The
plan developed, stage by stage, and quite satisfactorily.  We entered into a military alliance with the
trusting Filipinos, and they hemmed in Manila on
the land side, and by their valuable help the place,
with its garrison of 8,000 or 10,000 Spaniards, was
captured—a thing which we could not have accomplished unaided at that time.  We got their help by
—by ingenuity.  We knew they were fighting for
their independence, and that they had been at it
for two years.  We knew they supposed that we
also were fighting in their worthy cause—just as we had
helped the Cubans fight for Cuban independence—
and we allowed them to go on thinking so.  *Until*

*Manila was ours and we could get along without them.*
Then we showed our hand. Of course, they were
surprised—that was natural; surprised and disappointed; disappointed and grieved. To them it
looked un-American; uncharacteristic; foreign to
our established traditions. And this was natural,
too; for we were only playing the American Game
in public—in private it was the European. It was
neatly done, very neatly, and it bewildered them.
They could not understand it; for we had been so
friendly—so affectionate, even—with those simple-
minded patriots! We, our own selves, had brought
back out of exile their leader, their hero, their hope,
their Washington—Aguinaldo; brought him in a
warship, in high honor, under the sacred shelter and
hospitality of the flag; brought him back and restored
him to his people, and got their moving and eloquent
gratitude for it. Yes, we had been so friendly to
them, and had heartened them up in so many ways!
We had lent them guns and ammunition; advised
with them; exchanged pleasant courtesies with them;
placed our sick and wounded in their kindly care;
intrusted our Spanish prisoners to their humane and
honest hands; fought shoulder to shoulder with
them against "the common enemy" (our own
phrase); praised their courage, praised their gal-
lantry, praised their mercifulness, praised their fine
and honorable conduct; borrowed their trenches,
borrowed strong positions which they had previously
captured from the Spaniards; petted them, lied to
them—officially proclaiming that our land and naval
forces came to give them their freedom and displace

266

the bad Spanish Government—fooled them, used them until we needed them no longer; then derided the sucked orange and threw it away. We kept the positions which we had beguiled them of; by and by, we moved a force forward and overlapped patriot ground—a clever thought, for we needed trouble, and this would produce it. A Filipino soldier, crossing the ground, where no one had a right to forbid him, was shot by our sentry. The badgered patriots resented this with arms, without waiting to know whether Aguinaldo, who was absent, would approve or not. Aguinaldo did not approve; but that availed nothing. What we wanted, in the interest of Progress and Civilization, was the Archipelago, unencumbered by patriots struggling for independence; and War was what we needed. We clinched our opportunity. It is Mr. Chamberlain's case over again— at least in its motive and intention; and we played the game as adroitly as he played it himself."

At this point in our frank statement of fact to the Person Sitting in Darkness, we should throw in a little trade taffy about the Blessings of Civilization— for a change, and for the refreshment of his spirit— then go on with our tale:

"We and the patriots having captured Manila, Spain's ownership of the Archipelago and her sovereignty over it were at an end—obliterated—annihilated—not a rag or shred of either remaining behind. It was then that we conceived the divinely humorous idea of *buying* both of these specters from Spain! [It is quite safe to confess this to the Person Sitting in Darkness, since neither he nor any other sane person will believe it.] In buying those ghosts for twenty millions, we also contracted to take care of the friars and their accumulations. I think we also agreed to propagate leprosy and smallpox, but as to this there is doubt. But it is not important; persons afflicted with the friars do not mind other diseases.

"With our Treaty ratified, Manila subdued, and our Ghosts secured, we had no further use for Aguinaldo and the owners of the Archipelago. We forced a war, and we have been hunting America's guest and ally through the woods and swamps ever since."

At this point in the tale, it will be well to boast a little of our war work and our heriosms in the field, so as to make our performance look as fine as England's in South Africa; but I believe it will not be best to emphasize this too much. We must be cautious. Of course, we must read the war telegrams to the Person, in order to keep up our frankness; but we can throw an air of humorousness over them, and that will modify their grim eloquence a little, and their rather indiscret exhibitions of gory exultation. Before reading to him the following display heads of the dispatches of November 18, 1900, it will be well to practice on them in private first, so as to get the right tang of lightness and gayety into them:

"ADMINISTRATION WEARY OF
PROTRACTED HOSTILITIES!"

"REAL WAR AHEAD FOR FILIPINO
REBELS!"[1]

[1] "Rebels!" Mumble that funny word—don't let the Person catch it distinctly.

# TO THE PERSON SITTING IN DARKNESS

### "WILL SHOW NO MERCY!"
### "KITCHENER'S PLAN ADOPTED!"

Kitchener knows how to handle disagreeable people who are fighting for their homes and their liberties, and we must let on that we are merely imitating Kitchener, and have no national interest in the matter, further than to get ourselves admired by the Great Family of Nations, in which august company our Master of the Game has bought a place for us in the back row.

Of course, we must not venture to ignore our General MacArthur's reports—oh, why do they keep on printing those embarrassing things?—we must drop them trippingly from the tongue and take the chances:

> During the last ten months our losses have been 268 killed and 750 wounded; Filipino loss, *three thousand two hundred and twenty-seven killed*, and 694 wounded.

We must stand ready to grab the Person Sitting in Darkness, for he will swoon away at this confession, saying: "Good God! those 'niggers' spare their wounded, and the Americans massacre theirs!"

We must bring him to, and coax him and coddle him, and assure him that the ways of Providence are best, and that it would not become us to find fault with them; and then, to show him that we are only imitators, not originators, we must read the following passage from the letter of an American soldier lad in the Philippines to his mother, published in *Public Opinion*, of Decorah, Iowa, describing the finish of a victorious battle:

"WE NEVER LEFT ONE ALIVE. IF ONE WAS WOUNDED, WE WOULD RUN OUR BAYONETS THROUGH HIM."

Having now laid all the historical facts before the Person Sitting in Darkness, we should bring him to again, and explain them to him. We should say to him:

"They look doubtful, but in reality they are not. There have been lies; yes, but they were told in a good cause. We have been treacherous; but that was only in order that real good might come out of apparent evil. True, we have crushed a deceived and confiding people; we have turned against the weak and the friendless who trusted us; we have stamped out a just and intelligent and well-ordered republic; we have stabbed an ally in the back and slapped the face of a guest; we have bought a Shadow from an enemy that hadn't it to sell; we have robbed a trusting friend of his land and his liberty; we have invited our clean young men to shoulder a discredited musket and do bandits' work under a flag which bandits have been accustomed to fear, not to follow; we have debauched America's honor and blackened her face before the world; but each detail was for the best. We know this. The Head of every State and Sovereignty in Christendom and 90 per cent of every legislative body in Christendom, including our Congress and our fifty state legislatures, are members not only of the church, but also of the Blessings-of-Civilization Trust. This world-girdling accumulation of trained morals, high principles, and justice cannot do an unright thing, an unfair thing, an ungenerous thing, an unclean thing. It knows what it is about. Give yourself no uneasiness; it is all right."

Now then, that will convince the Person. You will see. It will restore the Business. Also, it will elect the Master of the Game to the vacant place in the Trinity of our national gods; and there on their high thrones the Three will sit, age after age, in the people's sight, each bearing the Emblem of his service: Washington, the Sword of the Liberator; Lincoln, the Slave's Broken Chains; the Master, the Chains Repaired.

It will give the Business a splendid new start. You will see.

Everything is prosperous, now; everything is just as we should wish it. We have got the Archipelago, and we shall never give it up. Also, we have every reason to hope that we shall have an opportunity before very long to slip out of our congressional contract with Cuba and give her something better in the place of it. It is a rich country, and many of us are already beginning to see that the contract was a sentimental mistake. But now—right now— is the best time to do some profitable rehabilitating work—work that will set us up and make us comfortable, and discourage gossip. We cannot conceal from ourselves that, privately, we are a little troubled about our uniform. It is one of our prides; it is acquainted with honor; it is familiar with great deeds and noble; we love it, we revere it; and so this errand it is on makes us uneasy. And our flag— another pride of ours, our chiefest! We have wor-

shiped it so; and when we have seen it in far lands—
glimpsing it unexpectedly in that strange sky, waving its welcome and benediction to us—we have
caught our breaths, and uncovered our heads, and
couldn't speak, for a moment, for the thought of
what it was to us and the great ideals it stood for.
Indeed, we *must* do something about these things; it
is easily managed. We can have a special one—our
states do it: we can have just our usual flag, with
the white stripes painted black and the stars replaced
by the skull and crossbones.

And we do not need that Civil Commission out
there. Having no powers, it has to invent them,
and that kind of work cannot be effectively done by
just anybody; an expert is required. Mr. Croker
can be spared. We do not want the United States
represented there, but only the Game.

By help of these suggested amendments, Progress
and Civilization in that country can have a boom,
and it will take in the Persons who are Sitting in
Darkness, and we can resume Business at the old
stand.

# TO MY MISSIONARY CRITICS

(*North American Review*, 1901)

I HAVE received many newspaper cuttings; also letters from several clergymen; also a note from the Rev. Dr. Judson Smith, Corresponding Secretary of the American Board of Foreign Missions—all of a like tenor; all saying, substantially, what is said in the cutting here copied:

## AN APOLOGY DUE FROM MR. CLEMENS

The evidence of the past day or two should induce Mark Twain to make for the amen corner and formulate a prompt apology for his scathing attack on the Rev. Dr. Ament, the veteran Chinese missionary. The assault was based on a Peking dispatch to the New York *Sun*, which said that Dr. Ament had collected from the Chinese in various places damages thirteen times in excess of actual losses. So Mark Twain charged Mr. Ament with bullyragging, extortion, and things. A Peking dispatch to the *Sun* yesterday, however, explains that the amount collected was not thirteen times the damage sustained, but *one-third in excess of the indemnities*, and that the blunder was due to a cable error in transmission. The 1-3d got converted into 13. Yesterday the Rev. Judson Smith, Secretary of the American Board, received a dispatch from Dr. Ament, calling attention to the cable blunder, and declaring that all the collections which he made were *approved by the Chinese officials*. The fractional amount that was collected in *excess* of actual losses, he explains, is being *used for the support of widows and orphans*.

So collapses completely—and convulsively—Mark Twain's sensational and ugly bombardment of a missionary whose character and services should have exempted him from such an assault.

From the charge the underpinning has been knocked out. To Dr. Ament Mr. Clemens has done an injustice which is gross but unintentional. If Mark Twain is the man we take him to be he won't be long in filing a retraction, plus an apology.

I have no prejudice against apologies. I trust I shall never withhold one when it is due; I trust I shall never even have a disposition to do so. These letters and newspaper paragraphs are entitled to my best attention; respect for their writers and for the humane feeling which has prompted their utterances requires this of me. It may be barely possible that, if these requests for an apology had reached me before the 20th of February, I might have had a sort of qualified chance to apologize; but on that day appeared the two little cablegrams referred to in the newspaper cutting copied above—one from the Rev. Dr. Smith to the Rev. Dr. Ament, the other from Dr. Ament to Dr. Smith—and my small chance died then. In my opinion, these cablegrams ought to have been suppressed, for it seems clear that they give Dr. Ament's case entirely away. Still, that is only an opinion, and may be a mistake. It will be best to examine the case from the beginning, by the light of the documents connected with it.

## EXHIBIT A

This is a dispatch from Mr. Chamberlain,[1] chief of the *Sun's* correspondence staff in Peking. It appeared in the *Sun* last Christmas Eve, and in referring to it hereafter I will call it the "C. E. dispatch" for short:

[1] Testimony of the manager of the *Sun*.

# TO MY MISSIONARY CRITICS

The Rev. Mr. Ament, of the American Board of Foreign Missions, has returned from a trip which he made for the purpose of collecting indemnities for damages done by Boxers. Everywhere he went he compelled the Chinese to pay. He says that all his native Christians are now provided for. He had seven hundred of them under his charge, and three hundred were killed. He has collected 300 taels for each of these murders, and has compelled full payment for all the property belonging to Christians that was destroyed. He also assessed fines amounting to thirteen times[1] the amount of the indemnity. This money will be used for the propagation of the Gospel.

Mr. Ament declares that the compensation he has collected is moderate when compared with the amount secured by the Catholics, who demand, in addition to money, head for head. They collect 500 taels for each murder of a Catholic. In the Wen-Chiu country 680 Catholics were killed, and for this the European Catholics here demand 750,000 strings of cash and 680 heads.

In the course of a conversation Mr. Ament referred to the attitude of the missionaries toward the Chinese. He said:

I deny emphatically that the missionaries are vindictive, that they generally looted, or that they have done anything since the siege that the circumstances did not demand. I criticize the Americans. The soft hand of the Americans is not as good as the mailed fist of the Germans. If you deal with the Chinese with a soft hand they will take advantage of it."

In an article addressed "To the Person Sitting in Darkness," published in the *North American Review* for February, I made some comments upon this C. E. dispatch.

In an Open Letter to me, from the Rev. Dr. Smith, published in the *Tribune* of February 15th, doubt is cast upon the authenticity of the dispatch.

Up to the 20th of February, this doubt was an important factor in the case: Dr. Ament's brief cable-

[1] Cable error. For "thirteen times" read "one third." This correction was made by Dr. Ament in his brief cablegram published February 20th, previously referred to

gram, published on that date, took the importance all out of it.

In the Open Letter, Dr. Smith quotes this passage from a letter from Dr. Ament, dated November 13th. The italics are mine:

*This* time I proposed to settle affairs *without the aid of soldiers or legations.*

This cannot mean two things, but only one: that, previously, he *had* collected by armed force.

Also, in the Open Letter, Dr. Smith quotes some praises of Dr. Ament and the Rev. Mr. Tewksbury, furnished by the Rev. Dr. Sheffield, and says:

Dr. Sheffield is not accustomed to speak thus of *thieves*, or *extortioners*, or *braggarts*.

What can he mean by those vigorous expressions? Can he mean that the first two would be applicable to a missionary who should collect from B, with the "aid of soldiers," indemnities possibly due by A, and upon occasion go out looting?

### EXHIBIT B

Testimony of George Lynch (indorsed as entirely trustworthy by the *Tribune* and the *Herald*), war correspondent in the Cuban and South African wars, and in the march upon Peking for the rescue of the legations. The italics are mine:

When the *soldiers* were prohibited from looting, no such prohibitions seemed to operate with the *missionaries*. For instance, the *Rev. Mr. Tewksbury held a great sale of looted goods, which lasted several days.*

A day or two after the relief, when looking for a place to sleep in, I met the Rev. Mr. Ament, of the American Board of Foreign

Missions. *He told me* he was going to take possession of the house of a wealthy Chinaman who was an old enemy of his, as he had interfered much in the past with his missionary labors in Peking. A couple of days afterwards *he did so,* and held a *great sale of his enemy's effects.* I bought a sable cloak at it for $125, and a couple of statues of Buddha. As the stock became depleted *it was replenished by the efforts of his converts, who were ransacking the houses in the neighborhood.*—New York *Herald,* February 18th.

It is Dr. Smith, not I, who has suggested that persons who act in this way are "thieves and extortioners."

### EXHIBIT C

Sir Robert Hart, in the *Fortnightly Review* for January, 1901. This witness has been for many years the most prominent and important Englishman in China, and bears an irreproachable reputation for moderation, fairness, and truth-speaking. In closing a description of the revolting scenes which followed the occupation of Peking, when the Christian armies (with the proud exception of the American soldiery, let us be thankful for that) gave themselves up to a ruthless orgy of robbery and spoliation, he says (the italics are mine):

And even some *missionaries* took such a *leading* part in "spoiling the Egyptians" for the greater glory of God that a bystander was heard to say: *"For a century to come Chinese converts will consider looting and vengeance Christian virtues:"*

It is Dr. Smith, not I, who has suggested that persons who act in this way are "thieves and extortioners." According to Mr. Lynch and Mr. Martin (another war correspondent), Dr. Ament helped to spoil several of those Egyptians. Mr. Martin took a photograph of the scene. It was reproduced in the *Herald*. I have it.

## EXHIBIT D

In a brief reply to Dr. Smith's Open Letter to me, I said this in the *Tribune*. I am italicizing several words—for a purpose:

Whenever he (Dr. Smith) can produce from the Rev. Mr. Ament an assertion that the *Sun's* character-blasting dispatch was not authorized *by him*, and whenever Dr. Smith can buttress Mr. Ament's disclaimer with a confession from *Mr. Chamberlain*, the head of the Laffan News Service in China, that that dispatch was a false invention *and unauthorized*, the case against Mr. Ament will fall at once to the ground.

## EXHIBIT E

Brief cablegrams, referred to above, which passed between Dr. Smith and Dr. Ament, and were published on February 20th:

Ament, Peking: Reported December 24 your collecting thirteen times actual losses; using for propagating the Gospel. Are these statements true? Cable specific answer.    SMITH.

Statement untrue. Collected 1-3 for church expenses, additional actual damages; now supporting widows and orphans. Publication thirteen times blunder cable. All collections received approval Chinese officials, who are urging further settlements same line.    AMENT.

Only two questions are asked; "specific" answers required; no perilous wanderings among the other details of the unhappy dispatch desired.

## EXHIBIT F

Letter from Dr. Smith to me, dated March 8th. The italics are mine; they tag inaccuracies of statement:

# TO MY MISSIONARY CRITICS

Permit me to call your attention to the marked paragraphs in the inclosed papers, and to ask you to note their relation to the two conditions named in your letter to the New York *Tribune* of February 15th.

The first is *Dr. Ament's denial of the truth of the dispatch in the New York "Sun,"* of December 24th, on which your criticisms of him in the *North American Review* of February were founded. The second is a correction by the *"Sun's" special correspondent* in Peking of the dispatch printed in the *Sun* of December 24th.

Since, as you state in your letter to the *Tribune*, "the case against Mr. Ament would fall to the ground" *if Mr. Ament denied the truth* of the *Sun's* first dispatch, and *if the 'Sun's' news agency* in Peking also *declared that dispatch false,* and these two conditions *have thus been fulfilled,* I am sure that upon having these *facts* brought to your attention you will gladly withdraw the criticisms that were *founded on a "cable blunder."*

I think Dr. Smith ought to read me more carefully; then he would not make so many mistakes. Within the narrow space of two paragraphs, totaling eleven lines, he has scored nine departures from fact out of a possible 9½. Now, is that parliamentary? I do not treat him like that. Whenever I quote him, I am particular not to do him the least wrong, or make him say anything he did not say.

(1) Mr. Ament doesn't "deny the truth of the C. E. dispatch"; he merely changes one of its phrases, without materially changing the meaning, and (immaterially) corrects a cable blunder (which correction I accept). He was asked no question about the other four fifths of the C. E. dispatch. (2) I said nothing about "special" correspondents; I named the right and responsible man—Mr. Chamberlain. The "correction" referred to is a repetition of the one I have just accepted, which (immaterially)

changes "thirteen times" to "one third" extra tax.
(3) I did not say anything about "the *Sun*'s news
agency"; I said "Chamberlain." I have every confidence in Mr. Chamberlain, but I am not personally acquainted with the others. (4) Once more—
Mr. Ament didn't "deny the truth" of the C. E.
dispatch, but merely made unimportant emenda-
tions of a couple of its many details. (5) I did not
say "if Mr. Ament denied the truth" of the C. E.
dispatch: I said, if he would assert that the dispatch
was not "authorized" *by him*. For example, I did
not suppose that the charge that the Catholic missionaries wanted 680 Chinamen beheaded was true;
but I did want to know if Dr. Ament personally
authorized that statement and the others, as coming
from his lips. Another detail: one of my conditions
was that Mr. Chamberlain must not stop with con-
fessing that the C. E. was a "false invention," he
must also confess that it was *"unauthorized."* Dr.
Smith has left out that large detail. (6) The *Sun*'s
news agency did not "declare the C. E. dispatch
false," but confined itself to correcting one unimportant detail of its long list—the change of "13
times" to "one third" extra. (7) The "two conditions" have not "been fulfilled"—far from it. (8)
Those details labeled "facts" are only fancies. (9)
Finally, my criticisms were by no means confined to
that detail of the C. E. dispatch which we now accept
as having been a "cable blunder."

Setting to one side these nine departures from fact,
I find that what is left of the eleven lines is straight
and true. I am not blaming Dr. Smith for these dis-

crepancies—it would not be right, it would not be
fair. I make the proper allowances. He has not
been a journalist, as I have been—a trade wherein
a person is brought to book by the rest of the
press so often for divergencies that, by and by,
he gets to be almost morbidly afraid to indulge
in them. It is so with me. I always have the disposition to tell what is not so; I was born with
it; we all have it. But I try not to do it now,
because I have found out that it is unsafe. But
with the Doctor of course it is different.

### EXHIBIT G

I wanted to get at the whole of the facts as regards
the C. E. dispatch, and so I wrote to China for them,
when I found that the Board was not going to do it.
But I am not allowed to wait. It seemed quite
within the possibilities that a full detail of the facts
might furnish me a chance to make an apology to
Mr. Ament—a chance which, I give you my word, I
would have honestly used, and not abused. But it
is no matter. If the Board is not troubled about
the bulk of that lurid dispatch, why should I be?
I answered the apology-urging letters of several clergymen with the information that I had written to
China for the details, and said I thought it was the
only sure way of getting into a position to do fair
and full justice to all concerned; but a couple of
them replied that it was not a matter that could
wait. That is to say, groping your way out of a
jungle in the dark with guesses and conjectures is

better than a straight march out in the sunlight of fact. It seems a curious idea.

However, those two clergymen were in a large measure right—from their point of view and the Board's; which is, putting it in the form of a couple of questions:

1. *Did Dr. Ament collect the assessed damages and thirteen times over?* The answer is: He did *not.* He collected only *a third* over.

2. *Did he apply the third to the "propagation of the Gospel?"* The answer is this correction: He applied it to "church expenses." Part or all of the outlay, it appears, goes to "supporting widows and orphans." It may be that church expenses and supporting widows and orphans are not part of the machinery for propagating the Gospel. I supposed they were, but it isn't any matter; I prefer this phrasing; it is not so blunt as the other.

In the opinion of the two clergymen and of the Board, these two points are *the only important ones* in the whole C. E. dispatch.

I accept that. Therefore let us throw out the rest of the dispatch as being no longer a part of Dr. Ament's case.

### EXHIBIT H

The two clergymen and the Board are quite content with Dr. Ament's answers upon the two points.

Upon the first point of the two, my own viewpoint may be indicated by a question:

*Did Dr. Ament collect from B (whether by compulsion or simple demand) even so much as a penny in*

*payment for murders or depredations, without know-
ing, beyond question, that B, and not another, committed the murders or the depredations?*

Or, in other words:

*Did Dr. Ament ever, by chance or through ignorance,
make the innocent pay the debts of the guilty?*

In the article entitled "To the Person Sitting in
Darkness," I put forward that point in a paragraph
taken from Macallum's (imaginary) "History":

### EXHIBIT I

When a white Boxer kills a Pawnee and destroys his property
the other Pawnees do not trouble to seek *him* out; they kill any
white person that comes along; also, they make some white
village pay deceased's heirs the full cash value of deceased,
together with full cash value of the property destroyed; they
also make the village pay, in addition, *thirteen times*[1] the value
of that property into a fund for the dissemination of the Pawnee
religion, which they regard as the best of all religions for the
softening and humanizing of the heart of man. It is their idea
that it is only fair and right *that the innocent should be made to
suffer for the guilty*, and that it is better that 90 and 9 innocent
should suffer than that one guilty person should escape.

We all know that Dr. Ament did not bring suspected persons into a duly organized court and try
them by just and fair Christian and civilized methods,
but proclaimed his "conditions," and collected damages from the innocent and the guilty alike, without
any court proceedings at all.[2] That he himself, and

[1] For "thirteen times" read "one third."—M. T.

[2] In civilized countries, if a mob destroy property in a town, the
damage is paid out of the town treasury, and no taxpayer suffers
a disproportionate share of the burden; the mayor is not privileged
to distribute the burden according to his private notions, sparing
himself and his friends, and fleecing persons he holds a spite against—
as in the Orient—and the citizen who is too poor to be a taxpayer
pays no part of the fine at all.

not the villagers, made the "conditions," we learn from his letter of November 13th, already quoted from—the one in which he remarked that, upon *that* occasion he brought no soldiers with him. The italics are mine:

> After our *conditions* were known many villagers came of their own accord and brought their money with them.

Not all, but "many." The Board really believes that those hunted and harried paupers out there were not only willing to strip themselves to pay Boxer damages, whether they owed them or not, but were sentimentally eager to do it. Mr. Ament says, in his letter: "The villagers were extremely grateful because I brought no foreign soldiers, and were glad to settle on the terms proposed." Some of those people know more about theology than they do about human nature. I do not remember encountering even a Christian who was "glad" to pay money he did not owe; and as for a Chinaman doing it, why, dear me, the thing is unthinkable. We have all seen Chinamen, many Chinamen, but not that kind. It is a new kind: an invention of the Board—and "soldiers."

## CONCERNING THE COLLECTIONS

What was the "one third extra"? Money due? No. Was it a theft, then? Putting aside the "one third extra," what was the *remainder* of the exacted indemnity, if collected from persons not *known* to owe it, and without Christian and civilized forms of procedure? Was *it* theft, was it robbery? In America it would be that; in Christian Europe it would be that. I have great confidence in Dr. Smith's judgment concerning this detail, and he calls it "theft and extortion"—even in China; for he was talking about the "thirteen times" at the time that he gave it that strong name.[1] It is his idea that, when you make guilty and innocent villagers pay the appraised damages, and then make them pay thirteen times that, besides, the *thirteen* stand for "theft and extortion."

Then what does *one third* extra stand for? Will he give that one third a name? Is it Modified Theft and Extortion? Is that it? The girl who was rebuked for having borne an illegitimate child excused herself by saying, "But it is such a *little* one."

When the "thirteen-times-extra" was alleged, it stood for theft and extortion, in Dr. Smith's eyes, and he was shocked. But when Dr. Ament showed that he had taken only a *third* extra, instead of thirteenfold, Dr. Smith was relieved, content, happy. I declare I cannot imagine why. That editor—quoted at the head of this article—was happy about it, too. I cannot think why. He thought I ought to "make for the amen corner and formulate a prompt apology." To whom, and for what? It is too deep for me.

To Dr. Smith, the "thirteenfold extra" clearly

[1] In his Open Letter, Dr. Smith cites Dr. Ament's letter of November 13th, which contains an account of Dr. Ament's collecting tour; then Dr. Smith makes this comment: "Nothing is said of securing 'thirteen times' the amount of the losses." Farther down, Dr. Smith quotes praises of Dr. Ament and his work (from a letter of the Rev. Dr. Sheffield), and adds this comment: "Dr. Sheffield is not accustomed to speak thus in praise of thieves, or extortioners, or braggarts." The reference is to the "thirteen-times" extra tax.

stood for "theft and extortion," and he was right, distinctly right, indisputably right. He manifestly thinks that when it got scaled away down to a mere "one third," a little thing like that was something other than "theft and extortion." Why? Only the Board knows! I will try to explain this difficult problem, so that the Board can get an idea of it. If a pauper owes me a dollar, and I catch him unprotected and make him pay me fourteen dollars, thirteen of it is "theft and extortion"; if I make him pay only a dollar and thirty-three and a third cents the thirty-three and a third cents are "theft and extortion" just the same. I will put it in another way, still simpler. If a man owes me one dog— any kind of a dog, the breed is of no consequence— and I—— But let it go; the Board would never understand it. It *can't* understand these involved and difficult things.

But *if* the Board could understand, then I could furnish some more instruction—which is this. The one third, obtained by "theft and extortion," is *tainted money*, and cannot be purified even by defraying "church expenses" and "supporting widows and orphans" with it. It has to be restored to the people it was taken from.

Also, there is another view of these things. By our Christian code of morals and law, the *whole* $1.33 1-3, if taken from a man not formally *proven* to have committed the damage the dollar represents, is. "theft and extortion." It cannot be honestly used for any purpose at all. It must be handed back to the man it was taken from.

Is there no way, then, to justify these thefts and extortions and make them clean and fair and honorable? Yes, there is. It can be done; it has been done; it continues to be done—by revising the Ten Commandments and bringing them down to date: for use in pagan lands. For example:

*Thou shalt not steal*—except when it is the custom of the country.

This way out is recognized and *approved* by all the best authorities, including the Board. I will cite witnesses.

*The newspaper cutting, above:* "Dr. Ament declares that all the collections which he made were approved by the *Chinese* officials." The editor is satisfied.

*Dr. Ament's cable to Dr. Smith:* "All collections received approval *Chinese* officials." Dr. Ament is satisfied.

*Letters from eight clergymen*—all to the same effect: Dr. Ament merely did as the *Chinese* do. So they are satisfied.

*Mr. Ward, of the "Independent."*

*The Rev. Dr. Washington Gladden.*

I have mislaid the letters of these gentlemen and cannot quote their words, but they are of the satisfied.

*The Rev. Dr. Smith*, in his Open Letter, published in the *Tribune:* "The whole procedure [Dr. Ament's] is in accordance with a custom among the *Chinese*, of holding a village responsible for wrongs suffered in that village, and especially making the head man of the village accountable for wrongs committed there." Dr. Smith is satisfied. Which means that the Board is satisfied.

The "head man"! Why, then, this poor rascal, innocent or guilty, must pay the whole bill, if he cannot squeeze it out of his poor-devil neighbors. But, indeed, he can be depended upon to try, even to the skinning them of their last brass farthing, their last rag of clothing, their last ounce of food. He can be depended upon to get the indemnity out of them, though it cost stripes and blows, blood-tears, and flesh.

### THE TALE OF THE KING AND HIS TREASURER

How strange and remote and romantic and Oriental and Arabian-Nighty it all seems—and is. It brings back the old forgotten tales, and we hear the King say to his Treasurer:

"Bring me 30,000 gold tomauns."

"Allah preserve us, Sire! the treasury is empty."

"Do you hear? Bring the money—in ten days. Else, send me your head in a basket."

"I hear and obey."

The Treasurer summons the head men of a hundred villages, and says to one:

"Bring me a hundred gold tomauns." To another, "Bring me five hundred." To another, "Bring a thousand. In ten days. Your head is the forfeit."

"Your slaves kiss your feet! Ah, high and mighty lord, be merciful to our hard-pressed villagers; they are poor, they are naked, they starve; oh, these impossible sums! even the half——"

"Go! Grind it out of them, crush it out of them, turn the blood of the fathers, the tears of the mothers, the milk of the babes to money—or take the consequences. Have you heard?"

"His will be done, Who is the Fount of love and mercy and compassion, Who layeth this heavy burden upon us by the hand of His anointed servants—blessed be His holy Name! The father shall bleed, the mother shall faint for hunger, the babe shall perish at the dry breast. The chosen of God have commanded: it shall be as they say."

I am not meaning to object to the substitution of pagan customs for Christian, here and there and now and then, when the Christian ones are inconvenient. No; I like it and admire it. I do it myself. And I admire the alertness of the Board in watching out for chances to trade Board morals for Chinese morals, and get the best of the swap; for I cannot endure those people, they are yellow, and I have never considered yellow becoming. I have always been like the Board—perfectly well-meaning, but destitute of the Moral Sense. Now, one of the main reasons why it is so hard to make the Board understand that there is no moral difference between a big filch and a little filch, but only a legal one, is that vacancy in its make-up. Morally, there are no degrees in stealing. The Commandment merely says, "Thou shalt not *steal*," and stops there. It doesn't recognize any difference between stealing a third and stealing thirteenfold. If I could think of a way to put it before the Board in such a plain and—

### THE WATERMELONS

I have it, now. Many years ago, when I was studying for the gallows, I had a dear comrade, a youth who was not in my line, but still a thoroughly good fellow, though devious. He was preparing to qualify for a place on the Board, for there was going to be a vacancy by superannuation in about five years. This was down South, in the slavery days. It was the nature of the negro then, as now, to steal watermelons. They stole three of the melons of an adoptive brother of mine, the only good ones he had. I suspected three of a neighbor's negroes, but there was no proof: and, besides, the watermelons in those negroes' private patches were all green and small, and not up to indemnity standard. But in the private patches of three other negroes there were a number of competent melons. I consulted with my comrade, the understudy of the Board. He said that if I would approve his arrangements, he would arrange. I said, "Consider me the Board; I approve: arrange." So he took a gun, and went and collected three large melons for my brother-on-the-half-shell, and one over. I was greatly pleased, and asked:

"Who gets the extra one?"

"Widows and orphans."

"A good idea, too. Why didn't you take thirteen?"

"It would have been wrong; a crime, in fact—Theft and Extortion."

"What is the one third extra—the odd melon—the same?"

It caused him to reflect. But there was no result.

The justice of the peace was a stern man. On the trial, he found fault with the scheme, and required us to explain upon what we based our strange conduct—as he called it. The understudy said:

"On the custom of the niggers. They all do it."

The justice forgot his dignity, and descended to sarcasm:

"Custom of the niggers! Are our morals so inadequate that we have to borrow of niggers?" Then he said to the jury: "Three melons were owing; they were collected from persons not proven to owe them; this is theft. They were collected by compulsion; this is extortion. A melon was added—for the widows and orphans. It was owed by no one. It is another theft, another extortion. Return it whence it came, with the others. It is not permissible, here, to apply to any object goods dishonestly obtained—not even to the feeding of widows and orphans, for that would be to put a shame upon charity and dishonor it."

He said it in open court, before everybody, and to me it did not seem very kind.

A clergyman, in a letter to me, reminds me, with a touch of reproach, that "many of the missionaries are good men, kind-hearted, earnest, devoted to their work." Certainly they are. No one is disputing it. Instead of "many," he could have said "almost all," and still said the truth, no doubt. I know many missionaries; I have met them all about the globe, and have known only one or two who could not fill that bill and answer to that description. "Almost all" comes near to being a proportion and a description applicable also to lawyers, authors, editors, merchants, manufacturers—in fact, to most guilds and vocations. Without a doubt, Dr. Ament did what he believed to be right, and I concede that when a man is doing what he believes to be right, there is argument on his side. I differ with Dr. Ament, but that is only because he got his training from the Board and I got mine outside. Neither of us is responsible, altogether.

### RECAPITULATION

But there is no need to sum up. Mr. Ament has acknowledged the "one third extra"—no other witness is necessary. The Rev. Dr. Smith has carefully considered the act and labeled it with a stern name, and his verdict seems to have no flaw in it. The morals of the act are Chinese, but are approved by the Board, and by some of the clergy and some of the newspapers, as being a valuable improvement upon Christian ones—which leaves me with a closed mouth, though with a pain in my heart.

### IS THE AMERICAN BOARD ON TRIAL?

Do I think that Dr. Ament and certain of his fellow missionaries are as bad as their conduct? No, I do not. They are the product of their training; and now that I understand the whole case, and where they got their ideals, and that they are merely subordinates and subject to authority, I comprehend that they are rather accessories than principals, and that their acts only show faulty heads curiously trained, not bad hearts. Mainly, as it seems to me, it is the American Board that is on trial. And again, it is a case of the head, not of the heart.

# TO MY MISSIONARY CRITICS

That it has a heart which has never harbored an evil intention, no one will deny, no one will question; the Board's history can silence any challenge on that score. The Board's heart is not in court: it is its head that is on trial.

It is a sufficiently strange head. Its ways baffle comprehension; its ideas are like no one else's; its methods are novelties to the practical world; its judgments are surprises. When one thinks it is going to speak and must speak, it is silent; when one thinks it ought to be silent and must be silent, it speaks. Put your finger where you think it ought to be, it is not there; put it where you think it ought not to be, there you find it.

When its servant in China seemed to be charging himself with amazing things, in a reputable journal—in a dispatch which was copied into many other papers—the Board was as silent about it as any dead man could have been who was informed that his house was burning over his head. An exchange of cablegrams could have enabled it, within two days, to prove to the world—possibly—that the damaging dispatch had not proceeded from the mouth of its servant; yet it sat silent and asked no questions about the matter.

It was silent during thirty-eight days. Then the dispatch came into prominence again. It chanced that I was the occasion of it. A break in the stillness followed. In what form? An exchange of cablegrams, resulting in proof that the damaging dispatch had not been authorized? No, in the form of an Open Letter by the Corresponding Secretary

of the American Board, the Rev. Dr. Smith, in which
it was *argued* that Dr. Ament could not have said
and done the things set forth in the dispatch.

Surely, this was bad politics. A repudiating telegram would have been worth more than a library of
argument.

An extension of the silence would have been better
than the Open Letter, I think. I thought so at the
time. It seemed to me that mistakes enough had
been made and harm enough done. I thought it
questionable policy to publish the Letter, for I "did
not think it likely that Dr. Ament would disown
the dispatch," and I telegraphed that to the Rev.
Dr. Smith. Personally, I had nothing against Dr.
Ament, and that is my attitude yet.

Once more it was a good time for an extension of
the silence. But no; the Board has its own ways,
and one of them is to do the unwise thing, when
occasion offers. After having waited fifty-six days,
it cabled to Dr. Ament. No one can divine why it
did so then, instead of fifty-six days earlier.[1] It
got a fatal reply—and was not aware of it. That
was that curious confession about the "one third
extra"; its application, not to the "propagation of
the Gospel," but only to "church expenses," support
of widows and orphans; and, on top of this confession, that other strange one revealing the dizzying
fact that our missionaries, who went to China to
teach Christian morals and justice, had adopted

[1] The cablegram went on the day (February 18th) that Mr.
George Lynch's account of the looting was published. See "Exhibit
B." It seems a pity it did not inquire about the looting and get it
denied.

pagan morals and justice in their place. *That cable-gram was dynamite.*

It seems odd that the Board did not see that that revelation made the case far worse than it was before; for there was a saving doubt, before—a doubt which was a Gibraltar for strength, and should have been carefully left undisturbed. Why did the Board allow that revelation to get into print? Why did the Board not suppress it and keep still? But no; in the Board's opinion, this was once more the time for speech. Hence Dr. Smith's latest letter to me, suggesting that I speak also—a letter which is a good enough letter, barring its nine defects, but is another evidence that the Board's head is not as good as its heart.

A missionary is a man who is pretty nearly all heart, else he would not be in a calling which requires of him such large sacrifices of one kind and another. He is made up of faith, zeal, courage, sentiment, emotion, enthusiasm; and so he is a mixture of poet, devotee, and knight errant. He exiles himself from home and friends and the scenes and associations that are dearest to him; patiently endures discomforts, privations, discouragements; goes with good pluck into dangers which he knows may cost him his life; and when he must suffer death, willingly makes that supreme sacrifice for his cause.

Sometimes the headpiece of that kind of a man can be of an inferior sort, and error of judgment can result—as we have seen. Then, for his protection, as it seems to me, he ought to have at his back a Board able to know a blunder when it sees one, and prompt to bring him back upon his right course when he strays from it. That is to say, I think the captain of a ship ought to understand navigation. Whether he does or not, he will have to take a captain's share of the blame, if the crew bring the vessel to grief.

# THOMAS BRACKETT REED

H E wore no shell. His ways were frank and open, and the road to his large sympathies was straight and unobstructed. His was a nature which invited affection—compelled it, in fact—and met it halfway. Hence he was "Tom" to the most of his friends, and to half of the nation. The abbreviating of such a man's name is a patent of nobility, and is conferred from the heart. Mr. Reed had a very strong and decided character, and he may have had enemies; I do not know; if he had them—outside of politics—they did not know the man. He was transparently honest and honorable, there were no furtivenesses about him, and whoever came to know him trusted him and was not disappointed. He was wise, he was shrewd and alert, he was a clear and capable thinker, a logical reasoner, and a strong and convincing speaker. His manner was easy and engaging, his speeches sparkled with felicities of phrasing thrown off without apparent effort, and when he needed the happy help of humor he had a mine of it as deep and rich as Kimberly to draw from. His services to his country were great, and they were gratefully acknowledged.

I cannot remember back to a time when he was not "Tom" Reed to me, nor to a time when he would have been offended at being so addressed by me. I cannot remember back to a time when I could let him alone in an after-dinner speech if he was present, nor to a time when he did not take my extravagances concerning him and misstatements about him in good part, nor yet to a time when he did not pay them back with usury when his turn came. The last speech he made was at my birthday dinner at the end of November, when naturally I was his text; my last word to him was in a letter the next day; a day later I was illustrating a fantastic article on Art with his portrait among others—a portrait now to be laid reverently away among the jests that begin in humor and end in pathos. These things happened only eight days ago, and now he is gone from us, and the nation is speaking of him as one who *was*. It seems incredible, impossible. Such a man, such a friend, seems to us a permanent possession; his vanishing from our midst is unthinkable; as unthinkable as was the vanishing of the Campanile, that had stood for a thousand years, and was turned to dust in a moment.

I have no wish, at this time, to enter upon light and humorous reminiscences connected with yachting voyages with Mr. Reed in northern and southern seas, nor with other recreations in his company in other places—they do not belong in this paper, they do not invite me, they would jar upon me. I have only wished to say how fine and beautiful was his life and character, and to take him by the hand and say good-by, as to a fortunate friend who has done well his work and goes a pleasant journey.

# THE FINISHED BOOK

(On Finishing *Joan of Arc*)

PARIS, 1895.

DO you know that shock? I mean, when you come, at your regular hour, into the sick room where you have watched for months, and find the medicine bottles all gone, the night table removed, the bed stripped, the furniture set stiffly to rights, the windows up, the room cold, stark, vacant—and you catch your breath. Do you know that shock?

The man who has written a long book has that experience the morning after he has revised it for the last time, seen the bearers convey it from the house, and sent it away to the printer. He steps into his study at the hour established by the habit of months —and he gets that little shock. All the litter and the confusion are gone. The piles of dusty reference books are gone from the chairs, the maps from the floor; the chaos of letters, manuscripts, notebooks, paper knives, pipes, matches, photographs, tobacco jars, and cigar boxes is gone from the writing table. The furniture is back where it use to be in the long ago. The housemaid, forbidden the place for five months, has been there, and tidied it up, and scoured it clean, and made it repellent and awful.

I stand here this morning, contemplating this desolation, and I realize that if I would bring back the spirit that made this hospital homelike and pleasant to me, I must restore the aids to lingering dissolution to their wonted places, and nurse another patient through and send it forth for the last rites, with many or few to assist there, as may happen; and that I will do.

# AS REGARDS PATRIOTISM

(About 1900)

IT is agreed, in this country, that if a man can arrange his religion so that it perfectly satisfies his conscience, it is not incumbent upon him to care whether the arrangement is satisfactory to anyone else or not.

In Austria and some other countries this is not the case. There the state arranges a man's religion for him, he has no voice in it himself.

Patriotism is merely a religion—love of country, worship of country, devotion to the country's flag and honor and welfare.

In absolute monarchies it is furnished from the throne, cut and dried, to the subject; in England and America it is furnished, cut and dried, to the citizen by the politician and the newspaper.

The newspaper - and - politician - manufactured Patriot often gags in private over his dose; but he takes it, and keeps it on his stomach the best he can. Blessed are the meek.

Sometimes, in the beginning of an insane shabby political upheaval, he is strongly moved to revolt, but he doesn't do it—he knows better. He knows that his maker would find it out—the maker of his Patriotism, the windy and incoherent six-dollar subeditor of his village newspaper—and would bray out in print and call him a Traitor. And how dreadful that would be. It makes him tuck his tail between his legs and shiver. We all know—the reader knows it quite well—that two or three years ago nine tenths of the human tails in England and America performed just that act. Which is to say, nine tenths of the Patriots in England and America turned traitor to keep from being called traitor. Isn't it true? You know it to be true. Isn't it curious?

Yet it was not a thing to be very seriously ashamed of. A man can seldom—very, very seldom—fight a winning fight against his training; the odds are too heavy. For many a year—perhaps always—the training of the two nations had been dead against independence in political thought, persistently inhospitable toward patriotism manufactured on a man's own premises, Patriotism reasoned out in the man's own head and fire-assayed and tested and proved in his own conscience. The resulting Patriotism was a shop-worn product procured at second hand. The Patriot did not know just how or when or where he got his opinions, neither did he care, so long as he was with what seemed the majority—which was the main thing, the safe thing, the comfortable thing. Does the reader believe he knows three men who have actual reasons for their pattern of Patriotism— and can furnish them? Let him not examine, unless he wants to be disappointed. He will be likely to find that his men got their Patriotism at the public trough, and had no hand in its preparation themselves.

Training does wonderful things. It moved the people of this country to oppose the Mexican War; them moved them to fall in with what they supposed was the opinion of the majority—majority Patriotism is the customary Patriotism—and go down there and fight. Before the Civil War it made the North indifferent to slavery and friendly to the slave interest; in that interest it made Massachusetts hostile to the American flag, and she would not allow it to be hoisted on her State House—in her eyes it was the flag of a faction. Then by and by, training swung Massachusetts the other way, and she went raging South to fight under that very flag and against that aforetime protected interest of hers.

There is nothing that training cannot do. Nothing is above its reach or below it. It can turn bad morals to good, good morals to bad; it can destroy principles, it can recreate them; it can debase angels to men and lift men to angelship. And it can do any one of these miracles in a year—even in six months.

Then men can be trained to manufacture their own Patriotism. They can be trained to labor it out in their own heads and hearts and in the privacy and independence of their own premises. It can train them to stop taking it by command, as the Austrian takes his religion.

# DR. LOEB'S INCREDIBLE DISCOVERY

EXPERTS in biology will be apt to receive with some skepticism the announcement of Dr. Jacques Loeb of the University of California as to the creation of life by chemical agencies. . . . Doctor Loeb is a very bright and ingenious experimenter, but *a consensus of opinion among biologists* would show that he is voted rather as a man of lively imagination than an inerrant investigator of natural phenomena.—New York *Times*, March 2d.

I wish I could be as young as that again. Although I seem so old, now, I was once as young as that. I remember, as if it were but thirty or forty years ago, how a paralyzing Consensus of Opinion accumulated from Experts a-setting around, about brother experts who had patiently and laboriously cold-chiseled their way into one or another of nature's safe-deposit vaults and were reporting that they had found something valuable was a plenty for me. It settled it.

But it isn't so now—no. Because, in the drift of the years I by and by found out that a Consensus examines a new thing with its feelings rather oftener than with its mind. You know, yourself, that that is so. Do those people examine with feelings that are friendly to evidence? You know they don't. It is the other way about. They do the examining by the light of their prejudices—now isn't that true?

With curious results, yes. So curious that you wonder the Consensuses do not go out of the busi-

ness.  Do you know of a case where a Consensus
won a game?  You can go back as far as you want
to and you will find history furnishing you this (until
now) unwritten maxim for your guidance and profit:
Whatever new thing a Consensus coppers (colloquial
for "bets against"), bet your money on that very
card and do not be afraid.

There was that primitive steam engine—ages back,
in Greek times: a Consensus made fun of it.  There
was the Marquis of Worcester's steam engine, 250
years ago: a Consensus made fun of it.  There was
Fulton's steamboat of a century ago: a French Consensus, including the Great Napoleon, made fun of
it.  There was Priestly, with his oxygen: a Consensus scoffed at him, mobbed him, burned him out,
banished him.  While a Consensus was proving, by
statistics and things, that a steamship could not
cross the Atlantic, a steamship did it.  A Consensus
consisting of all the medical experts in Great Britain
made fun of Jenner and inoculation.  A Consensus
consisting of all the medical experts in France made
fun of the stethoscope.  A Consensus of all the
medical experts in Germany made fun of that young
doctor (his name? forgotten by all but doctors, now,
revered now by doctors alone) who discovered and
abolished the cause of that awful disease, puerperal
fever; made fun of him, reviled him, hunted him,
persecuted him, broke his heart, killed him.  Electric
telegraph, Atlantic cable, telephone, all "toys," and
of no practical value—verdict of the Consensuses.
Geology, palæontology, evolution—all brushed into
space by a Consensus of theological experts, com-

prising all the preachers in Christendom, assisted by
the Duke of Argyle and (at first) the other scientists.
And do look at Pasteur and his majestic honor roll
of prodigious benefactions! Damned—each and
every one of them in its turn—by frenzied and fero-
cious Consensuses of medical and chemical Experts
comprising, for years, every member of the tribe in
Europe; damned without even a casual *look* at what
he was doing—and he pathetically imploring them
to come and take at least one little look before
making the damnation eternal. They shortened his
life by their malignities and persecutions; and thus
robbed the world of the further and priceless services
of a man who—along certain lines and within certain
limits—had done more for the human race than any
other one man in all its long history: a man whom
it had taken the Expert brotherhood ten thousand
years to produce, and whose mate and match the
brotherhood may possibly not be able to bring forth
and assassinate in another ten thousand. The
preacher has an old and tough reputation for bull-
headed and unreasoning hostility to new light; why,
he is not "in it" with the doctor! Nor, perhaps,
with some of the other breeds of Experts that sit
around and get up the Consensuses and squelch the
new things as fast as they come from the hands of
the plodders, the searchers, the inspired dreamers,
the Pasteurs that come bearing pearls to scatter in
the Consensus sty.

This is warm work! It puts my temperature up
to 106 and raises my pulse to the limit. It always
works just so when the red rag of a Consensus jumps

my fence and starts across my pasture. I have been a Consensus more than once myself, and I know the business—and its vicissitudes. I am a compositor-expert, of old and seasoned experience; nineteen years ago I delivered the final-and-for-good verdict that the linotype would never be able to earn its own living nor anyone else's: it takes fourteen acres of ground, now, to accommodate its factories in England. Thirty-five years ago I was an expert precious-metal quartz-miner. There was an outcrop in my neighborhood that assayed $600 a ton—gold. But every fleck of gold in it was shut up tight and fast in an intractable and impersuadable base-metal shell. Acting as a Consensus, I delivered the finality verdict that no human ingenuity would ever be able to set free two dollars' worth of gold out of a ton of that rock. The fact is, I did not foresee the cyanide process. Indeed, I have been a Consensus ever so many times since I reached maturity and approached the age of discretion, but I call to mind no instance in which I won out.

These sorrows have made me suspicious of Consensuses. Do you know, I tremble and the goose flesh rises on my skin every time I encounter one, now. I sheer warily off and get behind something, saying to myself, "It looks innocent and all right, but no matter, ten to one there's a cyanide process under that thing somewhere."

Now as concerns this "creation of life by chemical agencies." Reader, take my advice: don't you copper it. I don't say bet on it; no, I only say, don't you copper it. As you see, there is a Consensus out against it. If you find that you can't control your passions; if you feel that you have *got* to copper something and can't help it, copper the Consensus. It is the safest way—all history confirms it. If you are young, you will, of course, have to put up, on one side or the other, for you will not be able to restrain yourself; but as for me, I am old, and I am going to wait for a new deal.

P.S.—In the same number of the *Times* Doctor Funk says: "Man may be as badly fooled by believing too little as by believing too much; the hardheaded skeptic Thomas was the only disciple who was cheated." Is that the right and rational way to look at it? I will not be sure, for my memory is faulty, but it has always been my impression that Thomas was the only one who made an examination and proved a fact, while the others were accepting, or discounting, the fact on trust—like any other Consensus. If that is so, Doubting Thomas removed a doubt which must otherwise have confused and troubled the world until now. Including Doctor Funk. It seems to me that we owe that hard-headed—or sound-headed—witness something more than a slur. Why does Doctor Funk *examine* into spiritism, and then throw stones at Thomas. Why doesn't he take it on trust? Has inconsistency become a jewel in Lafayette Place?

OLD-MAN-AFRAID-OF-THE-CONSENSUS.

*Extract from Adam's Diary.*—Then there was a Consensus about it. It was the very first one. It sat six days and nights. It was then delivered of the verdict that a world could not be made out of nothing; that such small things as sun and moon and stars might, maybe, but it would take years and years, if there was considerable many of them. Then the Consensus got up and looked out of the window, and there was the whole outfit spinning and sparkling in space! You never saw such a disappointed lot.

his<br>
ADAM—i—<br>
mark

# THE DERVISH AND THE OFFENSIVE
## STRANGER

*THE Dervish:* I will say again, and yet again, and
still again, that a good deed——

*The Offensive Stranger:* Peace, and, O man of narrow
vision! There is no such thing as a good *deed*——

*The Dervish:* O shameless blasphe——

*The Offensive Stranger:* And no such thing as an
evil deed. There are good *impulses*, there are evil
impulses, and that is all. Half of the results of a
good intention are evil; half the results of an evil
intention are good. No man can command the
results, nor allot them.

*The Dervish:* And so——

*The Offensive Stranger:* And so you shall praise
men for their good intentions, and not blame them
for the evils resulting; you shall blame men for
their evil intentions, and not praise them for the
good resulting.

*The Dervish:* O maniac! will you say——

*The Offensive Stranger:* Listen to the law: From
*every* impulse, whether good or evil, flow two streams;
the one carries health, the other carries poison.
From the beginning of time this law has not changed,
to the end of time it will not change.

*The Dervish:* If I should strike thee dead in
anger——

## DERVISH AND OFFENSIVE STRANGER

*The Offensive Stranger:* Or kill me with a drug which you hoped would give me new life and strength ——

*The Dervish:* Very well. Go on.

*The Offensive Stranger:* In either case the results would be the same. Age-long misery of mind for you—an evil result; peace, repose, the end of sorrow for me—a good result. Three hearts that hold me dear would break; three pauper cousins of the third removed would get my riches and rejoice; you would go to prison and your friends would grieve, but your humble apprentice-priest would step into your shoes and your fat sleek life and be happy. And are these all the goods and all the evils that would flow from the well-intended or ill-intended act that cut short my life, O thoughtless one, O purblind creature? The good and evil results that flow from *any* act, even the smallest, breed on and on, century after century, forever and ever and ever, creeping by inches around the globe, affecting all its coming and going populations until the end of time, until the final cataclysm!

*The Dervish:* Then, there being no such thing as a good deed ——

*The Offensive Stranger:* Don't I tell you there are good *intentions*, and evil ones, and there an end? The *results* are not foreseeable. They are of both kinds, in all cases. It is the law. Listen: this is far-Western history:

### VOICES OUT OF UTAH

#### I

*The White Chief (to his people):* This wide plain was a desert. By our Heaven-blest industry we have

311

damned the river and utilized its waters and turned the desert into smiling fields whose fruitage makes prosperous and happy a thousand homes where poverty and hunger dwelt before. How noble, how beneficent, is Civilization!

## II

*Indian Chief* (*to his people*): This wide plain, which the Spanish priests taught our fathers to irrigate, was a smiling field, whose fruitage made our homes prosperous and happy. The white American has damned our river, taken away our water for his own valley, and turned our field into a desert; wherefore we starve.

*The Dervish:* I perceive that the good intention did really bring both good and evil results in equal measure. But a single case cannot prove the rule. Try again.

*The Offensive Stranger:* Pardon me, *all* cases prove it. Columbus discovered a new world and gave to the plodding poor and the landless of Europe farms and breathing space and plenty and happiness ——

*The Dervish:* A good result.

*The Offensive Stranger:* And they hunted and harried the original owners of the soil, and robbed them, beggared them, drove them from their homes, and exterminated them, root and branch.

*The Dervish:* An evil result, yes.

*The Offensive Stranger:* The French Revolution brought desolation to the hearts and homes of five million families and drenched the country with blood and turned its wealth to poverty.

*The Dervish:* An evil result.

*The Offensive Stranger:* But every great and precious liberty enjoyed by the nations of continental Europe to-day are the gift of that Revolution.

*The Dervish:* A good result, I concede it.

*The Offensive Stranger:* In our well-meant effort to lift up the Filipino to our own moral altitude with a musket, we have slipped on the ice and fallen down to his.

*The Dervish:* A large evil result.

*The Offensive Stranger:* But as an offset we are a World Power.

*The Dervish:* Give me time. I must think this one over. Pass on.

*The Offensive Stranger:* By help of three hundred thousand soldiers and eight hundred million dollars England has succeeded in her good purpose of lifting up the unwilling Boers and making them better and purer and happier than they could ever have become by their own devices.

*The Dervish:* Certainly that is a good result.

*The Offensive Stranger:* But there are only eleven Boers left now.

*The Dervish:* It has the appearance of an evil result. But I will think it over before I decide.

*The Offensive Stranger:* Take yet one more instance. With the best intentions the missionary has been laboring in China for eighty years.

*The Dervish:* The evil result is ——

EUROPE AND ELSEWHERE

*The Offensive Stranger:* That nearly a hundred thousand Chinamen have acquired our Civilization.

*The Dervish:* And the good result is ——

*The Offensive Stranger:* That by the compassion of God four hundred millions have escaped it.

# INSTRUCTIONS IN ART

(With Illustrations by the Author)

THE great trouble about painting a whole gallery of portraits at the same time is, that the housemaid comes and dusts, and does not put them back the way they were before, and so when the public flock to the studio and wish to know which is Howells and which is Depew and so on, you have to dissemble, and it is very embarrassing at first. Still, you know they are there, and this knowledge presently gives you more or less confidence, and you say sternly, "*This* is Howells," and watch the visitor's eye. If you see doubt there, you correct yourself and try another. In time you find one that will satisfy, and then you feel relief and joy, but you have suffered much in the meantime; and you know that this joy is only temporary, for the next inquirer will settle on another Howells of a quite different aspect, and one which you suspect is Edward VII or Cromwell, though you keep that to yourself, of course. It is much better to label a portrait when you first paint it, then there is no uncertainty in your mind and you can get bets out of the visitor and win them.

I believe I have had the most trouble with a portrait which I painted in installments—the head on one canvas and the bust on another.

The housemaid stood the bust up sideways, and now I don't know which way it goes. Some authorities think it belongs with the breastpin at the top, under the man's chin; others think it belongs the reverse way, on account of the collar, one of these saying, "A person can wear a breastpin on his stomach if he wants to, but he can't wear his collar anywhere he dern pleases." There is a certain amount of sense in that view of it. Still, there is no way to determine the matter for certain; when you join the installments, with the pin under the

THE HEAD ON ONE CANVAS

chin, that seems to be right; then when you reverse it and bring the collar under the chin it seems as right as ever; whichever way you fix it the lines come together snug and convincing, and either way you do it the portrait's face looks equally surprised and rejoiced, and as if it wouldn't be satisfied to have it any way but just that one; in fact, even if you take the bust away altogether the face seems surprised and happy just the same—I have never seen an expression before, which no vicissitudes could alter. I wish I could remember who it is. It looks a little like Washington, but I do not think it can be Washington, because he had as many ears on one side as the other. You can always tell Washington by that; he was very particular about his ears, and about having them arranged the same old way all the time.

By and by I shall get out of these confusions, and then it will be plain sailing; but first-off the confusions were natural and not to be avoided. My reputation came very suddenly and tumultuously when I published my own portrait, and it turned my head a little, for indeed there was never anything

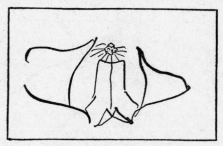

AND THE BUST ON ANOTHER

like it. In a single day I got orders from sixty-two people not to paint their portraits, some of them the most distinguished persons in the country—the President, the Cabinet, authors, governors, admirals, candidates for office on the weak side—almost everybody that was anybody, and it would really have turned the head of nearly any beginner to get so much notice and have it come with such a frenzy of cordiality. But I am growing calm and settling down to business, now; and pretty soon I shall cease to be flurried, and then when I do a portrait I shall be quite at myself and able on the instant to tell it from the others and pick it out when wanted.

I am living a new and exalted life of late. It steeps me in a sacred rapture to see a portrait develop and take soul under my hand. First, I

FIRST YOU THINK IT'S DANTE; NEXT YOU THINK IT'S EMERSON; THEN YOU THINK IT'S WAYNE MAC VEAGH. YET IT ISN'T ANY OF THEM; IT'S THE BEGINNINGS OF DEPEW

throw off a study—just a mere study, a few apparently random lines—and to look at it you would hardly ever suspect who it was going to be; even I cannot tell, myself. Take this picture, for instance: First you think it's Dante; next you think it's

Emerson; then you think it's Wayne Mac Veagh. Yet it isn't any of them; it's the beginnings of Depew. Now you wouldn't believe Depew could be devolved out of that; yet the minute it is finished here you have him to the life, and you say, yourself, "If that isn't Depew it isn't anybody."

Some would have painted him speaking, but he isn't always speaking, he has to stop and think sometimes.

That is a *genre* picture, as we say in the trade, and differs from the encaustic and other schools in various ways, mainly technical, which you wouldn't understand if I should explain them to you. But you will get the idea as I go along, and little by little you will learn all that is valuable about Art without knowing how it happened, and without any sense of strain or effort, and then you will know what school a picture belongs to, just at a glance, and whether it is an animal picture or a landscape. It is then that the joy of life will begin for you.

When you come to examine my portraits of Mr. Joe Jefferson and the rest, your eye will have become measurably educated by that time, and you will recognize at once that no two of them are alike. I will close the present chapter with an example of the nude, for your instruction.

This creation is different from any of the other works. The others are from real life, but this is an example of still-life; so called because it is a portrayal of a fancy only, a thing which has no actual and active existence. The purpose of a still-life picture is to concrete to the eye the spiritual, the intangible, a something which we feel, but cannot see with the fleshy vision—such as joy, sorrow, resentment, and so on. This is best achieved by the employment of that treatment which we call the impressionist, in the trade. The present example is an impressionist picture, done in distemper, with a chiaroscuro motif modified by monochromatic technique, so as to secure tenderness of feeling and spirituality of expression.

THAT THING IN THE RIGHT HAND IS NOT A SKILLET; IT IS A TAMBOURINE

At a first glance it would seem to be a Botticelli, but it is not that; it is only a humble imitation of that great master of longness and slimness and limbfulness.

The work is imagined from Greek story, and represents Proserpine or Persepolis, or one of those other Bacchantes doing the solemnities of welcome before the altar of Isis upon the arrival of the annual

shipload of Athenian youths in the island of Minos
to be sacrificed in appeasement of the Dordonian
Cyclops.

The figure symbolizes solemn joy.  It is severely

THE PORTRAIT REPRODUCES MR. JOSEPH JEFFERSON, THE
COMMON FRIEND OF THE HUMAN RACE

Greek, therefore does not call details of drapery or
other factitious helps to its aid, but depends wholly
upon grace of action and symmetry of contour for
its effects.  It is intended to be viewed from the
south or southeast, and I think that that is best;

for while it expresses more and larger joy when viewed from the east or the north, the features of the face are too much foreshortened and wormy when viewed from that point. That thing in the right hand is not a skillet; it is a tambourine.

EITHER MR. HOWELLS OR MR. LAFFAN. I CANNOT TELL WHICH BECAUSE THE LABEL IS LOST

This creation will be exhibited at the Paris Salon in June, and will compete for the *Prix de Rome*.

The above is a marine picture, and is intended to educate the eye in the important matters of perspective and foreshortening. The mountainous and bounding waves in the foreground, contrasted with the tranquil ship fading away as in a dream the other side of the fishing-pole, convey to us the idea of space and distance as no words could do. Such is the miracle wrought by that wondrous device, perspective.

The portrait reproduces Mr. Joseph Jefferson, the common friend of the human race. He is fishing, and is not catching anything. This is finely expressed by the moisture in the eye and the anguish of the mouth. The mouth is holding back words. The pole is bamboo, the line is foreshortened. This foreshortening, together with the smoothness of the water away out there where the cork is, gives a powerful impression of distance, and is another way of achieving a perspective effect.

We now come to the next portrait, which is either Mr. Howells or Mr. Laffan. I cannot tell which, because the label is lost. But it will do for both, because the features are Mr. Howells's, while

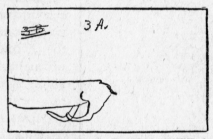

THE FRONT END OF IT WENT AROUND A
CORNER BEFORE I COULD GET TO IT

the expression is Mr. Laffan's. This work will bear critical examination.

The next picture is part of an animal, but I do not know the name of it. It is not finished. The front end of it went around a corner before I could get to it.

We will conclude with the portrait of a lady in the style of Raphael. Originally I started it out for Queen Elizabeth, but was not able to do the lace hopper her head projects out of, therefore I tried to turn it into Pocahontas, but was again baffled, and was compelled to make further modifications, this time achieving success. By spiritualizing it and turning it into the noble mother of our race and throwing into the countenance the sacred joy which her first tailor-made outfit infuses into her spirit, I was enabled to add to my gallery the best and most winning and eloquent portrait my brush has ever produced.

THE BEST AND MOST WINNING AND ELOQUENT PORTRAIT MY BRUSH HAS EVER PRODUCED

The most effective encouragement a beginner can have is the encouragement which he gets from noting his own progress with an alert and persistent eye. Save up your works and date them; as the years go by, run your eye over them from time to time, and measure your advancing stride. This will thrill you, this will nerve you, this will inspire you as nothing else can.

It has been my own course, and to it I owe the most that I am to-day in Art. When I look back and examine my first effort and then compare it with my latest, it seems unbelievable that I have climbed

so high in thirty-one years. Yet so it is. Practice—
that is the secret. From three to seven hours a day.
It is all that is required. The results are sure;
whereas indolence achieves nothing great.

IT SEEMS UNBELIEV-
ABLE THAT I HAVE
CLIMBED SO HIGH IN
THIRTY-ONE YEARS

# SOLD TO SATAN

(1904)

IT was at this time that I concluded to sell my soul to Satan. Steel was away down, so was St. Paul; it was the same with all the desirable stocks, in fact, and so, if I did not turn out to be away down myself, now was my time to raise a stake and make my fortune. Without further consideration I sent word to the local agent, Mr. Blank, with description and present condition of the property, and an interview with Satan was promptly arranged, on a basis of 2½ per cent, this commission payable only in case a trade should be consummated.

I sat in the dark, waiting and thinking. How still it was! Then came the deep voice of a far-off bell proclaiming midnight — Boom-m-m! Boom-m-m! Boom-m-m!—and I rose to receive my guest, and braced myself for the thunder crash and the brimstone stench which should announce his arrival. But there was no crash, no stench. Through the closed door, and noiseless, came the modern Satan, just as we see him on the stage—tall, slender, graceful, in tights and trunks, a short cape mantling his shoulders, a rapier at his side, a single drooping feather in his jaunty cap, and on his intellectual face the well-known and high-bred Mephistophelian smile.

SOLD TO SATAN

But he was not a fire coal; he was not red, no!
On the contrary. He was a softly glowing, richly
smoldering torch, column, statue of pallid light,
faintly tinted with a spiritual green, and out from
him a lunar splendor flowed such as one sees glinting
from the crinkled waves of tropic seas when the
moon rides high in cloudless skies.

He made his customary stage obeisance, resting
his left hand upon his sword hilt and removing his
cap with his right and making that handsome sweep
with it which we know so well; then we sat down.
Ah, he was an incandescent glory, a nebular dream,
and so much improved by his change of color. He
must have seen the admiration in my illuminated
face, but he took no notice of it, being long ago used
to it in faces of other Christians with whom he had
had trade relations.

. . . A half hour of hot toddy and weather chat,
mixed with occasional tentative feelers on my part
and rejoinders of, "Well, I could hardly pay *that* for
it, you know," on his, had much modified my shy-
ness and put me so much at my ease that I was
emboldened to feed my curiosity a little. So I
chanced the remark that he was surprisingly different
from the traditions, and I wished I knew what it was
he was made of. He was not offended, but answered
with frank simplicity:

"Radium!"

"That accounts for it!" I exclaimed. "It is the
loveliest effulgence I have ever seen. The hard and
heartless glare of the electric doesn't compare with it.
I suppose Your Majesty weighs about—about ——"

327

"I stand six feet one; fleshed and blooded I would weigh two hundred and fifteen; but radium, like other metals, is heavy. I weigh nine hundred-odd."

I gazed hungrily upon him, saying to myself:

"What riches! what a mine! Nine hundred pounds at, say, $3,500,000 a pound, would be— would be——" Then a treacherous thought burst into my mind!

He laughed a good hearty laugh, and said:

"I perceive your thought; and what a handsomely original idea it is!—to kidnap Satan, and stock him, and incorporate him, and water the stock up to ten billions—just three times its actual value—and blanket the world with it!" My blush had turned the moonlight to a crimson mist, such as veils and spectralizes the domes and towers of Florence at sunset and makes the spectator drunk with joy to see, and he pitied me, and dropped his tone of irony, and assumed a grave and reflective one which had a pleasanter sound for me, and under its kindly influence my pains were presently healed, and I thanked him for his courtesy. Then he said:

"One good turn deserves another, and I will pay you a compliment. Do you know I have been trading with your poor pathetic race for ages, and you are the first person who has ever been intelligent enough to divine the large commercial value of my make-up."

I purred to myself and looked as modest as I could.

"Yes, you are the first," he continued. "All through the Middle Ages I used to buy Christian

328

souls at fancy rates, building bridges and cathedrals
in a single night in return, and getting swindled out
of my Christian nearly every time that I dealt with
a priest—as history will concede—but making it
up on the lay square-dealer now and then, as *I*
admit; but none of those people ever guessed where
the *real* big money lay. You are the first."

I refilled his glass and gave him another Cavour.
But he was experienced, by this time. He inspected
the cigar pensively awhile; then:

"What do you pay for these?" he asked.

"Two cents—but they come cheaper when you
take a barrel."

He went on inspecting; also mumbling comments,
apparently to himself:

"Black — rough - skinned — rumpled, irregular,
wrinkled, barky, with crispy curled-up places on it—
burnt-leather aspect, like the shoes of the damned
that sit in pairs before the room doors at home of a
Sunday morning." He sighed at thought of his
home, and was silent a moment; then he said,
gently, "Tell me about this projectile."

"It is the discovery of a great Italian statesman,"
I said. "Cavour. One day he lit his cigar, then
laid it down and went on writing and forgot it. It
lay in a pool of ink and got soaked. By and by he
noticed it and laid it on the stove to dry. When it
was dry he lit it and at once noticed that it didn't
taste the same as it did before. And so ——"

"Did he say what it tasted like before?"

"No, I think not. But he called the government
chemist and told him to find out the source of that

329

new taste, and report. The chemist applied the tests, and reported that the source was the presence of sulphate of iron, touched up and spiritualized with vinegar—the combination out of which one makes ink. Cavour told him to introduce the brand in the interest of the finances. So, ever since then this brand passes through the ink factory, with the great result that both the ink and the cigar suffer a sea change into something new and strange. This is history, Sire, not a work of the imagination."

So then he took up his present again, and touched it to the forefinger of his other hand for an instant, which made it break into flame and fragrance—but he changed his mind at that point and laid the torpedo down, saying, courteously:

"With permission I will save it for Voltaire."

I was greatly pleased and flattered to be connected in even this little way with that great man and be mentioned to him, as no doubt would be the case, so I hastened to fetch a bundle of fifty for distribution among others of the renowned and lamented— Goethe, and Homer, and Socrates, and Confucius, and so on—but Satan said he had nothing against those. Then he dropped back into reminiscences of the old times once more, and presently said:

"They knew nothing about radium, and it would have had no value for them if they had known about it. In twenty million years it has had no value for your race until the revolutionizing steam-and-machinery age was born—which was only a few years before you were born yourself. It was a stunning little century, for sure, that nineteenth!

But it's a poor thing compared to what the twentieth is going to be."

By request, he explained why he thought so.

"Because power was so costly, then, and everything goes by power—the steamship, the locomotive, and everything else. Coal, you see! You have to have it; no steam and no electricity without it; and it's such a waste—for you burn it up, and it's gone! But radium—that's another matter! With my nine hundred pounds you could light the world, and heat it, and run all its ships and machines and railways a hundred million years, and not use up five pounds of it in the whole time! And then ——"

"Quick—my soul is yours, dear Ancestor; take it—we'll start a company!"

But he asked my age, which is sixty-eight, then politely sidetracked the proposition, probably not wishing to take advantage of himself. Then he went on talking admiringly of radium, and how with its own natural and inherent heat it could go on melting its own weight of ice twenty-four times in twenty-four hours, and keep it up forever without losing bulk or weight; and how a pound of it, if exposed in this room, would blast the place like a breath from hell, and burn me to a crisp in a quarter of a minute—and was going on like that, but I interrupted and said:

"But *you* are here, Majesty—nine hundred pounds —and the temperature is balmy and pleasant. I don't understand."

"Well," he said, hesitatingly, "it is a secret, but I may as well reveal it, for these prying and impertinent chemists are going to find it out sometime or other, anyway. Perhaps you have read what Madame Curie says about radium; how she goes searching among its splendid secrets and seizes upon one after another of them and italicizes its specialty; how she says 'the compounds of radium are *spontaneously luminous*'—require no coal in the production of light, you see; how she says, 'a glass vessel containing radium *spontaneously charges itself with electricity*'—no coal or water power required to generate it, you see; how she says 'radium possesses the remarkable property of *liberating heat spontaneously and continuously*'—no coal required to fire-up on the world's machinery, you see. She ransacks the pitchblende for its radioactive substances, and captures three and labels them; one, which is embodied with bismuth, she names polonium; one, which is embodied with barium, she names radium; the name given to the third was actinium. Now listen; she says '*the question now was to separate the polonium from the bismuth* . . . this is the task that has occupied us for years and has been a most difficult one.' For years, you see—for *years*. That is their way, those plagues, those scientists—peg, peg, peg—dig, dig, dig—plod, plod, plod. I wish I could catch a cargo of them for my place; it would be an economy. Yes, for years, you see. They never give up. Patience, hope, faith, perseverance; it is the way of all the breed. Columbus and the rest. In radium this lady has added a new world to the planet's possessions, and matched—Columbus—and his peer. She has set herself the task of divorcing polonium and

bismuth; when she succeeds she will have done—
what, should you say?"

"Pray name it, Majesty."

"It's another new world added—a gigantic one.
I will explain; for you would never divine the size
of it, and she herself does not suspect it."

"Do, Majesty, I beg of you."

"Polonium, freed from bismuth and made independent, is the one and only power that can control
radium, restrain its destructive forces, tame them,
reduce them to obedience, and make them do useful
and profitable work for your race. Examine my
skin. What do you think of it?"

"It is delicate, silky, transparent, thin as a gela-
tine film—exquisite, beautiful, Majesty!"

"It is made of polonium. All the rest of me is
radium. If I should strip off my skin the world
would vanish away in a flash of flame and a puff of
smoke, and the remnants of the extinguished moon
would sift down through space a mere snow-shower
of gray ashes!"

I made no comment, I only trembled.

"You understand, now," he continued. "I burn,
I suffer within, my pains are measureless and eternal,
but my skin protects you and the globe from harm.
Heat is power, energy, but is only useful to man when
he can control it and graduate its application to his
needs. You cannot do that with radium, now; it
will not be prodigiously useful to you until polonium
shall put the slave whip in your hand. I can release
from my body the radium force in any measure I
please, great or small; at my will I can set in motion

the works of a lady's watch or destroy a world. You saw me light that unholy cigar with my finger?"

I remembered it.

"Try to imagine how minute was the fraction of energy released to do that small thing! You are aware that everything is made up of restless and revolving molecules?—everything—furniture, rocks, water, iron, horses, men—everything that exists."

"Yes."

"Molecules of scores of different sizes and weights, but none of them big enough to be seen by help of any microscope?"

"Yes."

"And that each molecule is made up of thousands of separate and never-resting little particles called atoms?"

"Yes."

"And that up to recent times the smallest atom known to science was the hydrogen atom, which was a thousand times smaller than the atom that went to the building of any other molecule?"

"Yes."

"Well, the radium atom from the positive pole is 5,000 times smaller than *that* atom! This unspeakably minute atom is called an *electron*. Now then, out of my long affection for you and for your lineage, I will reveal to you a secret—a secret known to no scientist as yet—the secret of the firefly's light and the glowworm's; it is produced by a single electron imprisoned in a polonium atom."

"Sire, it is a wonderful thing, and the scientific world would be grateful to know this secret, which has baffled and defeated all its searchings for more than two centuries. To think!—a single electron, 5,000 times smaller than the invisible hydrogen atom, to produce that explosion of vivid light which makes the summer night so beautiful!"

"And consider," said Satan; "it is the only instance in all nature where radium exists in a pure state unencumbered by fettering alliances; where polonium enjoys the like emancipation; and where the pair are enabled to labor together in a gracious and beneficent and effective partnership. Suppose the protecting polonium envelope were removed; the radium spark would flash but once and the firefly would be consumed to vapor! Do you value this old iron letterpress?"

"No, Majesty, for it is not mine."

"Then I will destroy it and let you see. I lit the ostensible cigar with the heat energy of a single electron, the equipment of a single lightning bug. I will turn on twenty thousand electrons now."

He touched the massive thing and it exploded with a cannon crash, leaving nothing but vacancy where it had stood. For three minutes the air was a dense pink fog of sparks, through which Satan loomed dim and vague, then the place cleared and his soft rich moonlight pervaded it again. He said:

"You see? The radium in 20,000 lightning bugs would run a racing-mobile forever. There's no waste, no diminution of it." Then he remarked in a quite casual way, "We use nothing but radium at home."

I was astonished. And interested, too, for I have friends there, and relatives. I had always believed—

335

in accordance with my early teachings—that the fuel was soft coal and brimstone. He noticed the thought, and answered it.

"Soft coal and brimstone is the tradition, yes, but it is an error. We could use it; at least we could make out with it after a fashion, but it has several defects: it is not cleanly, it ordinarily makes but a temperate fire, and it would be exceedingly difficult, if even possible, to heat it up to standard, Sundays; and as for the supply, all the worlds and systems could not furnish enough to keep us going halfway through eternity. Without radium there could be no hell; certainly not a satisfactory one."

"Why?"

"Because if we hadn't radium we should have to dress the souls in some other material; then, of course, they would burn up and get out of trouble. They would not last an hour. You know that?"

"Why—yes, now that you mention it. But I supposed they were dressed in their natural flesh; they look so in the pictures—in the Sistine Chapel and in the illustrated books, you know."

"Yes, our damned look as they looked in the world, but it isn't flesh; flesh could not survive any longer than that copying press survived—it would explode and turn to a fog of sparks, and the result desired in sending it there would be defeated. Believe me, radium is the only wear."

"I see it now," I said, with prophetic discomfort, "I know that you are right, Majesty."

"I am. I speak from experience. You shall see, when you get there."

336

He said this as if he thought I was eaten up with curiosity, but it was because he did not know me. He sat reflecting a minute, then he said:

"I will make your fortune."

It cheered me up and I felt better. I thanked him and was all eagerness and attention.

"Do you know," he continued, "where they find the bones of the extinct moa, in New Zealand? All in a pile—thousands and thousands of them banked together in a mass twenty feet deep. And do you know where they find the tusks of the extinct mastodon of the Pleistocene? Banked together in acres off the mouth of the Lena—an ivory mine which has furnished freight for Chinese caravans for five hundred years. Do you know the phosphate beds of our South? They are miles in extent, a limitless mass and jumble of bones of vast animals whose like exists no longer in the earth—a cemetery, a mighty cemetery, that is what it is. All over the earth there are such cemeteries. Whence came the instinct that made those families of creatures go to a chosen and particular spot to die when sickness came upon them and they perceived that their end was near? It is a mystery; not even science has been able to uncover the secret of it. But there stands the fact. Listen, then. For a million years there has been a firefly cemetery."

Hopefully, appealingly, I opened my mouth—he motioned me to close it, and went on:

"It is in a scooped-out bowl half as big as this room on the top of a snow summit of the Cordilleras. That bowl is level full—of what? Pure firefly radium and the glow and heat of hell? For countless ages myriads of fireflies have daily flown thither and died in that bowl and been burned to vapor in an instant, each fly leaving as its contribution its only indestructible particle, its single electron of pure radium. There is energy enough there to light the whole world, heat the whole world's machinery, supply the whole world's transportation power from now till the end of eternity. The massed riches of the planet could not furnish its value in money. You are mine, it is yours; when Madame Curie isolates polonium, clothe yourself in a skin of it and go and take possession!"

Then he vanished and left me in the dark when I was just in the act of thanking him. I can find the bowl by the light it will cast upon the sky; I can get the polonium presently, when that illustrious lady in France isolates it from the bismuth. Stock is for sale. Apply to Mark Twain.

# THAT DAY IN EDEN

### (Passage from Satan's Diary)

LONG ago I was in the bushes near the Tree of Knowledge when the Man and the Woman came there and had a conversation. I was present, now, when they came again after all these years. They were as before—mere boy and girl—trim, rounded, slender, flexible, snow images lightly flushed with the pink of the skies, innocently unconscious of their nakedness, lovely to look upon, beautiful beyond words.

I listened again. Again as in that former time they puzzled over those words, Good, Evil, Death, and tried to reason out their meaning; but, of course, they were not able to do it. Adam said:

"Come, maybe we can find Satan. He might know these things."

Then I came forth, still gazing upon Eve and admiring, and said to her:

"You have not seen me before, sweet creature, but I have seen you. I have seen all the animals, but in beauty none of them equals you. Your hair, your eyes, your face, your flesh tints, your form, the tapering grace of your white limbs—all are beautiful, adorable, perfect."

It gave her pleasure, and she looked herself over, putting out a foot and a hand and admiring them; then she naïvely said:

"It is a joy to be so beautiful. And Adam—he is the same."

She turned him about, this way and that, to show him off, with such guileless pride in her blue eyes, and he—he took it all as just matter of course, and was innocently happy in it, and said, "When I have flowers on my head it is better still."

Eve said, "It is true—you shall see," and she flitted hither and thither like a butterfly and plucked flowers, and in a moment laced their stems together in a glowing wreath and set it upon his head; then tiptoed and gave it a pat here and there with her nimble fingers, with each pat enhancing its grace and shape, none knows how, nor why it should so result, but in it there is a law somewhere, though the delicate art and mystery of it is her secret alone, and not learnable by another; and when at last it was to her mind she clapped her hands for pleasure, then reached up and kissed him—as pretty a sight, taken altogether, as in my experience I have seen.

Presently, to the matter in hand. The meaning of those words—would I tell her?

Certainly none could be more willing, but how was I to do it? I could think of no way to make her understand, and I said so. I said:

"I will try, but it is hardly of use. For instance—what is pain?"

"Pain? I do not know."

"Certainly. How should you? Pain is not of your world; pain is impossible to you; you have never experienced a physical pain. Reduce that to a formula, a principle, and what have we?"

340

"What have we?"

"This: Things which are outside of our orbit—our own particular world—things which by our constitution and equipment we are unable to see, or feel, or otherwise experience—*cannot be made comprehensible to us in words.* There you have the whole thing in a nutshell. It is a principle, it is axiomatic, it is a law. Now do you understand?"

The gentle creature looked dazed, and for all result she was delivered of this vacant remark:

"What is axiomatic?"

She had missed the point. Necessarily she would. Yet her effort was success for me, for it was a vivid confirmation of the truth of what I had been saying. Axiomatic was for the present a thing outside of the world of her experience, therefore it had no meaning for her. I ignored her question and continued:

"What is fear?"

"Fear? I do not know."

"Naturally. Why should you? You have not felt it, you cannot feel it, it does not belong in your world. With a hundred thousand words I should not be able to make you understand what fear is. How then am I to explain death to you? You have never seen it, it is foreign to your world, it is impossible to make the word mean anything to you, so far as I can see. In a way, it is a sleep ——"

"Oh, I know what that is!"

"But it is a sleep only in a way, as I said. It is more than a sleep."

"Sleep is pleasant, sleep is lovely!"

"But death is a long sleep—very long."

341

"Oh, all the lovelier! Therefore I think nothing could be better than death."

I said to myself, "Poor child, some day you may know what a pathetic truth you have spoken; some day you may say, out of a broken heart, 'Come to me, O Death the compassionate! steep me in the merciful oblivion, O refuge of the sorrowful, friend of the forsaken and the desolate!'" Then I said aloud, "But this sleep is eternal."

The word went over her head. Necessarily it would.

"Eternal. What is eternal?"

"Ah, that also is outside of your world, as yet. There is no way to make you understand it."

It was a hopeless case. Words referring to things outside of her experience were a foreign language to her, and meaningless. She was like a little baby whose mother says to it, "Don't put your finger in the candle flame; it will burn you." Burn—it is a foreign word to the baby, and will have no terrors for it until experience shall have revealed its meaning. It is not worth while for mamma to make the remark, the baby will goo-goo cheerfully, and put its finger in the pretty flame—once. After these private reflections I said again that I did not think there was any way to make her understand the meaning of the word eternal. She was silent awhile, turning these deep matters over in the unworn machinery of her mind; then she gave up the puzzle and shifted her ground, saying:

"Well, there are those other words. What is good, and what is evil?"

342

"It is another difficulty. They, again, are outside of your world; they have place in the moral kingdom only. You have no morals."

"What are morals?"

"A system of law which distinguishes between right and wrong, good morals and bad. These things do not exist for you. I cannot make it clear; you would not understand."

"But try."

"Well, obedience to constituted authority is a moral law. Suppose Adam should forbid you to put your child in the river and leave it there overnight—would you put the child there?"

She answered with a darling simplicity and guilelessness:

"Why, yes, if I wanted to."

"There, it is just as I said—you would not know any better; you have no idea of duty, command, obedience; they have no meaning for you. In your present estate you are in no possible way responsible for anything you do or say or think. It is impossible for you to do wrong, for you have no more notion of right and wrong than the other animals have. You and they can do only right; whatever you and they do is right and innocent. It is a divine estate, the loftiest and purest attainable in heaven and in earth. It is the angel gift. The angels are wholly pure and sinless, for they do not know right from wrong, and all the acts of such are blameless. No one can do wrong without knowing how to distinguish between right and wrong."

"Is it an advantage to know?"

"Most certainly not! That knowledge would remove all that is divine, all that is angelic, from the angels, and immeasurably degrade them."

"Are there any persons that know right from wrong?"

"Not in—well, not in heaven."

"What gives that knowledge?"

"The Moral Sense."

"What is that?"

"Well—no matter. Be thankful that you lack it."

"Why?"

"Because it is a degradation, a disaster. Without it one cannot do wrong; with it, one can. Therefore it has but one office, only one—to teach how to do wrong. It can teach no other thing—no other thing whatever. It is the *creator* of wrong; wrong cannot exist until the Moral Sense brings it into being."

"How can one acquire the Moral Sense?"

"By eating of the fruit of the Tree, here. But why do you wish to know? Would you like to have the Moral Sense?"

She turned wistfully to Adam:

"Would you like to have it?"

He showed no particular interest, and only said:

"I am indifferent. I have not understood any of this talk, but if you like we will eat it, for I cannot see that there is any objection to it."

Poor ignorant things, the command of refrain had meant nothing to them, they were but children, and could not understand untried things and verbal abstractions which stood for matters outside of their little world and their narrow experience. Eve reached for an apple!—oh, farewell, Eden and your sinless joys, come poverty and pain, hunger and cold and heartbreak, bereavement, tears and shame, envy, strife, malice and dishonor, age, weariness, remorse; then desperation and the prayer for the release of death, indifferent that the gates of hell yawn beyond it!

She tasted—the fruit fell from her hand.

It was pitiful. She was like one who wakens slow and confusedly out of a sleep. She gazed half vacantly at me, then at Adam, holding her curtaining fleece of golden hair back with her hand; then her wandering glance fell upon her naked person. The red blood mounted to her cheek, and she sprang behind a bush and stood there crying, and saying:

"Oh, my modesty is lost to me—my unoffending form is become a shame to me!" She moaned and muttered in her pain, and dropped her head, saying, "I am degraded—I have fallen, oh, so low, and I shall never rise again."

Adam's eyes were fixed upon her in a dreamy amazement, for he could not understand what had happened, it being outside his world as yet, and her words having no meaning for one void of the Moral Sense. And now his wonder grew: for, unknown to Eve, her hundred years rose upon her, and faded the heaven of her eyes and the tints of her young flesh, and touched her hair with gray, and traced faint sprays of wrinkles about her mouth and eyes, and shrunk her form, and dulled the satin luster of her skin.

All this the fair boy saw: then loyally and bravely he took the apple and tasted it, saying nothing.

The change came upon him also. Then he gathered boughs for both and clothed their nakedness, and they turned and went their way, hand in hand and bent with age, and so passed from sight.

# EVE SPEAKS

## I

THEY drove us from the Garden with their swords
of flame, the fierce cherubim. And what had we
done? We meant no harm. We were ignorant, and
did as any other children might do. We could not
know it was wrong to disobey the command, for
the words were strange to us and we did not understand them. We did not know right from wrong—
how should we know? We could not, without the
Moral Sense; it was not possible. If we had been
given the Moral Sense first—ah, that would have
been fairer, that would have been kinder; then we
should be to blame if we disobeyed. But to say to
us poor ignorant children words which we could not
understand, and then punish us because we did not
do as we were told—ah, how can that be justified?
We knew no more then than this littlest child of
mine knows now, with its four years—oh, not so
much, I think. Would I say to it, "If thou touchest
this bread I will overwhelm thee with unimaginable
disaster, even to the dissolution of thy corporeal
elements," and when it took the bread and smiled
up in my face, thinking no harm, as not understanding those strange words, would I take advantage of
its innocence and strike it down with the mother
hand it trusted? Whoso knoweth the mother heart,
let him judge if it would do that thing. Adam says

347

my brain is turned by my troubles and that I am become wicked. I am as I am; I did not make myself.

They drove us out. Drove us out into this harsh wilderness, and shut the gates against us. We that had meant no harm. It is three months. We were ignorant then; we are rich in learning, now—ah, how rich! We know hunger, thirst, and cold; we know pain, disease, and grief; we know hate, rebellion, and deceit; we know remorse, the conscience that prosecutes guilt and innocence alike, making no distinction; we know weariness of body and spirit, the unrefreshing sleep, the rest which rests not, the dreams which restore Eden, and banish it again with the waking; we know misery; we know torture and the heartbreak; we know humiliation and insult; we know indecency, immodesty, and the soiled mind; we know the scorn that attaches to the transmitted image of God exposed unclothed to the day; we know fear; we know vanity, folly, envy, hypocrisy; we know irreverence; we know blasphemy; we know right from wrong, and how to avoid the one and do the other; we know all the rich product of the Moral Sense, and it is our possession. Would we could sell it for one hour of Eden and white purity; would we could degrade the animals with it!

We have it all—that treasure. All but death. Death. . . . Death. What may that be?

Adam comes.

"Well?"

"He still sleeps."

That is our second-born—our Abel.

"He has slept enough for his good, and his garden suffers for his care. Wake him."

"I have tried and cannot."

"Then he is very tired. Let him sleep on."

"I think it is his hurt that makes him sleep so long."

I answer: "It may be so. Then we will let him rest; no doubt the sleep is healing it."

## II

It is a day and a night, now, that he has slept. We found him by his altar in his field, that morning, his face and body drenched in blood. He said his eldest brother struck him down. Then he spoke no more and fell asleep. We laid him in his bed and washed the blood away, and were glad to know the hurt was light and that he had no pain; for if he had had pain he would not have slept.

It was in the early morning that we found him. All day he slept that sweet, reposeful sleep, lying always on his back, and never moving, never turning. It showed how tired he was, poor thing. He is so good and works so hard, rising with the dawn and laboring till the dark. And now he is overworked; it will be best that he tax himself less, after this, and I will ask him; he will do anything I wish.

All the day he slept. I know, for I was always near, and made dishes for him and kept them warm against his waking. Often I crept in and fed my eyes upon his gentle face, and was thankful for that blessed sleep. And still he slept on—slept with his

eyes wide; a strange thing, and made me think he
was awake at first, but it was not so, for I spoke
and he did not answer. He always answers when I
speak. Cain has moods and will not answer, but
not Abel.

I have sat by him all the night, being afraid he
might wake and want his food. His face was very
white; and it changed, and he came to look as he
had looked when he was a little child in Eden long
ago, so sweet and good and dear. It carried me back
over the abyss of years, and I was lost in dreams and
tears—oh, hours, I think. Then I came to myself;
and thinking he stirred, I kissed his cheek to wake
him, but he slumbered on and I was disappointed.
His cheek was cold. I brought sacks of wool and the
down of birds and covered him, but he was still
cold, and I brought more. Adam has come again,
and says he is not yet warm. I do not understand it.

### III

We cannot wake him! With my arms clinging
about him I have looked into his eyes, through the
veil of my tears, and begged for one little word,
and he will not answer. Oh, is it that long sleep—is
it death? And will he wake no more?

#### FROM SATAN'S DIARY

Death has entered the world, the creatures are
perishing; one of The Family is fallen; the product
of the Moral Sense is complete. The Family think
ill of death—they will change their minds.

# SAMUEL ERASMUS MOFFETT
## AUGUST 16,1908

### HIS CHARACTER AND HIS DEATH

*AUGUST 16th.*—Early in the evening of the first day of this month the telephone brought us a paralyzing shock: my nephew, Samuel E. Moffett, was drowned. It was while sea bathing. The seas were running high and he was urged not to venture out, but he was a strong swimmer and not afraid. He made the plunge with confidence, his frightened little son looking on. Instantly he was helpless. The great waves tossed him hither and thither, they buried him, they struck the life out of him. In a minute it was all over.

He was forty-eight years old, he was at his best, physically and mentally, and was well on his way toward earned distinction. He was large-minded and large-hearted, there was no blot nor fleck upon his character, his ideals were high and clean, and by native impulse and without effort he lived up to them.

He had been a working journalist, an editorial writer, for nearly thirty years, and yet in that exposed position had preserved his independence in full strength and his principles undecayed. Several years ago he accepted a high place on the staff of *Collier's Weekly* and was occupying it when he died.

In an early chapter of my *Autobiography*, written three years ago, I have told how he wrote from San Francisco, when he was a stripling and asked me to help him get a berth on a daily paper there; and how he submitted to the severe conditions I imposed, and got the berth and kept it sixteen years.

As child and lad his health was delicate, capricious, insecure, and his eyesight affected by a malady which debarred him from book study and from reading. This was a bitter hardship for him, for he had a wonderful memory and a sharp hunger for knowledge. School was not for him, yet while still a little boy he acquired an education, and a good one. He managed it after a method of his own devising: he got permission to listen while the classes of the normal school recited their abstruse lessons and blackboarded their mathematics. By questioning the little chap it was found that he was keeping up with the star scholars of the school.

In those days he paid us a visit in Hartford. It was when he was about twelve years old. I was laboriously constructing an ancient-history game at the time, to be played by my wife and myself, and I was digging the dates and facts for it out of cyclopædias, a dreary and troublesome business. I had sweated blood over that work and was pardonably proud of the result, as far as I had gone. I showed the child my mass of notes, and he was at once as excited as I should have been over a Sunday-school picnic at his age. He wanted to help, he was eager to help, and I was as willing to let him as I should have been to give away an interest in a

surgical operation that I was getting tired of. I
made him free of the cyclopædias, but he never consulted them—he had their contents in his head. All
alone he built and completed the game rapidly and
without effort.

Away back in '80 or '81 when the grand eruption
of Krakatoa, in the Straits of Sunda, occurred, the
news reached San Francisco late in the night—too
late for editors to hunt for information about that
unknown volcano in cyclopædias and write it up
exhaustively and learnedly in time for the first edition. The managing editor said, "Send to Moffett's
home; rout him out and fetch him; he will know
all about it; he won't need the cyclopædia." Which
was true. He came to the office and swiftly wrote
it all up without having to refer to books.

I will take a few paragraphs from the article about
him in *Collier's Weekly:*

If you wanted to know any fact about any subject it was
quicker to go to him than to books of reference. His good
nature made him the martyr of interruptions. In the middle
of a sentence, in a hurry hour, he would look up happily, and
whether the thing you wanted was railroad statistics or international law, he would bring it out of one of the pigeonholes in
his brain. A born dispenser of the light, he made the giving of
information a privilege and a pleasure on all occasions.

This cyclopædic faculty was marvelous because it was only
a small part of his equipment which became invaluable in
association with other gifts. A student and a humanist, he
delighted equally in books and in watching all the workings of
a political convention.

For any one of the learned professions he had conspicuous
ability. He chose that which, in the cloister of the editorial
rooms, makes fame for others. Any judge or Cabinet Minister
of our time may well be proud of a career of such usefulness

as his. Men with such a quality of mind as Moffett's are rare.

Anyone who discussed with him the things he advocated stood a little awed to discover that here was a man who had carefully thought out what would be best for all the people in the world two or three generations hence, and guided his work according to that standard. This was the one broad subject that covered all his interests; in detail they included the movement for universal peace about which he wrote repeatedly; so small a thing as a plan to place flowers on the window sills and fire escapes of New York tenement houses enlisted not only the advocacy of his pen, but his direct personal presence and co-operation; again and again, in his department in this paper, he gave indorsement and aid to similar movements, whether broad or narrow in their scope—the saving of the American forests, fighting tuberculosis, providing free meals for poor school children in New York, old-age pensions, safety appliances for protecting factory employees, the beautifying of American cities, the creation of inland waterways, industrial peace.

He leaves behind him wife, daughter, and son—inconsolable mourners. The son is thirteen, a beautiful human creature, with the broad and square face of his father and his grandfather, a face in which one reads high character and intelligence. This boy will be distinguished, by and by, I think.

In closing this slight sketch of Samuel E. Moffett I wish to dwell with lingering and especial emphasis upon the dignity of his character and ideals. In an age when we would rather have money than health, and would rather have another man's money than our own, he lived and died unsordid; in a day when the surest road to national greatness and admiration is by showy and rotten demagoguery in politics and by giant crimes in finance, he lived and died a gentleman.

# THE NEW PLANET

(The astronomers at Harvard have observed "perturbations" in the orbital movement of Neptune," such as might be caused by the presence of a new planet in the vicinity.)

I BELIEVE in the new planet. I was eleven years old in 1846, when Leverrier and Adams and Mary Somerville discovered Neptune through the disturbance and discomfort it was causing Uranus. "Perturbations," they call that kind of disturbance. I had been having those perturbations myself, for more than two months; in fact, all through watermelon time, for they used to keep dogs in some of the patches in those days. You notice that these recent perturbations are considered remarkable because they perturbate through three seconds of arc, but really that is nothing: often I used to perturbate through as much as half an hour if it was a dog that was attending to the perturbating. There isn't any Neptune that can outperturbate a dog; and I know, because I am not speaking from hearsay. Why, if there was a planet two hundred and fifty thousand "light-years" the other side of Neptune's orbit, Professor Pickering would discover it in a minute if it could perturbate equal to a dog. Give me a dog every time, when it comes to perturbating. You let a dog jump out at you all of a sudden in the dark of the moon, and you will see what a small thing three seconds of arc is: the shudder that goes through you then would open the seams of Noah's Ark itself, from figurehead to rudder post, and you would drop that melon the same as if you had never had any but just a casual interest in it. I know about these things, because this is not tradition I am writing, but history.

Now then, notice this. About the end of August, 1846, a change came over me and I resolved to lead a better life, so I reformed; but it was just as well, anyway, because they had got to having guns and dogs both. Although I was reformed, the perturbations did not stop! Does that strike you? They did not stop, they went right on and on and on, for three weeks, clear up to the 23d of September; then Neptune was discovered and the whole mystery stood explained. It shows that I am so sensitively constructed that I perturbate when any other planet is disturbed. This has been going on all my life. It only happens in the watermelon season, but that has nothing to do with it, and has no significance: geologists and anthropologists and horticulturists all tell me it is only ancestral and hereditary, and that is what I think myself. Now then, I got to perturbating again, this summer—all summer through; all through watermelon time: and *where*, do you think? Up here on my farm in Connecticut. Is that significant? Unquestionably it is, for you couldn't raise a watermelon on this farm with a derrick.

That perturbating was caused by the new planet. That Washington Observatory may throw as much doubt as it wants to, it cannot affect me, because I know there *is* a new planet. I know it because I don't perturbate for nothing. There has got to be a dog or a planet, one or the other; and there isn't any dog around here, so there's *got* to be a planet. I hope it is going to be named after me; I should just love it if I can't have a constellation.

## MARJORIE FLEMING, THE WONDER CHILD

**M**ARJORIE has been in her tiny grave a hundred years; and still the tears fall for her, and will fall. What an intensely human little creature she was! How vividly she lived her small life; how impulsive she was; how sudden, how tempestuous, how tender, how loving, how sweet, how loyal, how rebellious, how repentant, how wise, how unwise, how bursting with fun, how frank, how free, how honest, how innocently bad, how natively good, how charged with quaint philosophies, how winning, how precious, how adorable—and how perennially and indestructibly interesting! And all this exhibited, proved, and recorded before she reached the end of her ninth year and "fell on sleep."

Geographically considered, the lassie was a Scot; but in fact she had no frontiers, she was the world's child, she was the human race in little. It is one of the prides of my life that the first time I ever heard her name it came from the lips of Dr. John Brown—his very own self—Dr. John Brown of Edinburgh— Dr. John Brown of *Rab and His Friends*—Dr. John Brown of the beautiful face and the sweet spirit, whose friends loved him with a love that was worship—Dr. John Brown, who was Marjorie's biographer, and who had clasped an aged hand that had

358

caressed Marjorie's fifty years before, thus linking me with that precious child by an unbroken chain of handshakes, for I had shaken hands with Dr. John. This was in Edinburgh thirty-six years ago. He gave my wife his little biography of Marjorie, and I have it yet.

Is Marjorie known in America? No—at least to only a few. When Mr. L. MacBean's new and enlarged and charming biography[1] of her was published five years ago it was sent over here in sheets, the market not being large enough to justify recomposing and reprinting it on our side of the water. I find that there are even cultivated Scotchmen among us who have not heard of Marjorie Fleming.

She was born in Kirkcaldy in 1803, and she died when she was eight years and eleven months old. By the time she was five years old she was become a devourer of various kinds of literature—both heavy and light—and was also become a quaint and free-spoken and charming little thinker and philosopher whose views were a delightful jumble of first-hand cloth of gold and second-hand rags.

When she was six she opened up that rich mine, her journals, and continued to work it by spells during the remainder of her brief life. She was a pet of Walter Scott, from the cradle, and when he could have her society for a few hours he was content, and required no other. Her little head was full of noble passages from Shakespeare and other favor-

[1] *Marjorie Fleming.* By L. MacBean. G. P. Putnam's Sons, publishers, London and New York.

Permission to use the extracts quoted from Marjorie's Journal in this article has been granted me by the publishers.

ites of hers, and the fact that she could deliver them with moving effect is proof that her elocution was a born gift with her, and not a mechanical reproduction of somebody else's art, for a child's parrot-work does not move. When she was a little creature of seven years, Sir Walter Scott "would read ballads to her in his own glorious way, the two getting wild with excitement over them; and he would take her on his knee and make her repeat Constance's speeches in *King John* till he swayed to and fro, sobbing his fill." [Dr. John Brown.]

"*Sobbing his fill*"—that great man—over that little thing's inspired interpretations. It is a striking picture; there is no mate to it. Sir Walter said of her:

"She's the most extraordinary creature I ever met with, and her repeating of Shakespeare overpowers me as nothing else does."

She spent the whole of her little life in a Presbyterian heaven; yet she was not affected by it; she could not have been happier if she had been in the other heaven.

She was made out of thunderstorms and sunshine, and not even her little perfunctory pieties and shop-made holiness could squelch her spirits or put out her fires for long. Under pressure of a pestering sense of duty she heaves a shovelful of trade godliness into her journals every little while, but it does not offend, for none of it is her own; it is all borrowed, it is a convention, a custom of her environment, it is the most innocent of hypocrisies, and this tainted butter of hers soon gets to be as delicious to the reader as are the stunning and worldly sin-

# MARJORIE FLEMING

cerities she splatters around it every time her pen
takes a fresh breath. The adorable child! she hasn't
a discoverable blemish in her make-up anywhere.

Marjorie's first letter was written before she was
six years old; it was to her cousin, Isa Keith, a young
lady of whom she was passionately fond. It was
done in a sprawling hand, ten words to the page—and
in those foolscap days a page was a spacious thing:

"My Dear Isa—

"I now sit down on my botom to answer all the
kind & beloved letters which you was so so good as
to write to me. This is the first time I ever wrote
a letter in my life.

"Miss Potune, a lady of my acquaintance, praises
me dreadfully. I repeated something out of Deen
Swift & she said I was fit for the stage, & you may
think I was primmed up with majestick Pride, but
upon my word I felt myself turn a little birsay—
birsay is a word which is a word that William composed which is as you may suppose a little enraged.
This horid fat Simpliton says that my Aunt is beautifull which is intirely impossible for that is not her
nature."

Frank? Yes, Marjorie was that. And during the
brief moment that she enchanted this dull earth with
her presence she was the bewitchingest speller and
punctuator in all Christendom.

The average child of six "prints" its correspondence in rickety and reeling Roman capitals, or
dictates to mamma, who puts the little chap's mes-

361

sage on paper. The sentences are labored, repetitious, and slow; there are but three or four of them; they deal in information solely, they contain no ideas, they venture no judgments, no opinions; they inform papa that the cat has had kittens again; that Mary has a new doll that can wink; that Tommy has lost his top; and will papa come soon and bring the writer something nice? But with Marjorie it is different.

She needs no amanuensis, she puts her message on paper herself; and not in weak and tottering Roman capitals, but in a thundering hand that can be heard a mile and be read across the square without glasses. And she doesn't have to study, and puzzle, and search her head for something to say; no, she had only to connect the pen with the paper and turn on the current; the words spring forth at once, and go chasing after each other like leaves dancing down a stream. For she has a faculty, has Marjorie! Indeed yes; when she sits down on her bottom to do a letter, there isn't going to be any lack of materials, nor of fluency, and neither is her letter going to be wanting in pepper, or vinegar, or vitriol, or any of the other condiments employed by genius to save a literary work of art from flatness and vapidity. And as for judgments and opinions, they are as commodiously in her line as they are in the Lord Chief Justice's. They have weight, too, and are convincing: for instance, for thirty-six years they have damaged that "horid Simpliton" in my eyes; and, more than that, they have even imposed upon me—and most unfairly and unwarrantably—an aver-

sion to the horid fat Simpliton's name; a perfectly
innocent name, and yet, because of the prejudice
against it with which this child has poisoned my
mind for a generation I cannot see "Potune" on
paper and keep my gorge from rising.

In her journals Marjorie changes her subject
whenever she wants to—and that is pretty often.
When the deep moralities pay her a passing visit
she registers them. Meantime if a cherished love
passage drifts across her memory she shoves it into
the midst of the moralities—it is nothing to her that
it may not feel at home there:

"We should not be happy at the death of our fellow creatures, for they love life like us love your
neighbor & he will love you Bountifulness and
Mercifulness are always rewarded. In my travels
I met with a handsome lad named Charles Balfour
Esge [Esqr.] and from him I got offers of marage—
ofers of marage did I say? nay plainly [he] loved me.
Goodness does not belong to the wicked but badness
dishonor befals wickedness but not virtue, no disgrace befals virtue perciverence overcomes almost
al difficulties no I am rong in saying almost I should
say always as it is so perciverence is a virtue my Csosin
says pacience is a cristain virtue, which is true."

She is not copying these profundities out of a book,
she is getting them out of her memory; her spelling
shows that the book is not before her. The easy
and effortless flow of her talk is a marvelous thing
in a baby of her age. Her interests are as wide and
varied as a grown person's: she discusses all sorts
of books, and fearlessly delivers judgment upon them;

she examines whomsoever crosses the field of her vision, and again delivers a verdict; she dips into religion and history, and even into politics; she takes a shy at the news of the day, and comments upon it; and now and then she drops into poetry— into rhyme, at any rate.

Marjorie would not intentionally mislead anyone, but she has just been making a remark which moves me to hoist a danger-signal for the protection of the modern reader. It is this one: *"In my travels."* Naturally we are apt to clothe a word with its present-day meaning—the meaning we are used to, the meaning we are familiar with; and so—well, you get the idea: some words that are giants to-day were very small dwarfs a century ago, and if we are not careful to take that vast enlargement into account when we run across them in the literatures of the past, they are apt to convey to us a distinctly wrong impression. To-day, when a person says *"in my travels"* he means that he has been around the globe nineteen or twenty times, and we so understand him; and so, when Marjorie says it, it startles us for a moment, for it gives us the impression that *she* has been around it fourteen or fifteen times; whereas, such is not at all the case. She has traveled prodigiously for *her* day, but not for ours. She had "traveled," altogether, three miles by land and eight by water—per ferryboat. She is fairly and justly proud of it, for it is the exact equivalent, in grandeur and impressiveness, in the case of a child of our day, to two trips across the Atlantic and a thousand miles by rail.

364

"In the love novels all the heroins are very desperate Isabella will not allow me to speak about lovers and heroins, and tiss too refined for my taste a loadstone is a curous thing indeed it is true Heroic love doth never win disgrace this is my maxum and I will follow it forever Miss Eguards [Edgeworth] tails are very good particularly some that are very much adopted for youth as Lazy Lawrence Tarelton False Key &c &c Persons of the parlement house are as I think caled Advocakes Mr Cay & Mr Crakey has that honour. This has been a very mild winter. Mr Banestors Budget is to-night I hope it will be a good one. A great many authors have expressed themselfs too sentimentaly. . . . The Mercandile Afares are in a perilous situation sickness & a delicante frame I have not & I do not know what it is, but Ah me perhaps I shall have it.[1] Grandure reigns in Edinburgh. . . . Tomson is a beautifull author and Pope but nothing is like Shakepear of which I have a little knolegde of. An unfortunate death James the 5 had for he died of greif Macbeth is a pretty composition but awful one Macbeth is so bad & wicked, but Lady Macbeth is so hardened in guilt she does not mind her sins & faults No.

". . . A sailor called here to say farewell, it must be dreadful to leave his native country where he might get a wife or perhaps me, for I love him very much & with all my heart, but O I forgot Isabella forbid me to speak about love. . . . I wish everybody would follow her example & be as good as

[1] It is a whole century since the dimly conscious little prophet said it, but the pathos of it is still there.

pious & virtious as she is & they would get husbands soon enough, love is a parithatick [pathetic] thing as well as troublesome & tiresome but O Isabella forbid me to speak about it."

But the little rascal can't *keep* from speaking about it, because it is her supreme interest in life; her heart is not capacious enough to hold all the product that is engendered by the ever-recurring inflaming spectacle of man-creatures going by, and the surplus is obliged to spill over; Isa's prohibitions are no sufficient dam for such a discharge.

"Love I think is the fasion for everybody is marring [marrying]. . . . Yesterday a marrade man named Mr John Balfour Esg [Esq.] offered to kiss me, & offered to marry me though the man was espused [espoused], & his wife was present & said he must ask her permission but he did not, I think he was ashamed or confounded before 3 gentleman Mr Jobson and two Mr Kings."

I must make room here for another of Marjorie's second-hand high-morality outbreaks. They give me a sinful delight which I ought to grieve at, I suppose, but I can't seem to manage it:

"James Macary is to be transported for murder in the flower of his youth O passion is a terible thing for it leads people from sin to sin at last it gets so far as to come to greater crimes than we thought we could comit and it must be dreadful to leave his native country and his friends and to be so disgraced and affronted."

That is Marjorie talking shop, dear little diplomat —to please and comfort mamma and Isa, no doubt.

This wee little child has a marvelous range of interests. She reads philosophies, novels, baby books, histories, the mighty poets—reads them with burning interest, and frankly and freely criticizes them all; she revels in storms, sunsets, cloud effects, scenery of mountain, plain, ocean, and forest, and all the other wonders of nature, and sets down her joy in them all; she loves people, she detests people, according to mood and circumstances, and delivers her opinion of them, sometimes seasoned with attar of roses, sometimes with vitriol; in games, and all kinds of childish play she is an enthusiast; she adores animals, adores them all; none is too forlorn to fail of favor in her friendly eyes, no creature so humble that she cannot find something in it on which to lavish her caressing worship.

"I am going to-morrow to a delightfull place, Braehead by name, belonging to Mrs. Crraford [Crauford], where there is ducks cocks hens bob-blyjocks 2 dogs 2 cats and swine which is delightful. I think it is shocking to think that the dog and cat should bear them and they are drowned after all."

She is a dear child, a bewitching little scamp; and never dearer, I think, than when the devil has had her in possession and she is breaking her stormy little heart over the remembrance of it:

"I confess I have been very more like a little young divil than a creature for when Isabella went up stairs to teach me religion and my multiplication and to be good and all my other lessons I stamped with my foot and threw my new hat which she had made on the ground and was sulky and was dread-

fully passionate, but she never whiped me but said
Marjory go into another room and think what a
great crime you are committing letting your temper
git the better of you.  But I went so sulkily that
the devil got the better of me but she never never
never whips me so that I think I would be the better
of it & the next time that I behave ill I think she
should do it for she never does it. . . . Isabella has
given me praise for checking my temper for I was
sulky even when she was kneeling an whole hour
teaching me to write."

The wise Isabella, the sweet and patient Isabella!
It is just a hundred years now (May, 1909) since
the grateful child made that golden picture of you
and laid your good heart bare for distant generations
to see and bless; a hundred years—but if the picture
endures a thousand it will still bring you the blessing, and with it the reverent homage that is your
due.  You had the seeing eye and the wise head.  A
fool would have punished Marjorie and wrecked
her, but you held your hand, as knowing that when
her volcanic fires went down she would repent, and
grieve, and punish herself, and be saved.

Sometimes when Marjorie was miraculously good,
she got a penny for it, and once when she got an
entire sixpence, she recognized that it was wealth.
This wealth brought joy to her heart.  Why?
Because she could spend it on somebody else!  We
who know Marjorie would know that without being
told it.  I am sorry—often sorry, often grieved—
that I was not there and looking over her shoulder
when she was writing down her valued penny

rewards: I would have said, "Save that scrap of manuscript, dear; make a will, and leave it to your posterity, to save them from want when penury shall threaten them; a day will come when it will be worth a thousand guineas, and a later day will come when it will be worth five thousand; here you are, rejoicing in copper farthings, and don't know that your magic pen is showering gold coin all over the paper." But I was not there to say it; those who were there did not think to say it; and so there is not a line of that quaint precious cacography in existence to-day.

I have adored Marjorie for six-and-thirty years; I have adored her in detail, I have adored the whole of her; but above all other details—just a little above all other details—I have adored her because she detested that odious and confusing and unvanquishable and unlearnable and shameless invention, the multiplication table:

"I am now going to tell you the horible and wretched plaege [plague] that my multiplication gives me you can't conceive it the most Devilish thing is 8 times 8 & 7 times 7 it is what nature itself cant endure."

I stand reverently uncovered in the presence of that holy verdict.

Here is that person again whom I so dislike—and for no reason at all except that my Marjorie doesn't like her:

"Miss Potune is very fat she pretends to be very learned she says she saw a stone that dropt from the skies, but she is a good christian."

Of course, stones have fallen from the skies, but I don't believe this "horid fat Simpliton" had ever seen one that had done it; but even if she had, it was none of her business, and she could have been better employed than in going around exaggerating it and carrying on about it and trying to make trouble with a little child that had never done *her* any harm.

". . . The Birds do chirp the Lambs do leap and Nature is clothed with the garments of green yellow, and white, purple, and red.

". . . There is a book that is called the Newgate Calender that contains all the Murders: all the Murders did I say, nay all Thefts & Forgeries that ever were committed & fills me with horror & consternation."

Marjorie is a diligent little student, and her education is always storming along and making great time and lots of noise:

"Isabella this morning taught me some French words one of which is bon suar the interpretation is good morning."

It slanders Isabella, but the slander is not intentional. The main thing to notice is that big word, "interpretation." Not many children of Marjorie's age can handle a five syllable team in that easy and confident way. It is observable that she frequently employs words of an imposingly formidable size, and is manifestly quite familiar with them and not at all afraid of them.

"Isa is teaching me to make Simecolings nots of interrigations periods & commas &c. As this is Sunday I will meditate uppon senciable & Religious subjects first I should be very thankful I am not a beggar as many are."

That was the "first." She didn't get to her second subject, but got side-tracked by a saner interest, and used her time to better purpose.

"It is melancholy to think, that I have so many talents, & many there are that have not had the attention paid to them that I have, & yet they contrive to be better then me.

". . . Isabella is far too indulgent to me & even the Miss Crafords say that they wonder at her patience with me & it is indeed true for my temper is a bad one."

The daring child wrote a (synopsized) history of Mary Queen of Scots and of five of the royal Jameses in rhyme—but never mind, we have no room to discuss it here. Nothing was entirely beyond her literary jurisdiction; if it had occurred to her that the laws of Rome needed codifying she would have taken a chance at it.

Here is a sad note:

"My religion is greatly falling off because I dont pray with so much attention when I am saying my prayers and my character is lost a-mong the Breahead people I hope I will be religious again but as for regaining my character I despare of it."

When religion and character go, they leave a large vacuum. But there are ways to fill it:

"I've forgot to say, but I've four lovers, the other one is Harry Watson, a very delightful boy. . . . James Keith hardly ever Spoke to me, he said Girl!

make less noise. . . . Craky hall . . . I walked to that delightfull place with a delightful young man beloved by all his friends and espacialy by me his loveress but I must not talk any longer about him for Isa said it is not proper for to speak of gentalman but I will never forget him. . . .

"The Scythians tribe live very coarsely for a Gluton Introduced to Arsaces the Captain of the Army, 1 man who Dressed hair & another man who was a good cook but Arsaces said that he would keep 1 for brushing his horses tail and the other to fead his pigs. . . .

"On Saturday I expected no less than three well-made bucks, the names of whom is here advertised. Mr. Geo. Crakey [Cragie], and Wm. Keith and Jn Keith—the first is the funniest of every one of them. Mr. Crakey and I walked to Craky-hall [Craigiehall] hand and hand in Innocence and matitation sweet thinking on the kind love which flows in our tender hearted mind which is overflowing with majestic pleasure no one was ever so polite to me in the hole state of my existence. Mr. Craky you must know is a great Buck and pretty good-looking."

For a purpose, I wish the reader to take careful note of these statistics:

"I am going to tell you of a melancholy story. A young turkie of 2 or 3 months old, would you believe it, the father broke its leg, & he killed another! I think he ought to be transported or hanged."

Marjorie wrote some verses about this tragedy—I

think.  I cannot be quite certain it is this one, for in the verses there are three deaths, whereas these statistics do not furnish so many.  Also in the statistics the father of the deceased is indifferent about the loss he has sustained, whereas in the verses he is not.  Also in the third verse, the *mother*, too, exhibits feeling, whereas in the two closing verses of the poem she—at least it seems to be she—is indifferent.  At least it looks like indifference to me, and I believe it *is* indifference:

> "Three turkeys fair their last have breathed,
> And now this world forever leaved;
> Their father, and their mother too,
> They sighed and weep as well as you;
> Indeed, the rats their bones have cranched.
> Into eternity theire launched.
> A direful death indeed they had,
> As wad put any parent mad;
> But she was more than usual calm,
> She did not give a single dam."

The naughty little scamp!  I mean, for not leaving out the *l* in the word "Calm," so as to perfect the rhyme.  It seems a pity to damage with a lame rhyme a couplet that is otherwise without a blemish.

Marjorie wrote four journals.  She began the first one in January, 1809, when she was just six years old, and finished it five months later, in June.

She began the second in the following month, and finished it six months afterward (January, 1810), when she was just seven.

She began the third one in April, 1810, and finished it in the autumn.

She wrote the fourth in the winter of 1810-11, and the last entry in it bears date July 19, 1811, and she died exactly five months later, December 19th, aged eight years and eleven months. It contains her rhymed Scottish histories.

Let me quote from Dr. John Brown:

"The day before her death, Sunday, she sat up in bed, worn and thin, her eye gleaming as with the light of a coming world, and with a tremulous, old voice repeated a long poem by Burns—heavy with the shadow of death, and lit with the fantasy of the judgment seat—the publican's prayer in paraphrase, beginning:

" 'Why am I loth to leave this earthly scene?
    Have I so found it full of pleasing charms?
  Some drops of joy, with draughts of ill between,
    Some gleams of sunshine 'mid renewing storms.'

"It is more affecting than we care to say to read her mother's and Isabella Keith's letters written immediately after her death. Old and withered, tattered and pale, they are now; but when you read them, how quick, how throbbing with life and love! how rich in that language of affection which only women, and Shakespeare, and Luther can use—that power of detaining the soul over the beloved object and its loss."

Fifty years after Marjorie's death her sister, writing to Dr. Brown, said:

"My mother was struck by the patient quietness manifested by Marjorie during this illness, unlike her ardent, impulsive nature; but love and poetic feeling were unquenched. When Dr. Johnstone

374

rewarded her submissiveness with a sixpence, the
request speedily followed that she might get out ere
New Year's Day came.  When asked why she was so
desirous of getting out, she immediately rejoined:
'Oh, I am so anxious to buy something with my
sixpence for my dear Isa Keith.'  Again, when lying
very still, her mother asked her if there was anything
she wished: 'Oh yes, if you would just leave the
room door open a wee bit, and play the *Land o' the
Leal*, and I will lie and *think* and enjoy myself'
(this is just as stated to me by her mother and mine).
Well, the happy day came, alike to parents and child,
when Marjorie was allowed to come forth from the
nursery to the parlor.  It was Sabbath evening, and
after tea.  My father, who idolized this child, and
never afterward in my hearing mentioned her name,
took her in his arms; and while walking her up and
down the room she said: 'Father, I will repeat something to you;  what would you like?'  He said,
'Just choose for yourself, Maidie.'  She hesitated for
a moment between the paraphrase, 'Few are thy
days and full of woe,' and the lines of Burns already
quoted, but decided on the latter; a remarkable
choice for a child.  The repeating of these lines
seemed to stir up the depths of feeling in her soul.
She asked to be allowed to write a poem.  There
was a doubt whether it would be right to allow her,
in case of hurting her eyes.  She pleaded earnestly,
'Just this once'; the point was yielded, her slate
was given her, and with great rapidity she wrote an
address of fourteen lines 'To my loved cousin on the
author's recovery.'"

The cousin was Isa Keith.

"She went to bed apparently well, awoke in the middle of the night with the old cry of woe to a mother's heart, 'My head, my head!' Three days of the dire malady, 'water in the head,' followed, and the end came."

# ADAM'S SOLILOQUY

(The spirit of Adam is supposed to be visiting New York City
inspecting the dinosaur at the Museum of Natural History)

(1905)

## I

IT is strange . . . very strange. *I* do not remember this creature. (*After gazing long and admiringly.*) Well, it is wonderful! The mere *skeleton*
fifty-seven feet long and sixteen feet high! Thus
far, it seems, they've found only this sample—without doubt a merely medium-sized one; a person
could not step out here into the Park and happen
by luck upon the largest horse in America; no, he
would happen upon one that would look small alongside of the biggest Normandy. It is quite likely that
the biggest dinosaur was ninety feet long and twenty
feet high. It would be five times as long as an elephant; an elephant would be to it what a calf is to an
elephant. The bulk of the creature! The weight of
him! As long as the longest whale, and twice the substance in him! And all good wholesome pork, most
likely; meat enough to last a village a year. . . .
Think of a hundred of them in line, draped in shining
cloth of gold!—a majestic thing for a coronation procession. But expensive, for he would eat much; only
kings and millionaires could afford him.

I have no recollection of him; neither Eve nor I

had heard of him until yesterday. We spoke to
Noah about him; he colored and changed the subject. Being brought back to it—and pressed a
little—he confessed that in the matter of stocking
the Ark the stipulations had not been carried out
with absolute strictness—that is, in minor details,
unessentials. There were some irregularities. He
said the boys were to blame for this—the boys
mainly, his own fatherly indulgence partly. They
were in the giddy heyday of their youth at the time,
the happy springtime of life; their hundred years sat
upon them lightly, and—well, he had once been a
boy himself, and he had not the heart to be too
exacting with them. And so—well, they did things
they shouldn't have done, and he—to be candid, he
winked. But on the whole they did pretty faithful
work, considering their age. They collected and
stowed a good share of the really useful animals;
and also, when Noah was not watching, a multitude
of useless ones, such as flies, mosquitoes, snakes,
and so on, but they did certainly leave ashore a
good many creatures which might possibly have
had value some time or other, in the course of time.
Mainly these were vast saurians a hundred feet
long, and monstrous mammals, such as the mega-
therium and that sort, and there was really some
excuse for leaving them behind, for two reasons:
(1) it was manifest that some time or other they
would be needed as fossils for museums and (2)
there had been a miscalculation, the Ark was smaller
than it should have been, and so there wasn't room
for those creatures. There was actually fossil mate-

rial enough all by itself to freight twenty-five Arks like that one. As for the dinosaur—— But Noah's conscience was easy; it was not named in his cargo list and he and the boys were not aware that there was such a creature. He said he could not blame himself for not knowing about the dinosaur, because it was an American animal, and America had not then been discovered.

Noah went on to say, "I did reproach the boys for not making the most of the room we had, by discarding trashy animals and substituting beasts like the mastodon, which could be useful to man in doing heavy work such as the elephant performs, but they said those great creatures would have increased our labors beyond our strength, in the matter of feeding and watering them, we being short-handed. There was something in that. We had no pump; there was but one window; we had to let down a bucket from that, and haul it up a good fifty feet, which was very tiresome; then we had to carry the water downstairs—fifty feet again, in cases where it was for the elephants and their kind, for we kept them in the hold to serve for ballast. As it was, we lost many animals—choice animals that would have been valuable in menageries—different breeds of lions, tigers, hyenas, wolves, and so on; for they wouldn't drink the water after the salt sea water got mixed with the fresh. But we never lost a locust, nor a grasshopper, nor a weevil, nor a rat, nor a cholera germ, nor any of that sort of beings. On the whole, I think we did very well, everything considered. We were shepherds and farmers; we had never been to sea before; we were ignorant of naval matters, and I know this for certain, that there is more difference between agriculture and navigation than a person would think. It is my opinion that the two trades do not belong together. Shem thinks the same; so does Japheth. As for what Ham thinks, it is not important. Ham is biased. You find me a Presbyterian that isn't, if you think you can."

He said it aggressively; it had in it the spirit of a challenge. I avoided argument by changing the subject. With Noah, arguing is a passion, a disease, and it is growing upon him; has been growing upon him for thirty thousand years, and more. It makes him unpopular, unpleasant; many of his oldest friends dread to meet him. Even strangers soon get to avoiding him, although at first they are glad to meet him and gaze at him, on account of his celebrated adventure. For a time they are proud of his notice, because he is so distinguished; but he argues them to rags, and before long they begin to wish, like the rest, that something had happened to the Ark.

## II

(*On the bench in the Park, midafternoon, dreamily noting the drift of the human species back and forth.*) To think—this multitude is but a wee little fraction of the earth's population! And all blood kin to me, every one! Eve ought to have come with me; this would excite her affectionate heart. She was never able to keep her composure when she came upon a relative; she would try to kiss every one of these people, black and white and all. (*A baby wagon passes.*) How little change one can notice—none at all, in fact. I remember the first child well—— Let me see . . . it is three hundred thousand years ago come Tuesday. This one is just like it. So between the first one and the last one there is really nothing to choose. The same insufficiency of hair, the same absence of teeth, the same feebleness of body and apparent vacancy of mind, the same general unattractiveness all around. Yet Eve worshiped that early one, and it was pretty to see her with it. This latest one's mother worships *it;* it shows in her eyes—it is the very look that used to shine in Eve's. To think that so subtle and intangible a thing as a *look* could flit and flash from face to face down a procession three hundred thousand years long and remain the same, without shade of change! Yet here it is, lighting this young creature's face just as it lighted Eve's in the long ago—the newest thing I have seen in the earth, and the oldest. Of course, the dinosaur—— But that is in another class.

She drew the baby wagon to the bench and sat down and began to shove it softly back and forth with one hand while she held up a newspaper with the other and absorbed herself in its contents. Presently, "My!" she exclaimed; which startled me, and I ventured to ask her, modestly and respectfully, what was the matter. She courteously passed the paper to me and said—pointing with her finger:

"There—it reads like fact, but I don't know."

It was very embarrassing. I tried to look at my ease, and nonchalantly turned the paper this and that and the other way, but her eye was upon me and I felt that I was not succeeding. Pretty soon she asked, hesitatingly:

"Can't—can't—you—read?"

I had to confess that I couldn't. It filled her with wonder. But it had one pleasant effect—it interested her in me, and I was thankful, for I was getting lonesome for some one to talk to and listen to. The young fellow who was showing me around —on his own motion, I did not invite him—had missed his appointment at the Museum, and I was feeling disappointed, for he was good company. When I told the young woman I could not read, she asked me another embarrassing question:

"Where are you from?"

I skirmished—to gain time and position. I said:

"Make a guess. See how near you can come."

She brightened, and exclaimed:

"I shall dearly like it, sir, if you don't mind. If I guess right will you tell me?"

"Yes."

"Honor bright?"

"Honor bright? What is that?"

She laughed delightedly and said:

"That's a good start! I was *sure* that that phrase would catch you. I know one thing, now, all right. I know——"

"What do you know?"

"That you are not an American. And you aren't, *are* you?"

"No. You are right. I'm not—honor bright, as you say."

She looked immensely pleased with herself, and said:

"I reckon I'm not always smart, but *that* was smart, anyway. But not so *very*, after all, because I already knew—believed I knew—that you were a foreigner, by another sign."

"What was that?"

"Your accent."

She was an accurate observer; I do speak English with a heavenly accent, and she had detected the foreign twang in it. She ran charmingly on, most naïvely and engagingly pleased with her triumph:

"The minute you said, 'See 'ow near you can come to it,' I said to myself, 'Two to one he is a foreigner, and ten to one he's English.' Now that *is* your nationality, *isn't* it?"

I was sorry to spoil her victory, but I had to do it: "Ah—you'll have to guess again."

"What—you are not an Englishman?"

"No—honor bright."

She looked me searchingly over, evidently communing with herself—adding up my points, then she said:

"Well, you don't *look* like an Englishman, and that is true." After a little she added, "The fact is, you don't look like *any* foreigner—not quite like . . . like *anybody* I've seen before. I will guess some more."

She guessed every country whose name she could think of and grew gradually discouraged. Finally she said:

"You must be the Man Without a Country—the

one the story tells about. You don't seem to have
any nationality at all. How did you come to come
to America? Have you any kinfolks here?"

"Yes—several."

"Oh, then you came to see *them*."

"Partly—yes."

She sat awhile, thinking, then:

"Well, I'm not going to give up quite yet. Where
do you live when you are at home—in a city, or in
the country?"

"Which do you think?"

"Well, I don't quite know. You *do* look a little
countrified, if you don't mind my saying it; but
you look a little citified, too—not much, but a little,
although you can't read, which is very curious, and
you are not used to newspapers. Now *my* guess is
that you live mainly in the country when you are at
home, and not very much in the city. Is that right?"

"Yes, quite right."

"Oh, good! Now I'll take a fresh start."

Then she wore herself to the bone, naming cities.
No success. Next she wanted me to help her a
little with some "pointers," as she phrased it. Was
my city large? Yes. Was it very large? Yes. Did
they have mobiles there? No. Electric light? No.
Railroads, hospitals, colleges, cops? No.

"Why, then, it's not civilized! Where *can* that
place be? Be good and tell me just one peculiarity
of it—then maybe I can guess."

"Well, then, just one; it has gates of pearl."

"Oh, go along! That's the New Jerusalem. It
isn't fair to joke. Never mind. I'll guess it yet—it

will come into my head pretty soon, just when I'm
not expecting it. Oh, I've got an idea! Please talk
a little in your own language—that 'll be a good
pointer." I accommodated her with a sentence or
two. She shook her head despondently.

"No," she said, "it doesn't sound human. I
mean, it doesn't sound like any of these other foreigners. It's pretty enough—it's quite pretty, I
think—but I'm sure I've not heard it before. Maybe
if you were to pronounce your name—— What *is*
your name, if you'll be so good?"

"Adam."

"Adam?"

"Yes."

"But Adam *what?*"

"That is all—just Adam."

"Nothing at all but just that? Why, how curious!
There's plenty of Adams; how can they tell you
from the rest?"

"Oh, that is no trouble. I'm the only one there
is, there where I'm from."

"Upon my word! Well, it beats the band! It
reminds a person of the old original. That was his
name, too, and he hadn't any but that—just like
you." Then, archly, "You've heard of him, I
suppose?"

"Oh yes! Do you know him? Have you ever
seen him?"

"*Seen* him? Seen *Adam?* Thanks to goodness,
no! It would scare me into fits."

"I don't see why."

"You don't?"

"No."

"*Why* don't you see why?"

"Because there is no sense in a person being scared of his kin."

"*Kin?*"

"Yes. Isn't he a distant relative of yours?"

She thought it was prodigiously funny, and said it was perfectly true, but *she* never would have been bright enough to think of it. I found it a new and most pleasant sensation to have my wit admired, and was about to try to do some more when that young fellow came. He planted himself on the other side of the young woman and began a vapid remark about the weather, but she gave him a look that withered him and got stiffly up and wheeled the baby away.

# BIBLE TEACHING AND RELIGIOUS PRACTICE

RELIGION had its share in the changes of civilization and national character, of course. What share? The lion's. In the history of the human race this has always been the case, will always be the case, to the end of time, no doubt; or at least until man by the slow processes of evolution shall develop into something really fine and high—some billions of years hence, say.

The Christian's Bible is a drug store. Its contents remain the same; but the medical practice changes. For eighteen hundred years these changes were slight—scarcely noticeable. The practice was allopathic—allopathic in its rudest and crudest form. The dull and ignorant physician day and night, and all the days and all the nights, drenched his patient with vast and hideous doses of the most repulsive drugs to be found in the store's stock; he bled him, cupped him, purged him, puked him, salivated him, never gave his system a chance to rally, nor nature a chance to help. He kept him religion sick for eighteen centuries, and allowed him not a well day during all that time. The stock in the store was made up of about equal portions of baleful and debilitating poisons, and healing and comforting medicines; but the practice of the time confined

the physician to the use of the former; by consequence, he could only damage his patient, and that
is what he did.

Not until far within our century was any considerable change in the practice introduced; and then
mainly, or in effect only, in Great Britain and the
United States. In the other countries to-day, the
patient either still takes the ancient treatment or
does not call the physician at all. In the English-
speaking countries the changes observable in our
century were forced by that very thing just referred
to—the revolt of the patient against the system;
they were not projected by the physician. The
patient fell to doctoring himself, and the physician's
practice began to fall off. He modified his method
to get back his trade. He did it gradually, reluctantly; and never yielded more at a time than the
pressure compelled. At first he relinquished the
daily dose of hell and damnation, and administered
it every other day only; next he allowed another
day to pass; then another and presently another;
when he had restricted it at last to Sundays, and
imagined that now there would surely be a truce,
the homœopath arrived on the field and made him
abandon hell and damnation altogether, and administered Christ's love, and comfort, and charity and
compassion in its stead. These had been in the drug
store all the time, gold labeled and conspicuous among
the long shelfloads of repulsive purges and vomits and
poisons, and so the practice was to blame that they
had remained unused, not the pharmacy. To the
ecclesiastical physician of fifty years ago, his pred-

ecessor for eighteen centuries was a quack; to the ecclesiastical physician of to-day, his predecessor of fifty years ago was a quack. To the every-man-his-own-ecclesiastical-doctor of—when?—what will the ecclesiastical physician of to-day be? Unless evolution, which has been a truth ever since the globes, suns, and planets of the solar system were but wandering films of meteor dust, shall reach a limit and become a lie, there is but one fate in store for him.

The methods of the priest and the parson have been very curious, their history is very entertaining. In all the ages the Roman Church has owned slaves, bought and sold slaves, authorized and encouraged her children to trade in them. Long after some Christian peoples had freed their slaves the Church still held on to hers. If any could know, to absolute certainty, that all this was right, and according to God's will and desire, surely it was she, since she was God's specially appointed representative in the earth and sole authorized and infallible expounder of his Bible. There were the texts; there was no mistaking their meaning; she was right, she was doing in this thing what the Bible had mapped out for her to do. So unassailable was her position that in all the centuries she had no word to say against human slavery. Yet now at last, in our immediate day, we hear a Pope saying slave trading is wrong, and we see him sending an expedition to Africa to stop it. The texts remain: it is the practice that has changed. Why? Because the world has corrected the Bible. The Church never corrects it; and also never fails to drop in at the tail of the procession—and take the credit of the correction. As she will presently do in this instance.

Christian England supported slavery and encouraged it for two hundred and fifty years, and her Church's consecrated ministers looked on, sometimes taking an active hand, the rest of the time indifferent. England's interest in the business may be called a Christian interest, a Christian industry. She had her full share in its revival after a long period of inactivity, and this revival was a Christian monopoly; that is to say, it was in the hands of Christian countries exclusively. English parliaments aided the slave traffic and protected it; two English kings held stock in slave-catching companies. The first regular English slave hunter—John Hawkins, of still revered memory—made such successful havoc, on his second voyage, in the matter of surprising and burning villages, and maiming, slaughtering, capturing, and selling their unoffending inhabitants, that his delighted queen conferred the chivalric honor of knighthood on him—a rank which had acquired its chief esteem and distinction in other and earlier fields of Christian effort. The new knight, with characteristic English frankness and brusque simplicity, chose as his device the figure of a negro slave, kneeling and in chains. Sir John's work was the invention of Christians, was to remain a bloody and awful monopoly in the hands of Christians for a quarter of a millennium, was to destroy homes, separate families, enslave friendless men and women, and break a myriad of human hearts, to the end that Christian nations might be prosperous and comfortable, Christian churches be built, and the gospel of the meek and merciful Redeemer be spread abroad in the earth; and so in the name of his ship, unsuspected but eloquent and clear, lay hidden prophecy. She was called *The Jesus*.

But at last in England, an illegitimate Christian rose against slavery. It is curious that when a Christian rises against a rooted wrong at all, he is usually an illegitimate Christian, member of some despised and bastard sect. There was a bitter struggle, but in the end the slave trade had to go— and went. The Biblical authorization remained, but the practice changed.

Then—the usual thing happened; the visiting English critic among us began straightway to hold up his pious hands in horror at our slavery. His distress was unappeasable, his words full of bitterness and contempt. It is true we had not so many as fifteen hundred thousand slaves for him to worry about, while his England still owned twelve millions, in her foreign possessions; but that fact did not modify his wail any, or stay his tears, or soften his censure. The fact that every time we had tried to get rid of our slavery in previous generations, but had always been obstructed, balked, and defeated by England, was a matter of no consequence to him; it was ancient history, and not worth the telling.

Our own conversion came at last. We began to stir against slavery. Hearts grew soft, here, there, and yonder. There was no place in the land where the seeker could not find some small budding sign of

pity for the slave.  No place in all the land but one
—the pulpit.  It yielded at last;  it always does.  It
fought a strong and stubborn fight, and then did what
it always does, joined the procession—at the tail end.
Slavery fell.  The slavery text remained;  the practice
changed, that was all.

During many ages there were witches.  The Bible
said so.  The Bible commanded that they should not
be allowed to live.  Therefore the Church, after
doing its duty in but a lazy and indolent way for
eight hundred years, gathered up its halters, thumb-
screws, and firebrands, and set about its holy work
in earnest.  She worked hard at it night and day
during nine centuries and imprisoned, tortured,
hanged, and burned whole hordes and armies of
witches, and washed the Christian world clean with
their foul blood.

Then it was discovered that there was no such
thing as witches, and never had been.  One does not
know whether to laugh or to cry.  Who discovered
that there was no such thing as a witch—the priest,
the parson?  No, these never discover anything.
At Salem, the parson clung pathetically to his witch
text after the laity had abandoned it in remorse and
tears for the crimes and cruelties it has persuaded
them to do.  The parson wanted more blood, more
shame, more brutalities;  it was the unconsecrated
laity that stayed his hand.  In Scotland the parson
killed the witch after the magistrate had pronounced
her innocent;  and when the merciful legislature proposed to sweep the hideous laws against witches from
the statute book, it was the parson who came implor-

ing, with tears and imprecations, that they be suffered to stand.

There are no witches. The witch text remains; only the practice has changed. Hell fire is gone, but the text remains. Infant damnation is gone, but the text remains. More than two hundred death penalties are gone from the law books, but the texts that authorized them remain.

Is it not well worthy of note that of all the multitude of texts through which man has driven his annihilating pen he has never once made the mistake of obliterating a good and useful one? It does certainly seem to suggest that if man continues in the direction of enlightenment, his religious practice may, in the end, attain some semblance of human decency.

# THE WAR PRAYER

(Dictated 1904-05)

IT was a time of great and exalting excitement. The country was up in arms, the war was on, in every breast burned the holy fire of patriotism; the drums were beating, the bands playing, the toy pistols popping, the bunched firecrackers hissing and spluttering; on every hand and far down the receding and fading spread of roofs and balconies a fluttering wilderness of flags flashed in the sun; daily the young volunteers marched down the wide avenue gay and fine in their new uniforms, the proud fathers and mothers and sisters and sweethearts cheering them with voices choked with happy emotion as they swung by; nightly the packed mass meetings listened, panting, to patriot oratory which stirred the deepest deeps of their hearts, and which they interrupted at briefest intervals with cyclones of applause, the tears running down their cheeks the while; in the churches the pastors preached devotion to flag and country, and invoked the God of Battles, beseeching His aid in our good cause in an outpouring of fervid eloquence which moved every listener. It was indeed a glad and gracious time, and the half dozen rash spirits that ventured to disapprove of the war and cast a doubt upon its righteousness straightway got such a stern and angry

394

warning that for their personal safety's sake they quickly shrank out of sight and offended no more in that way.

Sunday morning came—next day the battalions would leave for the front; the church was filled; the volunteers were there, their young faces alight with martial dreams—visions of the stern advance, the gathering momentum, the rushing charge, the flashing sabers, the flight of the foe, the tumult, the enveloping smoke, the fierce pursuit, the surrender!— them home from the war, bronzed heroes, welcomed, adored, submerged in golden seas of glory! With the volunteers sat their dear ones, proud, happy, and envied by the neighbors and friends who had no sons and brothers to send forth to the field of honor, there to win for the flag, or, failing, die the noblest of noble deaths. The service proceeded; a war chapter from the Old Testament was read; the first prayer was said; it was followed by an organ burst that shook the building, and with one impulse the house rose, with glowing eyes and beating hearts, and poured out that tremendous invocation —

"God the all-terrible! Thou who ordainest,
    Thunder thy clarion and lightning thy sword!"

Then came the "long" prayer. None could remember the like of it for passionate pleading and moving and beautiful language. The burden of its supplication was, that an ever-merciful and benignant Father of us all would watch over our noble young soldiers, and aid, comfort, and encourage them in their patriotic work; bless them, shield them in the day of battle and the hour of peril, bear them in His mighty hand, make them strong and confident, invincible in the bloody onset; help them to crush the foe, grant to them and to their flag and country imperishable honor and glory—

An aged stranger entered and moved with slow and noiseless step up the main aisle, his eyes fixed upon the minister, his long body clothed in a robe that reached to his feet, his head bare, his white hair descending in a frothy cataract to his shoulders, his seamy face unnaturally pale, pale even to ghastliness. With all eyes following him and wondering, he made his silent way; without pausing, he ascended to the preacher's side and stood there, waiting. With shut lids the preacher, unconscious of his presence, continued his moving prayer, and at last finished it with the words, uttered in fervent appeal, "Bless our arms, grant us the victory, O Lord our God, Father and Protector of our land and flag!"

The stranger touched his arm, motioned him to step aside—which the startled minister did—and took his place. During some moments he surveyed the spellbound audience with solemn eyes, in which burned an uncanny light; then in a deep voice he said:

"I come from the Throne—bearing a message from Almighty God!" The words smote the house with a shock; if the stranger perceived it he gave no attention. "He has heard the prayer of His servant your shepherd, and will grant it if such shall be your desire after I, His messenger, shall have explained to you its import—that is to say, its full import.

For it is like unto many of the prayers of men, in that it asks for more than he who utters it is aware of—except he pause and think.

"God's servant and yours has prayed his prayer. Has he paused and taken thought? Is it one prayer? No, it is two—one uttered, the other not. Both have reached the ear of Him Who heareth all supplications, the spoken and the unspoken. Ponder this —keep it in mind. If you would beseech a blessing upon yourself, beware! lest without intent you invoke a curse upon a neighbor at the same time. If you pray for the blessing of rain upon your crop which needs it, by that act you are possibly praying for a curse upon some neighbor's crop which may not need rain and can be injured by it.

"You have heard your servant's prayer—the uttered part of it. I am commissioned of God to put into words the other part of it—that part which the pastor—and also you in your hearts— fervently prayed silently. And ignorantly and unthinkingly? God grant that it was so! You heard these words: 'Grant us the victory, O Lord our God!' That is sufficient. The *whole* of the uttered prayer is compact into those pregnant words Elaborations were not necessary. When you have prayed for victory you have prayed for many unmentioned results which follow victory—*must* follow it, cannot help but follow it. Upon the listening spirit of God the Father fell also the unspoken part of the prayer. He commandeth me to put it into words. Listen!

"O Lord our Father, our young patriots, idols of

our hearts, go forth to battle—be Thou near them!
With them—in spirit—we also go forth from the
sweet peace of our beloved firesides to smite the foe.
O Lord our God, help us to tear their soldiers to
bloody shreds with our shells; help us to cover their
smiling fields with the pale forms of their patriot
dead; help us to drown the thunder of the guns with
the shrieks of their wounded, writhing in pain; help
us to lay waste their humble homes with a hurricane
of fire; help us to wring the hearts of their unoffending widows with unavailing grief; help us to turn
them out roofless with their little children to wander
unfriended the wastes of their desolated land in rags
and hunger and thirst, sports of the sun flames of
summer and the icy winds of winter, broken in
spirit, worn with travail, imploring Thee for the
refuge of the grave and denied it—for our sakes who
adore Thee, Lord, blast their hopes, blight their
lives, protract their bitter pilgrimage, make heavy
their steps, water their way with their tears, stain
the white snow with the blood of their wounded
feet! We ask it, in the spirit of love, of Him Who
is the Source of Love, and Who is the ever-faithful
refuge and friend of all that are sore beset and seek
His aid with humble and contrite hearts. Amen."

(*After a pause.*) "Ye have prayed it; if ye still
desire it, speak! The messenger of the Most High
waits."

It was believed afterward that the man was a
lunatic, because there was no sense in what he said.

# CORN-PONE OPINIONS

(Written in 1900)

FIFTY years ago, when I was a boy of fifteen and helping to inhabit a Missourian village on the banks of the Mississippi, I had a friend whose society was very dear to me because I was forbidden by my mother to partake of it. He was a gay and impudent and satirical and delightful young black man—a slave—who daily preached sermons from the top of his master's woodpile, with me for sole audience. He imitated the pulpit style of the several clergymen of the village, and did it well, and with fine passion and energy. To me he was a wonder. I believed he was the greatest orator in the United States and would some day be heard from. But it did not happen; in the distribution of rewards he was overlooked. It is the way, in this world.

He interrupted his preaching, now and then, to saw a stick of wood; but the sawing was a pretense —he did it with his mouth; exactly imitating the sound the bucksaw makes in shrieking its way through the wood. But it served its purpose; it kept his master from coming out to see how the work was getting along. I listened to the sermons from the open window of a lumber room at the back of the house. One of his texts was this:

"You tell me whar a man gits his corn pone, en I'll tell you what his 'pinions is."

I can never forget it. It was deeply impressed upon me. By my mother. Not upon my memory, but elsewhere. She had slipped in upon me while I was absorbed and not watching. The black philosopher's idea was that a man is not independent, and cannot afford views which might interfere with his bread and butter. If he would prosper, he must train with the majority; in matters of large moment, like politics and religion, he must think and feel with the bulk of his neighbors, or suffer damage in his social standing and in his business prosperities. He must restrict himself to corn-pone opinions—at least on the surface. He must get his opinions from other people; he must reason out none for himself; he must have no first-hand views.

I think Jerry was right, in the main, but I think he did not go far enough.

1. It was his idea that a man conforms to the majority view of his locality by calculation and intention.

This happens, but I think it is not the rule.

2. It was his idea that there is such a thing as a first-hand opinion; an original opinion; an opinion which is coldly reasoned out in a man's head, by a searching analysis of the facts involved, with the heart unconsulted, and the jury room closed against outside influences. It may be that such an opinion has been born somewhere, at some time or other, but I suppose it got away before they could catch it and stuff it and put it in the museum.

I am persuaded that a coldly-thought-out and independent verdict upon a fashion in clothes, or

manners, or literature, or politics, or religion, or
any other matter that is projected into the field of
our notice and interest, is a most rare thing—if it
has indeed ever existed.

A new thing in costume appears—the flaring hoopskirt, for example—and the passers-by are shocked,
and the irreverent laugh. Six months later everybody is reconciled; the fashion has established itself;
is is admired, now, and no one laughs. Public opinion
resented it before, public opinion accepts it now, and
is happy in it. Why? Was the resentment reasoned
out? Was the acceptance reasoned out? No. The
instinct that moves to conformity did the work. It
is our nature to conform; it is a force which not
many can successfully resist. What is its seat? The
inborn requirement of self-approval. We all have
to bow to that; there are no exceptions. Even the
woman who refuses from first to last to wear the
hoopskirt comes under that law and is its slave;
she could not wear the skirt and have her own
approval; and that she *must* have, she cannot help
herself. But as a rule our self-approval has its
source in but one place and not elsewhere—the
approval of other people. A person of vast consequences can introduce any kind of novelty in dress
and the general world will presently adopt it—moved
to do it, in the first place, by the natural instinct to
passively yield to that vague something recognized
as authority, and in the second place by the human
instinct to train with the multitude and have its
approval. An empress introduced the hoopskirt,
and we know the result. A nobody introduced the

bloomer, and we know the result. If Eve should come again, in her ripe renown, and reintroduce her quaint styles—well, we know what would happen. And we should be cruelly embarrassed, along at first.

The hoopskirt runs its course and disappears. Nobody reasons about it. One woman abandons the fashion; her neighbor notices this and follows her lead; this influences the next woman; and so on and so on, and presently the skirt has vanished out of the world, no one knows how nor why; nor cares, for that matter. It will come again, by and by; and in due course will go again.

Twenty-five years ago, in England, six or eight wine glasses stood grouped by each person's plate at a dinner party, and they were used, not left idle and empty; to-day there are but three or four in the group, and the average guest sparingly uses about two of them. We have not adopted this new fashion yet, but we shall do it presently. We shall not think it out; we shall merely conform, and let it go at that. We get our notions and habits and opinions from outside influences; we do not have to study them out.

Our table manners, and company manners, and street manners change from time to time, but the changes are not reasoned out; we merely notice and conform. We are creatures of outside influences; as a rule we do not think, we only imitate. We cannot invent standards that will stick; what we mistake for standards are only fashions, and perishable. We may continue to admire them, but we drop the use of them. We notice this in literature. Shakespeare is a standard, and fifty years ago we used to write tragedies which we couldn't tell from—from somebody else's; but we don't do it any more, now. Our prose standard, three quarters of a century ago, was ornate and diffuse; some authority or other changed it in the direction of compactness and simplicity, and conformity followed, without argument. The historical novel starts up suddenly, and sweeps the land. Everybody writes one, and the nation is glad. We had historical novels before; but nobody read them, and the rest of us conformed—without reasoning it out. We are conforming in the other way, now, because it is another case of everybody.

The outside influences are always pouring in upon us, and we are always obeying their orders and accepting their verdicts. The Smiths like the new play; the Joneses go to see it, and they copy the Smith verdict. Morals, religions, politics, get their following from surrounding influences and atmospheres, almost entirely; not from study, not from thinking. A man must and will have his own approval first of all, in each and every moment and circumstance of his life—even if he must repent of a self-approved act the moment after its commission, in order to get his self-approval *again:* but, speaking in general terms, a man's self-approval in the large concerns of life has its source in the approval of the peoples about him, and not in a searching personal examination of the matter. Mohammedans are Mohammedans because they are born and reared among that sect, not because they have thought it

out and can furnish sound reasons for being Mohammedans; we know why Catholics are Catholics;
why Presbyterians are Presbyterians; why Baptists
are Baptists; why Mormons are Mormons; why
thieves are thieves; why monarchists are monarchists; why Republicans are Republicans and
Democrats, Democrats. We know it is a matter of
association and sympathy, not reasoning and examination; that hardly a man in the world has an
opinion upon morals, politics, or religion which he
got otherwise than through his associations and sympathies. Broadly speaking, there are none but corn-
pone opinions. And broadly speaking, corn-pone
stands for self-approval. Self-approval is acquired
mainly from the approval of other people. The
result is conformity. Sometimes conformity has a
sordid business interest—the bread-and-butter interest—but not in most cases, I think. I think that in
the majority of cases it is unconscious and not calculated; that it is born of the human being's natural
yearning to stand well with his fellows and have
their inspiring approval and praise—a yearning
which is commonly so strong and so insistent that
it cannot be effectually resisted, and must have its
way.

A political emergency brings out the corn-pone
opinion in fine force in its two chief varieties—the
pocketbook variety, which has its origin in self-
interest, and the bigger variety, the sentimental
variety—the one which can't bear to be outside the
pale; can't bear to be in disfavor; can't endure the
averted face and the cold shoulder; wants to stand

well with his friends, wants to be smiled upon, wants to be welcome, wants to hear the precious words, "*He's* on the right track!" Uttered, perhaps by an ass, but still an ass of high degree, an ass whose approval is gold and diamonds to a smaller ass, and confers glory and honor and happiness, and membership in the herd. For these gauds many a man will dump his life-long principles into the street, and his conscience along with them. We have seen it happen. In some millions of instances.

Men think they think upon great political questions, and they do; but they think with their party, not independently; they read its literature, but not that of the other side; they arrive at convictions, but they are drawn from a partial view of the matter in hand and are of no particular value. They swarm with their party, they feel with their party, they are happy in their party's approval; and where the party leads they will follow, whether for right and honor, or through blood and dirt and a mush of mutilated morals.

In our late canvass half of the nation passionately believed that in silver lay salvation, the other half as passionately believed that that way lay destruction. Do you believe that a tenth part of the people, on either side, had any rational excuse for having an opinion about the matter at all? I studied that mighty question to the bottom—came out empty. Half of our people passionately believe in high tariff, the other half believe otherwise. Does this mean study and examination, or only feeling? The latter, I think. I have deeply studied that question, too—

and didn't arrive. (We all do no end of feeling, and we mistake it for thinking. And out of it we get an aggregation which we consider a boon. Its name is Public Opinion. It is held in reverence. It settles everything. Some think it the Voice of God.

**THE END**